An Introduction to
Statistics
using Microsoft **Excel**

BY

Dan Remenyi
George Onofrei
Joseph English

Published by ACPIL
Copyright © 2009, 2010, 2011, 2015 ACPIL
http://www.academic-publishing.org

Academic Conferences and Publishing International Ltd
33 Wood Lane
Sonning Common
Nr Reading
RG4 9SJ
UK
info@academic-publishing.org

Disclaimer: While every effort has been made by the authors and the publishers to ensure that all the material in this book is accurate and correct any error made by readers as a result of any of the material, formulae or other information in this book is the sole responsibility of the reader.

When you can measure what you are speaking about, and express it in numbers, you know something about it; but when you cannot measure it, when you cannot express it in numbers, your knowledge is of a meagre and unsatisfactory kind.
William Thomson later Lord Kelvin, Mathematician and Physicist 1824-1907

First edition 2010
ISBN 978-1-906638-55-9
Second printing April 2011
Third Printing June 2011
Fourth Printing June 2013

Second edition 2015
978-1-910810-16-3 (printed)
978-1-910810-17-0 (e-pub)
978-1-910810-18-7 (mobi)

Excel is a trade name registered by the Microsoft Corporation.

Cover artwork by Joshua McNutt, Letterkenny, Ireland

Preface to the First Edition

To illustrate the statistical functions and techniques within Excel we have used examples drawn for the world of research. We chose to do this because we believe this will clearly demonstrate some of the facilities within this spreadsheet. However, the statistical power of Excel will allow readers to use this software in a variety of ways, far beyond that of research. art. It is a science in that it is a body of knowledge which is built on a series of well established rules of applied mathematics. Rigorous statistical analysis is required for quantitative research. There is no argument about how statistical calculations or techniques are to be performed and if the rules are not followed then incorrect answers will most probably be produced. However statistics is also an art that requires a considerable amount of judgement on the part of a practitioner. Judgements and decisions have to be made that relate to deciding how a research question should be designed and the role of data and statistics in answering it. There are issues relating to which statistical technique to use, what level of significance to work at, and how the results can be interpreted.

What is also problematic in statistics, which is why it should be regarded as an art, is that there may be disagreements among practitioners about the meaning on these judgements and what answers could be given. It is indeed common to find different researchers taking quite different positions concerning which statistical technique is best to use. Not to mention the fact that the same statistical results can be understood differently.
Excel, with its built in statistical functions is a good tool to use to become familiar with statistics. There are many statistical functions in Excel but this book only addresses the functions required to perform the tasks most often required by researchers. Advanced functions are not used. It is also important to say that Excel has limitations as a statistical package and experienced researchers may well need to use a dedicated statistics package as well as Excel.

This book is not intended to cover all the possible statistical procedures or techniques that can be performed within Excel. The intention is that it will be an introduction to statistics which will facilitate readers to acquire the knowledge to understand the basics and to progress further if he or she so wishes. Furthermore for those who wish to use Excel in more advanced ways there is a list of add-in products in the Appendix.

Dan Remenyi

Dan.remenyi@gmail.com
June 2009

i

Preface to the Second Edition

Individual performance with respect to understanding numbers varies considerably. Some people appear to be able to handle arithmetic, mathematics and statistics with much greater ease than others. Some people believe that they just can't do any form of mathematical manipulation. Recently in a shop I bought three items which cost £2, £4 and £5. The shop attendant reached for a calculator. I said, "Don't worry, I owe you £11". She looked at me with a combination of alarm, suspicion and contempt and proceeded to key the numbers into the calculator anyway. "Yes. It was £11", she said. I suppose she could be described as being a victim of arithmophobia which is defined as a state of anxiety brought on by having to deal with numbers.

It has been thought for aeons that prowess with numbers was an innate ability which was sometimes described as having a "gift". The belief was that the brains of people who could do numbers were somehow differently wired to those who could not. In recent years it was said that there had to be a maths gene. However it is now believed that although clearly there is some variation in natural ability with respect to performance in these subjects the reason for the wide variation is more to do with how the subject was originally taught and the amount of encouragement which an individual received from his or her teachers, mentors and family.

The handling of numbers in arithmetic and the progression into the more abstract field of mathematics and statistics is generally approached poorly in our education system. The inadequacy is not necessarily in the teaching techniques or the books and other texts used but rather in the attitude towards these subjects. These subjects are seen as something which has to be taught because it is part of a preordained curriculum rather than a set of tools which are available to help people live a fuller, more productive and more interesting life. It is so enlightening when one hears people say, "I thought that when I left school I was leaving all the maths stuff behind me!" or "I was bored witless by all those numbers and formulas [sic] that were forced down my throat".

By the way these comments in no way imply that the inadequacy in handling numbers by these people is "all the teachers' fault". It is deeply embedded in our culture. Parents who never liked arithmetic and maths pass on their attitudes to their children as surely as they pass on other family beliefs and/or prejudices. We are often encouraged to believe that numbers are hard and that it is OK not to be able to be good with them. And to add to this, children's play culture can reinforce these problems in a number of different ways. I was quite startled to recently see a video of a little girl's talking plastic doll which among other things said "Maths is hard". But the gender issue is yet another story to be dealt with elsewhere.

This book was written out of a frustration at seeing statistics taught through formal methods using large scale statistics software packages. It seemed to me that very little was learned by this process and quite often both the teachers and the students were in denial. It is true that the students were generally able to pick up enough knowledge to pass an examination or to complete a piece of research. But I seldom saw anything which could be regarded as deep learning and the little which had been learned did not stay for any length of time in the heads of these learners. I know people who have passed several university level courses in statistics and they can hardly recall never mind use any of what was taught to them.

The purpose of the book was to get people involved with statistics gently, through the use of a very popular software package which although designed for general calculation had statistical features, mostly in the form of statistical functions, built into it. The book facilitates the reader in learning a material amount about this subject on a step by step basis. A lot of emphasis is placed on knowing the vocabulary and checking one's own progress as one proceeds.

This seems to have worked and I was truly delighted to receive positive feedback and especially an e-mail from a reader who told me that having the book nearby was almost as good as having a personal teacher in the room. I was also told that with the help of the book many of the long standing problems with the subject has been dissolved and washed away. The Self Test and the additional assignments are an important part of this.

As anyone can quickly see the book is intended to address most of the basic needs of those wanting to start out to learn to use statistics and it leaves the more esoteric aspects of the subject to other texts.

As a consequence of this we have only made one change to the 2nd Edition. We have added a prologue rather than a chapter at the beginning of the second edition of the book. This prologue we have called *Statistics and thinking statistically.* The main purpose of this prologue is to situate statistics and how it can help our thinking within the greater context of our daily lives. Statistics is too often seen like the way arithmetic has been described above as something we have to do because it is in the syllabus and it is expected of us but it does not have anything to do with our real lives. This should not be the case.

Thinking statistically plants this subject right in the middle of anyone's everyday life. It is effectively another more sophisticated way of seeing the world. It looks beyond the obvious. It encourages one to think about variation and association. It questions our current models of how things work and it allows us to bring a new level of reality into our view of what is going on around us. Thinking statistically requires sensitivity to numeric data and the level of this is more than reached by the content of this book.

We have therefore produced this book in the hope that it will not only facilitate the learning of the software package and the statistical formulae and functions used therein but that it will also help readers' ability to be more aware of variation and association in the world around them.

Dan Remenyi

Dan.remenyi@gmail.com
May 2015

How to use this book

This book starts with the assumption that little is known about statistics; however it does assume that the reader has some knowledge of Excel.

This book has been written as a tutorial and as such the techniques of statistics are illustrated through many examples. The mathematical equations required for statistical concepts such as the mean and the standard deviation have not been provided as these are easily performed with functions in Excel.

It is hoped that readers will follow the examples by using the techniques and for this reason the data referred to in the book is available to the reader by downloading files from the web.

For beginners to statistics it is preferable to start reading at the beginning i.e. Part 1 and proceed slowly through the book. For those who have a knowledge of statistics the book may be started at Part 2 or at Part 3.

A glossary has been provided at the start of each Part which covers the statistical terms used in that section of the book.

Self tests, assignments and exercises are provided and worked solutions to these are available on request.

Three types of files are available for use with this book. These are obtainable at the following website http://www.academic-publishing.org/intro_excel.htm. The first set of files contains data for the worked examples in the book. The second sets of files are Excel files which can be used as templates. The third set of files contains data which are used in the exercises at the end of each part.

Acknowledgements

We would like to acknowledge the contribution of many colleagues and students over the years who have all made a contribution to our understanding of the body of knowledge we call statistics.

Table of Contents

A Prologue

Statistics and thinking statistically, take nothing at face value, question your understanding of any numbers presented to you

Statistics and thinking statistically

This part of the book invites readers to pause for a few moments before diving into the statistical techniques and functions, and to consider what statistics and statistical thinking really have to offer. Some readers will like to do this at the outset while others would prefer to undertake this reflection after they have read the book. It doesn't matter much which approach a person would take.

Statistics can really help us better understand the world around us and facilitate our achievement of much better results. The application of the knowledge represented by statistics has time and again improved our ability to be both more efficient and more effective. It has also allowed us to acquire a deeper understanding of what is actually represented in a set of data. In this way there have been major advances in medical science, all forms of engineering as well as an understanding of our world in general. It is hard to imagine modern society without the knowledge which has been provided though access to statistical analysis and the interpretation thereof (Bernstein 1996). It is, of course, true to say that care has to be taken in the preparation of any statistics as numbers can misrepresent either through carelessness or ignorance. Statistics can also deliberately mislead but such behaviour is not the subject matter of this book.

When statistics is initially taught it is often in terms of an introduction to the basic tools required to manipulate numbers such as means and standard deviations and coefficients of correlation. Then ideas related to distributions, probability and hypothesis testing are presented. In this way the new comer to statistics is exposed to a world of ideas concerning calculation, functions and techniques. Fortunately computers have considerably reduced the labour required for this type of work and in so doing have made statistical analysis more accessible to a wider range of people.

The approach described in the above paragraph could be considered as formal statistical analysis but there is another aspect to analysis which is referred to as *thinking statistically* and has to do with acquiring a different mindset with which to understand what is going on about us. To accomplish this it is necessary to see statistics not as a separate field of study (Abelson 1995) but rather as a facilitator to our understanding. To become accomplished in this respect there is the need to stand back and look beyond the obvious and to ask provoking questions.

Thus before plunging into a book on the use of statistical techniques, functions and formulae it is perhaps worth the readers' while to pause and reflect on what is meant by the expression *thinking statistically*. This term has been to some extent popularised by a number of authors who have written extensively on this topic and therefore it is important to mention that it is the intention here to address the topic at a very high level using a small number of pages. If a high level definition is required then thinking statistically could be defined or perhaps described as introducing the element of reality into how we perceive and understand the world around us by reflecting on the situation and triggering questions that allow us to examine the uncertainty which is associated with most if not with all aspects of our lives. This manner of thought is associated with not accepting data at face value but rather encouraging scepticism, eliminating naivety and being open to new perspectives. Thinking statistically effectively opens up opportunities for learning - learning about our understanding of what we are doing and the impact we are having as well as acquiring a greater understanding of the complex environment in which we live.

To explore the concept of thinking statistically it is necessary reflect on the fact that we perceive the world around us through a series of mental models which mostly interconnect the phenomena we experience daily. These mental models not only make sense of our world but they provide access to the personal thoughts which determine how we can manage the variables that affect our lives. The models are composed of variables and relationships which we understand through our attempt at ordering or quantifying them in some sort of way.

Thinking statistically has a number of important components the first of which is the realisation that the measurement of the world around us is one of the very best ways of understanding the phenomena we encounter in everyday life. The results of this measurement are usually considered the data which we need to direct our thinking. The importance of measurement has been the basis of the thinking of many philosophers and scientists over the last few millennia but in relatively modern times it was popularised by a statement made by the famous Victorian scientist Lord Kelvin (1883) who said:

> When you can measure what you are speaking about, and express it in numbers, you know something about it; but when you cannot measure it,

when you cannot express it in numbers, your knowledge is of a meagre and unsatisfactory kind.

Few would disagree with Kelvin. Having the measure of something is indeed a crucial step in understanding it or more precisely acquiring a more comprehensive understanding of it. But stated on its own it is a rather over simplification as it does not take into account the range of knowledge which may be available about a particular phenomenon and which may not be amenable to measurement. Kelvin's statement can also be seen as important as it draws our attention to the fact that there are things and issues about which we are unable or at least have considerable difficulty to measure or express in numbers. It is important to point out that many would disagree with the proposition that knowledge about a phenomenon which could not be measured should be regarded as "*meagre and unsatisfactory*". It is often the case that the most important facts are descriptive in nature and thus not easily amenable to measurement, but this is another issue.

The idea of measurement can be deceptive in that it suggests that if the issue or phenomenon is measurable then there is always a unique answer to attempts to measure it. In practice there is, frequently if not always, some variation in the results we obtain when we attempt to measure the same item, issue or phenomenon even under controlled conditions. At a fundamental level variation is deeply built into the human experience.

Thinking statistically recognises this fact and provides us with the cognitive tools for dealing with the variation. To use these cognitive tools we need to have a positive attitude towards curiosity, or ability to be sceptical in our desire to engage with the subject and seek deeper understanding or meaning to the mental models which explain the world for us. Thinking statistically provides an ability to connect our experience to our models of the real world which we are trying to describe and therefore understand and manage.

Those individuals who are orientated to thinking statistically will:-

1. Appreciate the value of collecting appropriate data in as numeric a form as possible;
2. Realise the variation inherent in any form of measurement or data collection;
3. Be curious as to how the variation may be explained;
4. Be cognisant of the different ways the data may be analysed;
5. Look for a model that will optimise how the situation may be understood;

6. Be sceptical of any model and look for alternative explanations;
7. Be aware that any conclusions reached will always be contingents and may be over turned by the discovery of more or different data.

These 7 points could be summaries in the following few sentences. Have a broad awareness of the issue being studied and the environment in which they exist. Be careful with acquiring appropriate data and vigilant concerning variations. Look for multiple explanations and be sceptical of conclusions and be prepared to accept other explanations. Some authors have described this as applying common sense to any given analytical work and explanation of a phenomenon. But it is more than that. It is a type of common sense which is informed by a sensitivity to variation and association which is present in sets of numbers which are presented as evidence. The effect of this is to minimise the naive belief in the certainty of data especially numerical data and to trigger questions about their providence and what they might actually mean (Wild & Pfannkuch 1999).

Having said what thinking statistically is, it is now worthwhile saying what it is not. Thinking statistically does not imply an intimate knowledge of all the latest statistical techniques. It does not imply a mastery of powerful statistical software. It does not mean that a degree in statistics is necessary (Bram 2013). However it is correct to say that before thinking statistically can take on any real meaningful role in the way someone perceived his or her world they do need to have a level of numeracy which allows them to be comfortable with numbers. It is important to understand the order of numbers and proportions for example. Some knowledge of the language of statisticians and at least an elementary knowledge of the more basic concepts is also required especially those involving the concepts of variation and association. These are not especially challenging and many people who want to master them can do so without enormous difficulty. But it is also important to say that there are those who have great difficulty with numbers and for them the very name *thinking statistically* will be daunting. This is often an emotional rather than an intellectual response. By looking at the list of 7 factors above there is really nothing there which requires much by way of numeracy skills. However, this does not mean that fear of numbers is not truly real and a barrier to thinking statistically. This issue may be seen as another example of the famous Roosevelt (1933) aphorism "*The only thing to fear is fear itself*".

The opposite of fear, an excessive enthusiasm and belief that the subject has been fully understood can also be a problem. A little knowledge can be dangerous and it is important that someone who has acquired the habit of thinking statistically does not regard him or herself as being a statistician. This would be a completely inappropriate interpretation of the term.

In a sense thinking statistically could be seen as the bridge between the statistician and those completely inexperienced in the use of statistics to understand their world. One of the reasons this bridge is needed is that formal statistics can sometimes suggest explanations which are simply inappropriate and result in incorrect courses of action. This was well explained by Paulos (1998) when he wrote:-

> *Without an ambient story, background knowledge, and some indication of the providence of the statistics, it is impossible to evaluate their validity. Common sense and informal logic are as essential to the task as an understanding of the formal statistical notions.*

Paulos's comment is important because he cautions against the naive acceptance of the findings of numerical analysis without looking for a greater understanding and applying the scepticism which is the hallmark of thinking statistically.

In a sense Paulos agrees with Disraeli's infamous comment that there are "Lies, damn lies and statistics", but unlike Disraeli he tells us how statistics can be used so that we can extract from them the value which can give us so much more insight and can facilitate greater control over whatever we are concerned about.

With this in mind it is suggested that readers of this book should endeavour to cultivate the habit of thinking statistically. It will certainly open up new horizons for many people by helping them to ask different and more difficult questions in the hope of acquiring a better understanding of the issues under consideration. It will require readers to engage in a higher level of subtle thought. It will mean looking beyond the obvious for the lessons to be learnt from a situation which may be understood at a deeper level. It should allow better results to be achieved leading to a higher level of efficiency and effectiveness.

Part 1

**Descriptive Statistics, Processing a Short
Questionnaire and
Understanding the Data**

Working with Numbers

Working with numbers need not be difficult or daunting. If this subject is approached correctly an understanding of numbers comes naturally to many people and even those who have had bad experiences with mathematics or arithmetic at school sometimes surprise themselves with what they can achieve.

The exercises presented in this Part of the book focuses on a small set of numbers which is the data received from completed questionnaires and these numbers are used to help understand the attitudes of the people who answered the questionnaires.

Several concepts will be used in this Part including the idea of the average responses which shows what a typical person thinks; the spread of responses which shows how much diversity there is in the group who answered the questions and then the shape of the distribution of the data received.

Use of graphs to present data is demonstrated, as is the idea of combining data into numerical summaries so as to obtain a better understanding of what is being suggested by the numbers.

This book is for the novice in statistics. Some knowledge of Excel will be required. If you don't understand basic Excel you will need some help with this. One of the challenges for beginners to statistics is to learn the language of the subject. There will be new words to be learnt. For this reason a glossary of terms has been provided and users of this book should consult this whenever they encounter a new word which is not familiar to them.

Statistics is one of those subjects where it is necessary to practise the techniques in order to fully understand them. Some people have said that they have had to use a technique or a function a number of times before the "penny dropped". Therefore do not panic if it takes a while to become really comfortable with the contents of this book.

This book uses data for the exercises which could be entered into the computer by the reader. Alternatively we have placed some of the more important data files on the Web which may be downloaded. These files are at URL http://www.academic-publishing.org/intro_excel.htm
These data files are clearly named and may be down loaded when needed.

Glossary of terms

Central tendency	The "mid" point of a data set. It is a measure of location. There are three measures of central tendency which are the mean, the median and the mode.
Correlation	The correlation indicates the strength and direction of a linear relationship between two variables.
Cumulative relative frequency	A cumulative relative frequency is a tabular summary of a set of data showing the relative frequency of data points less than or equal to the upper class limit of each class.
Data	Observed value of one or more characteristics of the phenomenon under study. Any outcome which can be recorded which has stimulated any aspect of human senses which the researcher believes may be useful in answering the research question.
Descriptive statistics	Statistical summaries are used to describe and understand a situation through the use of data. In numeric terms these are means, medians, modes and other numbers to help in summarising the characteristics of a population.
Dispersion	The spread of data within a data set. It is a measure of how the data is scattered. There are two principal measures of spread and they are the range and the standard deviation.
Exploratory data analysis	The use of relatively simple techniques to facilitate the understanding of the data.
Heuristic	This is a rule of thumb or an experience based technique.

Histograms	A histogram is a graph type which uses a series of bars where the height of the bar is proportional to the number of observations (frequency) that fall in the interval represented by the bar.
Independent variable	A variable whose values are independent of changes in the values of other variables.
Interval data	Data where the interval between numbers has meaningful interpretation but where the division of these numbers is not meaningful.
Inter item correlation	The term inter item correlation is used to describe the process of examining constructs to ensure there is an appropriate degree of correlation between the elements within the construct.
Matrix	Data supplied in the form of rows and column are said to be in a matrix.
Nominal data	Data that refers to descriptions rather than numbers. In a questionnaire the indication that the respondent was English speaking, for example, would be an element of nominal data.
Non-response rate	The number of unreturned questionnaires divided by the total number of questionnaires distributed expressed as a percentage.
Ordinal data	Data which is presented in an ordered fashion usually indicating preference or importance. The numbers assigned to the outcomes indicate the order of importance.
Population	The total set of all possible elements from which a sample is drawn.
Questionnaire	In social science research a questionnaire is a list of questions which, when answered may deliver the data required to answer the research question – sometimes referred to as a measuring instrument.

Ratio data	Data that indicates both magnitude and degree of magnitude so that the differences between them and their ratios are apparent. An example would be the size of different cities. City A has 2 million people, City B 4 million people and City C has 8 million people. Thus city C is twice the size of city B and four times the size of city A.
Relative frequency	The relative frequency is the fraction or proportion of the number of occurrences observed for a specific category of a variable to the total number of items observed over all categories of the variable i.e. sample size.
Response rate	The number of completed questionnaires returned by the informants divided by the total number of questionnaires distributed.
Sample	A part of something larger such as a subset of a population. This sample is usually drawn from a sampling frame.
Sample frame	The group of data from which the actual sample is selected. It is a list or working subset of the population.
Statistic	A number which has relevance to a question being asked or a matter under consideration.
Statistics	Either a collection of numbers which have relevance or a method for handling and understanding a group of data usually in the form of numbers. Statistics is also a body of theoretical and practical knowledge which studies variation and uncertainty as expressed in numbers.
Usable returned questionnaire	A questionnaire which has been completed to an adequate level to be used as data to assist in answering the research question.

Descriptive statistical analysis using a spreadsheet

1.1 Introduction

This book continues worked example which illustrates the presentation and analysis of data. The example is based on data obtained from survey research that used a questionnaire. No details of the sampling frame are required or provided for this exercise. In order to increase the authenticity of this worked example, readers are shown how the data from the questionnaires needs to be carefully reviewed before the process of analysis begins. Thereafter a number of different Excel functions and commands are used to provide a basis for the interpretation of the data. Additionally this worked example introduces some of the vocabulary of questionnaire processing and descriptive statistics analysis.

1.2 From the research question to the questionnaire

Figure 1.1 shows the questionnaire used. The objective of the survey is to obtain an assessment of the views or opinions of students studying in the Faculty of Business and Accounting Studies at a university. These views or opinions will be used to answer the research question, *How are the services delivered by the Faculty perceived by the students and what differences are there between the two Schools in the Faculty?* To answer this question a number of variables are used. The variables used are a result of the researcher's practical and theoretical understanding of the issues involved in influencing the opinions of students with regards to the services delivered by the Faculty.

The questionnaire is in three parts.

Part A is a set of 12 Likert[1] type questions using a 9 point scale where respondents are asked to express the extent to which they agree or disagree with propositions about various aspects of the educational institu-

---

[1] A Likert Scale named after Rensis Likert, a founder of the University of Michigan's Institute for Social Research, is a psychometric measure frequently used in questionnaires and is the most commonly used scale in survey research. When completing a Likert scale questionnaire participants answer in levels of agreement with a statement. Each question is referred to as a Likert item, although it usually appears to be a scale of itself, and a Likert scale is the sum of a number of Likert items. Likert items may be graduated using 5, 7 or 9 positions of difference, and it is common to have an odd number of positions. The mid-position is regarded as neither supporting nor disagreeing with the proposition. Sometimes a forced opinion is gained by removing the mid-position. The questionnaire responses can be analysed individually or summed to create a score for the group. This group score is a Likert scale, and can be treated as interval data.

tion's services. All 12 aspects of the educational institution's services are considered to be variables and data will be captured and processed for each of these. A Likert scale is a widely used scale in opinion survey research. When responding to a Likert type question respondents specify their level of agreement to a statement. In the following questionnaire 1 denotes *strongly disagree* and 9 denotes *strongly agree*. Each variable will be analysed separately as well as together. Although the data obtained here is ordinal it is common practice to treat it as though it was interval and in the analysis described here this will be done.

Part B of the questionnaire asks respondents to indicate whether they are from the School of Business or the School of Accounting. Note the result of this question will provide nominal data which may be used to establish differences in views between the two groups under consideration.

In Part C of the questionnaire a final Likert type question is posed, asking respondents' overall opinions of the service delivery of the School/Institution. Note that the data collected in Part A and Part C is ordinal data and the data collected in Part B is Nominal.

Questionnaire

The Faculty of Business and Accounting Studies wishes to obtain an assessment of the views of the students as to the quality of the services delivered. All students are asked to complete the following questionnaire and return it to the Faculty Office.

This questionnaire should be completed anonymously and so please do not include your name, student number or any other indicator as to who you are. Your assistance is much appreciated.

Part A

Question 1
The quality of the lectures is excellent
Strongly Disagree   *Strongly Agree*
  1☐   2☐   3☐   4☐   5☐   6☐   7☐   8☐   9☐

Question 2
The quality of the handouts is excellent
Strongly Disagree   *Strongly Agree*
  1☐   2☐   3☐   4☐   5☐   6☐   7☐   8☐   9☐

Question 3
The quality of the class rooms is excellent
Strongly Disagree   *Strongly Agree*
  1☐   2☐   3☐   4☐   5☐   6☐   7☐   8☐   9☐

Question 4
The quality of the lecturers is excellent
Strongly Disagree   *Strongly Agree*
1☐   *2*☐   *3*☐   *4*☐   *5*☐   *6*☐   *7*☐   *8*☐   *9*☐

Question 5
The quality of the library is excellent
Strongly Disagree   *Strongly Agree*
1☐   *2*☐   *3*☐   *4*☐   *5*☐   *6*☐   *7*☐   *8*☐   *9*☐

Question 6
The quality of the canteen is excellent
Strongly Disagree   *Strongly Agree*
1☐   *2*☐   *3*☐   *4*☐   *5*☐   *6*☐   *7*☐   *8*☐   *9*☐

Question 7
The quality of the projection facilities is excellent
Strongly Disagree   *Strongly Agree*
1☐   *2*☐   *3*☐   *4*☐   *5*☐   *6*☐   *7*☐   *8*☐   *9*☐

Question 8
The quality of the residence is excellent
Strongly Disagree   *Strongly Agree*
1☐   *2*☐   *3*☐   *4*☐   *5*☐   *6*☐   *7*☐   *8*☐   *9*☐

Question 9
Examinations are professionally conducted
Strongly Disagree   *Strongly Agree*
1☐   *2*☐   *3*☐   *4*☐   *5*☐   *6*☐   *7*☐   *8*☐   *9*☐

Question 10
The quality of the feedback is excellent
Strongly Disagree   *Strongly Agree*
1☐   *2*☐   *3*☐   *4*☐   *5*☐   *6*☐   *7*☐   *8*☐   *9*☐

Question 11
The quality of the ICT is excellent
Strongly Disagree   *Strongly Agree*
1☐   *2*☐   *3*☐   *4*☐   *5*☐   *6*☐   *7*☐   *8*☐   *9*☐

Question 12
The quality of the recreational facilities is excellent
Strongly Disagree   *Strongly Agree*
1☐   *2*☐   *3*☐   *4*☐   *5*☐   *6*☐   *7*☐   *8*☐   *9*☐

```
┌─────────────────────────────────────────────────────────────┐
│ Part B                                                        │
│                                                               │
│ Of which School are you a member?                             │
│ School of Business          ☐                                 │
│ School of Accounting        ☐                                 │
│                                                               │
│                                                               │
│ Part C                                                        │
│                                                               │
│ Overall I regard the service delivery to be excellent         │
│ Strongly Disagree                        Strongly Agree       │
│   1☐   2☐   3☐   4☐   5☐   6☐   7☐   8☐   9☐                 │
│                                                               │
│ Thank you for completing this questionnaire.                  │
│                                                               │
│ Signed                                                        │
│ Researcher                                                    │
│ e-mail address                                                │
└─────────────────────────────────────────────────────────────┘
```

Figure 1.1: The questionnaire – A 9 point Likert Item type question set

1.3   The Sample

It is important to note that when using a questionnaire like this one it is highly unlikely that every appropriate student will respond. The questionnaires are distributed to a sample of students and the number of questionnaires received back is referred to as the response rate from that sample[2]. In order to be useful it is necessary to have a reasonably sized sample. The question of sample size will be addressed later in this book.

Furthermore the sample needs to be representative of the population[3].

1.4   Data capture

The first step is to transfer the respondents' scores into the spreadsheet. This requires some planning of the spreadsheet to decide how the data will best be positioned for the analysis to be performed. Often, as in this example, rows are allocated to each respondent and if this is the case then columns are used to record the results of each question.

In this example there were 30 completed questionnaires. Figure 1.2 shows the original data, which is referred to as the 'raw data'. Notice that

---

[2] The whole student group from which the sample originates is referred to as the population.
[3] Ideally a random sample should be taken when using a questionnaire. As there are both practical and theoretical problems associated with obtaining a random sample and thus researchers often compromise by taking what they believe to be a representative sample.

the responses to Part B, which asked for the School in which the respondent was studying, need to be coded, i.e. the ticks for the School of Business are entered as a 1 and the ticks for the School of Accounting are entered as a 2.

A primary overview of the data

Scores given to the individual questions ....

	Q-01	Q-02	Q-03	Q-04	Q-05	Q-06	Q-07	Q-08	Q-09	Q-10	Q-11	Q-12	School	Overall Rating
Respondent 1	3	5	2	7	0	9	5	2	6	7	6	9	2	7
Respondent 2	1	6	1	6	7	8	10	3	8	6	2	9	1	6
Respondent 3	2	2	2	4	4	4	3	3	5	7	5	9	2	5
Respondent 4	8	8	6		7	9	7	7	3	6	3	9	1	6
Respondent 5	1	1	3	2	3	1	9	4	7	1	7	9	1	3
Respondent 6	3	3	3	2	5	1	8	2	4		2	9	1	4
Respondent 7	6	6	5	6	5	6	10	99	4	8	4	9	1	4
Respondent 8	2	4	5	4	3	2	15	6	6		6	9	2	5
Respondent 9	7	9	7	6	5	4	10	9	5	3	5	9	1	0
Respondent 10	1	2	3	2	5	8	9	8	8	8	8	9	2	8
Respondent 11	3	1	9	1	5	6	6	8	3	3	2	5	1	3
Respondent 12	4	1	3	4	5	4	7	2	1	8	1	5	1	7
Respondent 13	1	3	4	2	3	1	4	3	6	6	6	5	1	7
Respondent 14	3	1	5	3	3	1	5	9	4	7	9	9	2	4
Respondent 15	4	2	8	4	2	4	3	8	8	5	8	9	2	5
Respondent 16	5	3	7	3	5	1	7	2	5	5	5	9	5	6
Respondent 17	6	3	0	1	2	1	5	6	1	0	1	9	1	6
Respondent 18	2	2	5	3	5	1	5	8	7	6	9	9	2	3
Respondent 19	6	2	8	6	3	2	3	8	4	3	4	9	2	7
Respondent 20	2	1	7	3	6	2	2	2	2	4	2	9	1	5
Respondent 21	1	2	3	2	5	8	3	8	8	8	8	9	2	8
Respondent 22	2	2	9	1	5	6	6	8	3	3	2	9	1	4
Respondent 23	4	1	3	4	5	4	7	2	1	8	1	9	1	7
Respondent 24	1	3	4	2	3	1	4	3	6	6	6	9	1	7
Respondent 25	3	1	5	3	3	1	5	9	4	7	9	9	2	4
Respondent 26	4	2	8	4	2	4	3	8	8	5	8	9	2	5
Respondent 27	5	3	7	3	5	1	7	2	5	5	5	9	5	6
Respondent 28	6	3	8	1	2	1	5	6	1	8	1	9	1	6
Respondent 29	2	2	5	3	5	1	5	8	7	6	9	9	2	3
Respondent 30	6	2	8	6	3	2	3	8	4	3	4	9	2	7

Figure 1.2: The raw data entered in a spreadsheet

On examination of this data it can be seen that some of the responses are invalid. For example Respondent 7's response to question 8 has been entered as 99, whereas the valid range for that question is 1 to 9.

Therefore the researcher needs to 'clean' the data. This is of critical importance because if errors made at the time of data entry are not corrected then the system will exhibit the phenomenon referred to as garbage-in-garbage-out (GIGO).

The first step is to go back to the questionnaires[4] to see if the error was made during the transcription of the data to the spreadsheet. If this is the case a correction can be made. If there is a missing data point,

---

[4] Note the Respondent number is entered with the rest of the data so that each line in the spreadsheet can be traced back to an original questionnaire.

where the respondent has failed to answer the question, a different approach is required. Although sometimes questionnaire results are processed in such a way as to ignore missing data points, sometimes it is thought to be better practice[5] to estimate a value. One way to achieve this is to use the average or mean of the scores the respondent gave to all other questions. This approach will be taken in this exercise.

The raw data can be downloaded from http://www.academic-publishing.org/intro_excel.htm. These data will be maintained on this website while the book is in print.

If Excel is loaded on the computer in use the file will be transferred and displayed in an Excel worksheet format as described in Figure 1.2.

Looking at Figure 1.2 it can be seen that the first missing data point is in cell E7. The formula to calculate the mean score for the questions of respondent 4 is as follows[6]:

=round(average(B7:D7,F7:M7),0)

Note that two separate cell ranges are required in the =average function. If the current cell (E7) were included in the range this would produce a circular reference and thus produce an incorrect result. As the informants were asked to express their views as whole numbers the =round() function has been used to round the result to the nearest whole number. After performing this calculation the formula should be replaced with the resulting value as the formula itself is no longer required. This is achieved by selecting **Edit Copy** and then without moving the cursor, select **Edit Paste Special** and tick the **Values** box.

Figure 1.3 is the data after the 'cleaning up' exercise has been completed.

---

5 Some researchers would strongly disagree with the necessity of making any such estimate and they would proceed without any adjustment. Some early software packages would not correctly function without a value in all the cells but this is no longer the case.

[6] This is only one of a number of different ways in which it is possible to estimate missing data. Another way is to calculate the average score obtained for that question from the rest of the informants and to use that average. Ultimately how missing data is estimated is always a subjective judgement. However if the approach shown in the text or the approach described in this footnote is used then the estimate will not have materially changed the outcome of the calculations.

	A	B	C	D	E	F	G	H	I	J	K	L	M	N	O
2		Scores given to the individual questions •••►													
3		Q - 01	Q - 02	Q - 03	Q - 04	Q - 05	Q - 06	Q - 07	Q - 08	Q - 09	Q - 10	Q - 11	Q - 12	School	O'all Rating
4	Respondent 1	3	5	2	7	8	9	5	2	6	7	6	9	2	7
5	Respondent 2	1	6	1	8	7	8	1	3	8	6	2	9	1	6
6	Respondent 3	2	2	2	4	4	4	3	3	5	7	6	9	2	5
7	Respondent 4	8	8	6	6	7	9	7	7	3	6	3	9	1	6
8	Respondent 5	1	1	3	2	3	1	9	4	7	1	7	9	1	3
9	Respondent 6	3	3	3	2	5	1	8	2	4	4	2	9	1	4
10	Respondent 7	6	6	5	6	5	6	1	9	4	8	4	9	1	4
11	Respondent 8	2	4	5	4	3	2	1	6	6	4	6	9	2	5
12	Respondent 9	7	9	7	6	5	4	1	9	5	3	6	9	1	8
13	Respondent 10	1	2	3	2	5	8	9	8	8	8	8	9	2	8
14	Respondent 11	3	1	9	1	5	6	6	8	3	3	2	5	1	3
15	Respondent 12	4	1	3	4	5	4	7	2	1	8	1	5	1	7
16	Respondent 13	1	3	4	2	3	1	4	3	6	6	6	5	1	7
17	Respondent 14	3	1	5	3	3	1	5	9	4	7	9	9	2	4
18	Respondent 15	4	2	8	4	2	4	3	8	8	5	8	9	2	6
19	Respondent 16	5	3	7	3	5	1	7	2	5	5	5	9	2	6
20	Respondent 17	6	3	8	1	2	1	5	6	1	8	1	9	1	6
21	Respondent 18	2	2	5	3	5	1	6	8	7	6	9	9	2	3
22	Respondent 19	6	2	8	6	3	2	3	8	4	3	4	9	2	7
23	Respondent 20	2	1	7	3	6	2	2	2	2	4	2	9	1	5
24	Respondent 21	1	2	3	2	5	8	3	8	8	8	8	9	2	8
25	Respondent 22	2	2	9	1	5	6	6	8	3	3	2	9	1	4
26	Respondent 23	4	1	3	4	5	4	7	2	1	8	1	9	1	7
27	Respondent 24	1	3	4	2	3	1	4	3	6	6	6	9	1	7
28	Respondent 25	3	1	5	3	3	1	5	9	4	7	9	9	2	4
29	Respondent 26	4	2	8	4	2	4	3	8	8	5	8	9	2	5
30	Respondent 27	5	3	7	3	5	1	7	2	5	5	5	9	2	6
31	Respondent 28	6	3	8	1	2	1	5	6	1	8	1	9	1	6
32	Respondent 29	2	2	5	3	5	1	5	8	7	6	9	9	2	3
33	Respondent 30	6	2	8	6	3	2	3	8	4	3	4	9	2	7
34															

Figure 1.3: The 'cleaned' data

Having made a suitable number of adjustments to the raw data it will be useful to move onto the next phase of the book and thus the cleaned data may now be downloaded from
http://www.academic-publishing.org/intro_excel.htm

1.5   Descriptive Statistics

Descriptive statistics, as the name suggests, are ways of describing what attributes a set of data is exhibiting. There are a number of different descriptive statistics functions in Excel.

Some exploratory data analysis is performed in order to help understand what the data suggests, or in other words what the sample of students who have completed the questionnaire are communicating as individuals as well as collectively to the researcher.

The first piece of analysis considers whether respondents' overall rating shown in column O is greater or less than the average of the individual ratings for each of the issues were given. This involves two steps. In the first place each respondent's overall average score is calculated, that is the average of the data in columns B through M, and then the result of this is subtracted from the overall rating in column O.

Figure 1.4 shows the results in columns Q and R. Where the overall rating exceeds the average rating this is recorded as a "*" in column S.

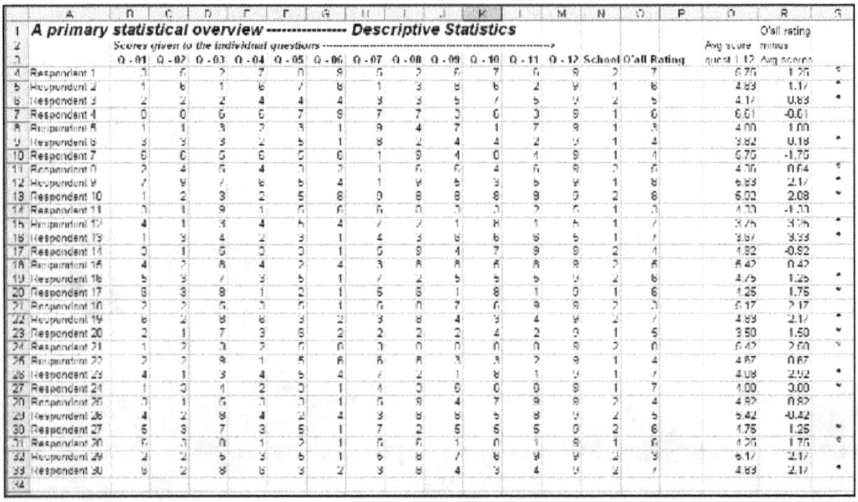

	A	B	C	D	E	F	G	H	I	J	K	L	M	N	O	P	Q	R	S
1	A primary statistical overview --------------- Descriptive Statistics																	O'all rating	
2		Scores given to the individual questions -->															Avg score	minus	
3		Q - 01	Q - 02	Q - 03	Q - 04	Q - 05	Q - 06	Q - 07	Q - 08	Q - 09	Q - 10	Q - 11	Q - 12	School	O'all Rating		quest 1 12	Avg scores	
4	Respondent 1	3	5	2	7	0	9	5	2	5	7	5	9	2	7		5.75	1.25	*
5	Respondent 2	1	6	1	6	7	8	1	3	8	6	2	9	1	6		4.83	1.17	*
6	Respondent 3	2	2	2	4	4	4	3	3	5	7	5	9	2	5		4.17	0.83	*
7	Respondent 4	0	0	6	6	7	9	7	7	3	6	3	9	1	6		6.61	-0.61	
8	Respondent 5	1	1	3	2	3	1	9	4	7	1	7	9	1	3		4.00	1.00	
9	Respondent 6	3	3	3	2	5	1	8	2	4	4	2	9	1	4		3.82	0.18	*
10	Respondent 7	6	0	5	6	5	6	1	9	4	0	4	9	1	4		5.75	-1.75	
11	Respondent 8	2	4	5	4	3	2	1	5	5	4	5	9	2	5		4.36	0.64	*
12	Respondent 9	7	9	7	6	5	4	1	9	5	3	5	9	1	8		5.83	2.17	*
13	Respondent 10	1	2	3	2	5	8	0	8	8	8	8	0	2	8		6.02	2.08	*
14	Respondent 11	3	1	9	1	5	6	5	0	3	3	2	5	1	3		4.33	-1.33	
15	Respondent 12	4	1	3	4	5	4	7	2	1	8	1	5	1	7		3.75	3.25	*
16	Respondent 13	1	3	4	2	3	1	4	3	6	6	6	5	1	7		3.67	3.33	*
17	Respondent 14	3	1	5	3	3	1	5	9	4	7	9	9	2	4		4.92	-0.92	
18	Respondent 15	4	2	8	4	2	4	3	8	8	6	8	9	2	6		5.42	0.42	
19	Respondent 16	5	3	7	3	5	1	7	2	5	5	5	9	2	6		4.75	1.25	*
20	Respondent 17	8	3	8	1	2	1	5	6	1	8	1	0	1	6		4.25	1.75	*
21	Respondent 18	2	2	5	3	5	1	5	0	7	6	9	9	2	3		5.17	2.17	
22	Respondent 19	6	2	8	8	3	2	3	8	4	3	4	9	2	7		4.83	2.17	*
23	Respondent 20	2	1	7	3	6	2	2	2	2	4	2	9	1	5		3.50	1.50	*
24	Respondent 21	1	2	3	2	5	0	3	0	0	0	0	9	2	0		5.42	2.60	*
25	Respondent 22	2	2	9	1	5	6	6	8	3	3	2	9	1	4		4.67	0.67	
26	Respondent 23	4	1	3	4	5	4	7	2	1	8	1	9	1	7		4.08	2.92	*
27	Respondent 24	1	3	4	2	3	1	4	3	6	0	0	9	1	7		4.00	3.00	*
28	Respondent 25	3	1	5	3	3	1	5	9	4	7	9	9	2	4		4.92	0.92	
29	Respondent 26	4	2	8	4	2	4	3	8	8	5	8	9	2	5		5.42	-0.42	
30	Respondent 27	5	3	7	3	5	1	7	2	5	5	5	0	2	6		4.75	1.25	*
31	Respondent 28	5	3	0	1	2	1	5	5	1	0	1	9	1	5		4.25	1.75	*
32	Respondent 29	2	2	5	3	5	1	5	8	7	8	9	9	2	3		5.17	2.17	
33	Respondent 30	8	2	8	6	3	2	3	8	4	3	4	9	2	7		4.83	2.17	*
34																			

Figure 1.4: Difference between the overall score to the average score of the 12 questions

To calculate the average score, the following formula is required in cell Q4:

=average(B4:M4)

This is then copied for the range Q5 through Q33.

To calculate how this score varies from the overall rating score the following formula is required in cell R4:

=O4-Q4

It is interesting to note how many respondents scored a higher overall rating than the average of the 12 questions in Part 1 of the questionnaire. This is shown by the positive values in column R. In column S a test has been performed to identify those respondents with an overall rating that exceeds the average score for the 12 questions. The formula in cell S4 is:

=if(R4>0,"*"," ")

This is expressed as 'if R4 is greater than zero then display an asterisk, otherwise leave the cell blank'. The formula can be copied into cells S5 through S33.

Figure 1.5 is a line chart showing the difference in the overall rating score against the average score of all the questions in part 1 of the questionnaire.

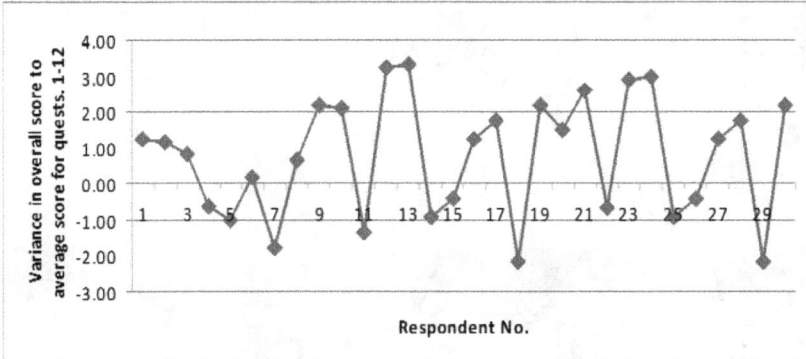

Figure 1.5: Line chart of average score by respondent

From the chart in Figure 1.5 it can be seen inter alia that respondents 12 and 13 showed the greatest positive difference between their overall score and the average of all their scores, whilst respondents 18 and 29 had the greatest negative difference between their overall score and the average of all their scores. Furthermore 19 out of the 30 respondents were prepared to give a higher overall rating for the facilities than the average of their individual scores. The interpretation of these facts is, of course, up to the researcher.

1.6 Sorting the data

Before moving on to discuss other descriptive statistics it is worth noting that it is possible to sort the data in terms of the average score for each question across the 30 respondents.

There are two steps in the process. Firstly the average[7] is calculated on a column by column basis by entering the following formula into cell B35 and copying it through to cell M35:

---

[7] Three types of average are described by statisticians. These are the arithmetic mean which in Excel is calculated by =average(), the median which is =median() and the mode which is =mode(). The mode is defined as the most frequently occurring data value and is primarily used with nominal data. It has only limited value in any quantitative analysis.

=average(B4:B33)

	A	B	C	D	E	F	G	H	I	J	K	L	M	N	O
1	**A primary statistical overview**														
2		Scores given to the individual questions ··>													
3		Q - 01	Q - 02	Q - 03	Q - 04	Q - 05	Q - 06	Q - 07	Q - 08	Q - 09	Q - 10	Q - 11	Q - 12	School	O'all Rating
4	Respondent 1	3	5	2	7	8	9	5	2	8	7	8	9	2	7
5	Respondent 2	1	6	1	6	7	0	1	0	0	0	2	9	1	0
6	Respondent 3	2	2	2	4	4	4	3	3	5	7	5	0	2	5
7	Respondent 4	8	8	6	6	7	9	7	7	3	6	3	9	1	6
8	Respondent 5	1	1	3	2	3	1	9	1	7	1	7	9	1	3
9	Respondent 6	3	3	3	2	5	1	8	2	4	4	2	9	1	4
10	Respondent 7	6	6	5	6	5	6	1	9	4	8	4	9	1	4
11	Respondent 8	2	4	5	4	0	2	1	0	6	4	0	9	2	0
12	Respondent 9	7	9	7	6	5	4	1	0	5	3	5	0	1	8
13	Respondent 10	1	2	3	2	6	8	9	8	8	8	8	9	2	8
14	Respondent 11	3	1	9	1	6	6	6	8	3	3	2	5	1	3
15	Respondent 12	4	1	3	4	5	4	7	2	1	8	1	5	1	7
16	Respondent 13	1	3	4	2	3	1	4	3	8	8	8	5	1	7
17	Respondent 14	3	1	5	0	0	1	5	9	4	7	9	9	2	4
18	Respondent 15	4	2	8	4	2	4	3	8	8	5	8	0	2	5
19	Respondent 16	5	3	7	3	5	1	7	2	5	5	5	0	2	6
20	Respondent 17	6	3	8	1	2	1	6	6	1	8	1	9	1	6
21	Respondent 18	2	2	5	3	6	1	6	8	7	6	9	9	2	3
22	Respondent 19	6	2	8	6	3	2	3	8	4	3	4	9	2	7
23	Respondent 20	2	1	7	3	8	2	2	2	2	4	2	9	1	5
24	Respondent 21	1	2	0	2	5	0	0	0	0	0	0	9	2	0
25	Respondent 22	2	2	9	1	5	6	6	8	3	3	2	0	1	4
26	Respondent 23	4	1	3	4	6	4	7	2	1	8	1	9	1	7
27	Respondent 24	1	3	4	2	3	1	4	3	6	6	6	9	1	7
28	Respondent 25	3	1	5	3	3	1	5	9	4	7	9	9	2	4
29	Respondent 26	4	2	8	4	2	4	3	8	8	5	8	9	2	5
30	Respondent 27	5	0	7	0	5	1	7	2	0	5	5	9	2	0
31	Respondent 28	6	3	8	1	2	1	5	6	1	8	1	0	1	6
32	Respondent 29	2	2	5	3	6	1	5	8	7	6	9	9	2	3
33	Respondent 30	6	2	8	6	3	2	3	8	4	3	4	9	2	7
34															
35	Mean score	3.47	2.67	5.37	3.48	4.30	3.47	4.67	5.70	4.80	5.61	4.93	8.60		5.53

Figure 1.6: Average score by question.

The next step requires the creation of a separate 3 column and 12 row matrix, which can be placed anywhere in the spreadsheet. For this example the matrix commences in cell S15 and is shown in Figure 1.7.

The main features of this matrix are that the question numbers and the question content are listed vertically and in the column next to them the average score for each of the answers to the questions is also listed. To convert the average scores currently in the range B35:M35 i.e. across row 35 to a range in a column i.e. column S, the **Copy – Paste Special - Transpose** command is used[8].

---

[8] If the reader is unfamiliar with these commands the Excel Help function may be of use.

	S	T	U	V
15	**Questionnaire variables with average scores**			
16	Q - 01	Quality of the lectures	3.47	
17	Q - 02	Quality of the handouts	2.87	
18	Q - 03	Quality of the class rooms	5.37	
19	Q - 04	Quality of the lecturers	3.47	
20	Q - 05	Quality of the library	4.30	
21	Q - 06	Quality of the canteen	3.47	
22	Q - 07	Quality of the projection facilities	4.67	
23	Q - 08	Quality of the residence	5.70	
24	Q - 09	Quality of the examination	4.80	
25	Q - 10	Quality of the feedback	5.60	
26	Q - 11	Quality of services ICT	4.93	
27	Q - 12	Quality of the recreational facilitie	8.60	
28				

Figure 1.7: The matrix prepared before sorting.

Once this matrix has been produced all that remains is to sort it on the average score column. This is achieved by selecting the **Data, Sort, Descending** option from the toolbar. Figure 1.8 shows the results.

	S	T	U	V	W
31	**Questionnaire variables sorted by average scores**				
32	Q - 12	Quality of the recreational facilitie	8.60		
33	Q - 08	Quality of the residence	5.70		
34	Q - 10	Quality of the feedback	5.60		
35	Q - 03	Quality of the class rooms	5.37		
36	Q - 11	Quality of services ICT	4.93		
37	Q - 09	Quality of the examination	4.80		
38	Q - 07	Quality of the projection facilities	4.67		
39	Q - 05	Quality of the library	4.30		
40	Q - 01	Quality of the lectures	3.47		
41	Q - 04	Quality of the lecturers	3.47		
42	Q - 06	Quality of the canteen	3.47		
43	Q - 02	Quality of the handouts	2.87		

Figure 1.8: The matrix sorted by average scores.

Figure 1.8 illustrates the issues respondents/informants thought to be best and worst. The interpretation of this sorted data list is an important aspect of the results of the questionnaire and will require considerable reflection.

1.7   Presenting Data using Charts

An important aspect of the analysis of data is how the results are presented. One of the more effective ways of presenting data in Excel is through charts. There is a wide range of chart/graph types to choose from and Excel has an easy to use charting facility. For example, the calculated data for the mean or average scores in Row 35 could be drawn as a bar chart, a line chart, or as a scatter diagram.

Figure 1.9 shows a bar chart of the average scores for questions 1 to 12, Figure 1.10 shows the same data as a line chart and Figure 1.11 is a scatter diagram of this data. These three graphs show the same data and an analyst would probably use one or two of these.

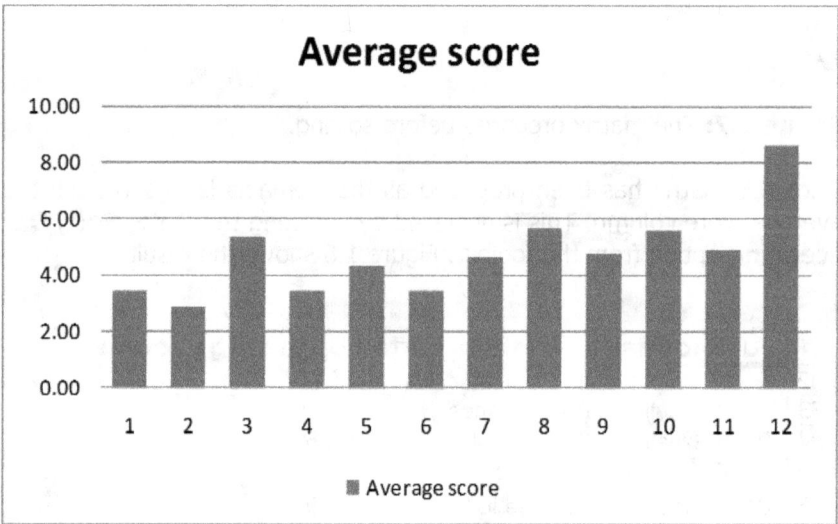

Figure 1.9: A bar chart showing average scores by question

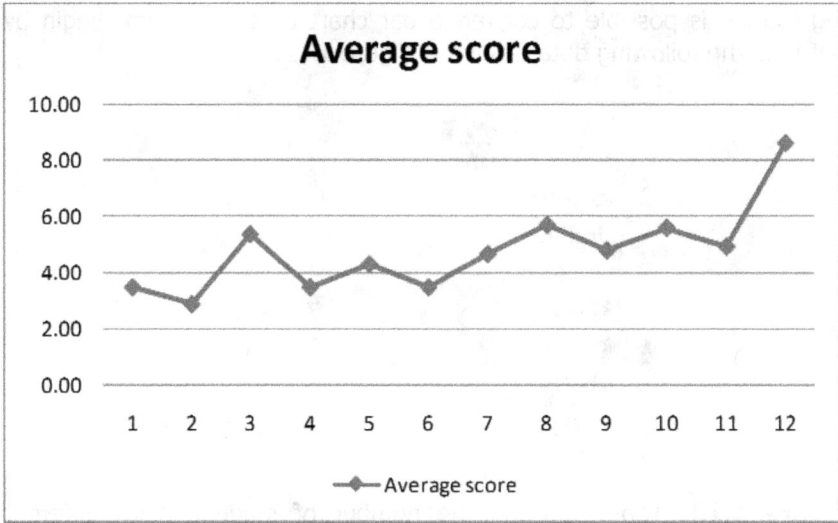

Figure 1.10: A line chart showing average scores by question

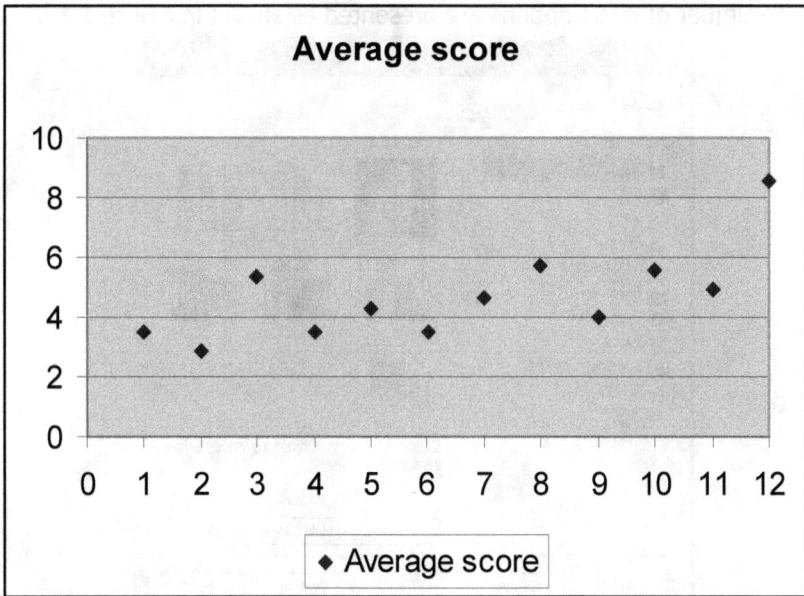

Figure 1.11: A scatter diagram showing average scores by question

Creating a histogram

There is no facility in Excel to produce a histogram directly from the chart wizard options. However, using the annotation options within the charting tools it is possible to convert a bar chart to a histogram. Begin by entering the following data, shown in Figure 1.12.

	A	B	C
1	No. of Months experience	No. of Students	
2	Under 25	1	
3	26-36	4	
4	37-48	7	
5	49-60	7	
6	61-72	4	
7	above 72	7	
8			

Figure 1.12: Table showing the number of students with different lengths of working experience

Highlight the range A1:B7 and click on the **Chart Wizard** from the toolbar. A number of chart options are presented as shown in Figure 1.13.

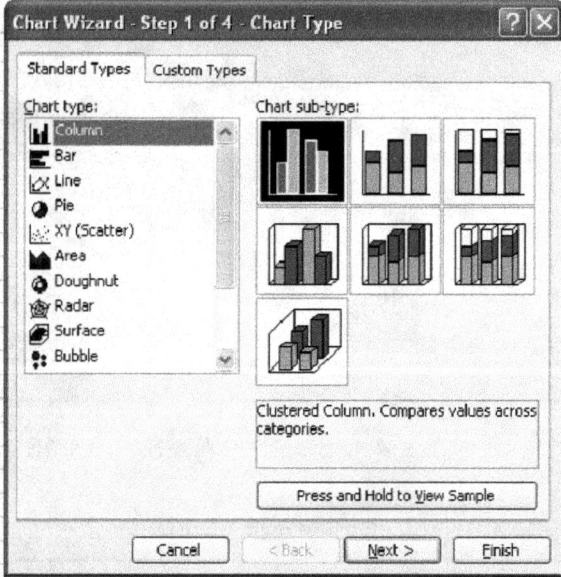

Figure 1.13: Chart type selection

As there is no option for histogram, at this point select **Column** from the chart type list and the basic bar graph (first icon) from the chart sub-types. This creates a vertical bar graph. Click **Next** and the screen will appear as shown in Figure 1.14.

Confirm that the Data Series is in a column in the spreadsheet by ensuring the columns button is highlighted as shown in Figure 1.14.

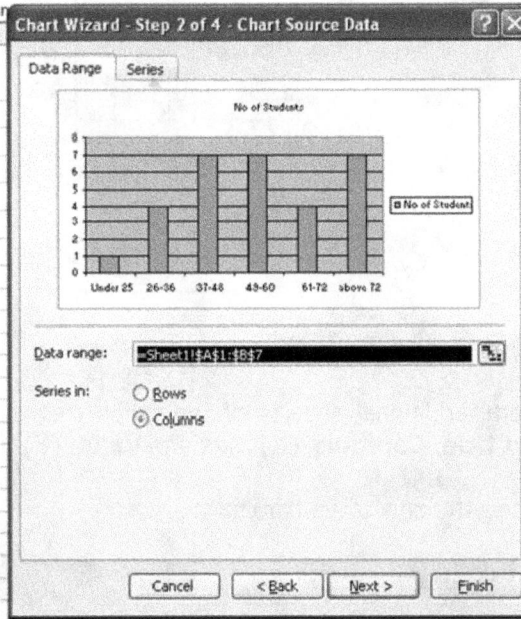

Figure 1.14: Preview of Basic Bar Chart

As the data range originally selected included the column descriptors in column A and the headings in row 1, these will automatically be set as the x-axis labels and the legend for the data. Click next and the enhanced preview in Figure 1.15 will be displayed.

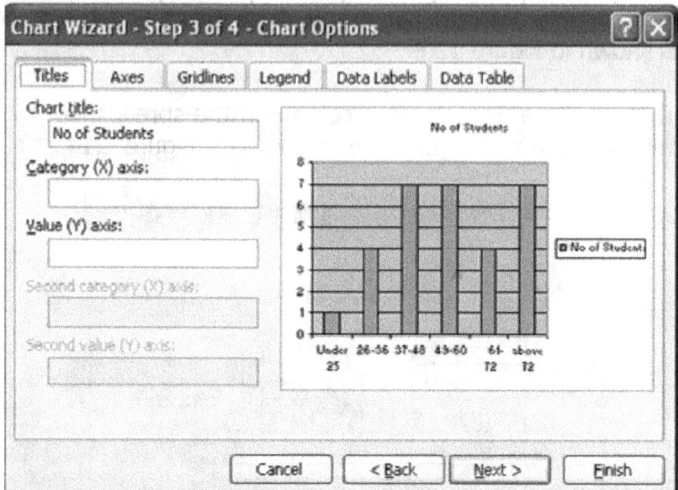

Figure 1.15: Enhanced preview showing

There are several additional aspects of the graph that can be entered such as a **Chart title**, **Category (X) axis** and **Value (Y) axis**.

Figure 1.16 shows the annotated bar chart.

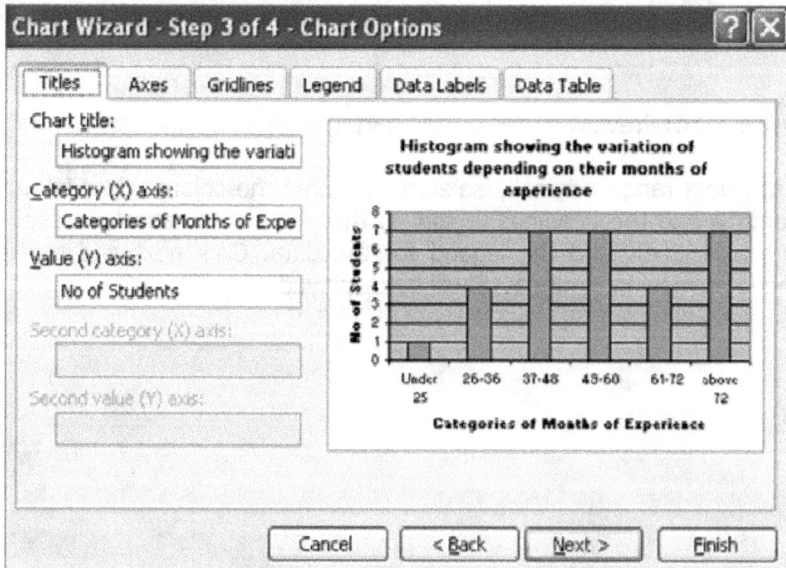

Figure 1.16: Preview of the annotated bar chart

Note that as this chart only has one series of data, the legend automatically created and shown in Figure 1.14 is not required. With the screen as shown in Figure 1.15 above, click on the **Legend** tab and take the tick off the **Show Legend** option.

Click **Next** and the final step is to decide whether the chart is to be positioned in a separate sheet within the workbook, or as an object in the current workbook. The options are shown in Figure 1.17.

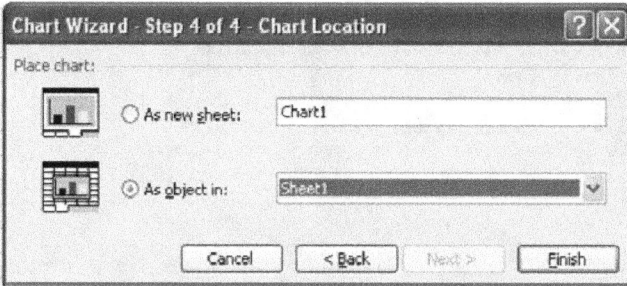

Figure 1.17: Chart positioning options

In this example the chart is placed in the current worksheet as an object and will appear as shown in Figure 1.18.

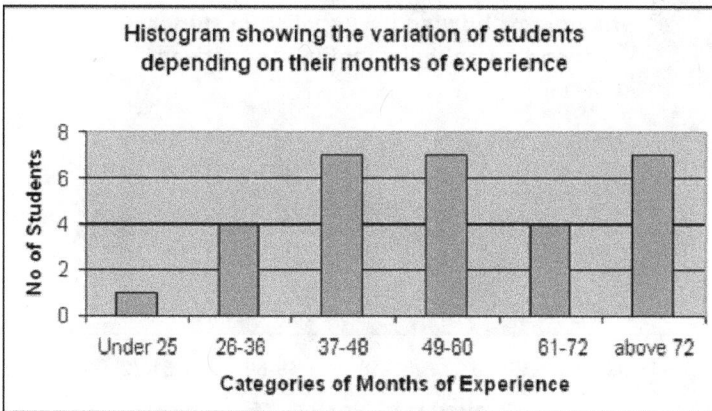

Figure 1.18: Completed bar chart

To convert the bar chart to a histogram it is necessary to remove the gaps between the bars. To do this, double-click on one of the bars in the graph, which will bring up the Format Data Series screen. Select the **Options** tab and set the gap width to 0, as shown in Figure 1.19

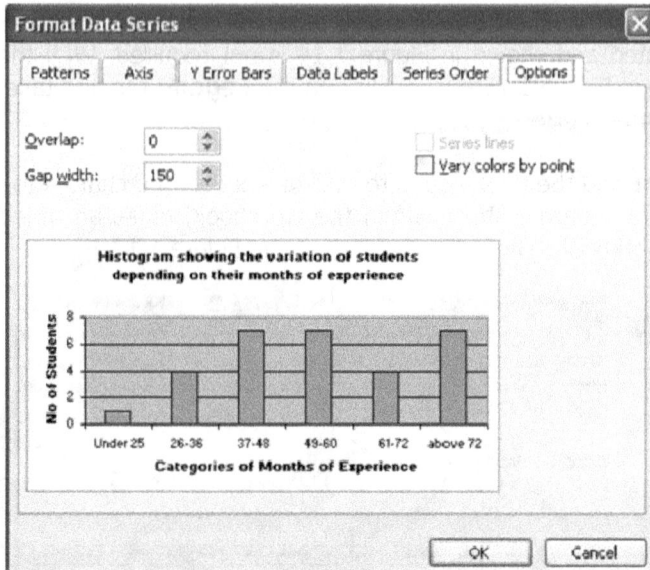

Figure 1.19: Removing the gap between the bars to produce a histogram – the gap of 150 will be reduced to zero

The completed histogram is shown in Figure 1.20.

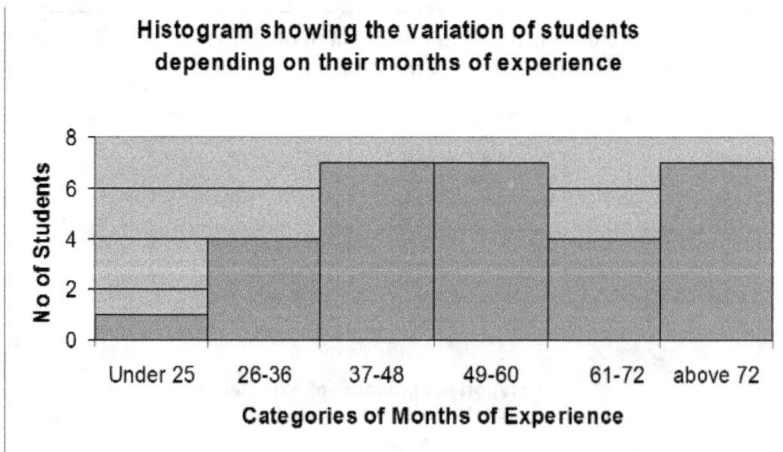

Figure 1.20: Completed histogram

Creating a Scatter Plot (XY) diagram

XY or Scatter Plot charts use a series of data points representing an x-value and a y-value, which are co-ordinates on the chart.

To illustrate the creation of an XY chart enter the data shown in Figure 1.21 into a spreadsheet. Note that the data in column A is referred to as the independent variable and the data in column B is referred to as the dependent variable.

	A	B	C
1	No of classes attended	Examination Mark	
2	10	65	
3	11	68	
4	4	39	
5	8	60	
6	12	65	
7	7	55	
8	2	35	
9	8	50	
10	10	60	
11	7	52	

Figure 1.21: Table showing the number of classes attended and the examination mark

Highlight all the data from A1:B11 and select the **Chart Wizard** from the toolbar. From the list of chart types choose **XY (Scatter)** and select the unconnected dots icon from the **Chart sub-types** as shown in Figure 1.22.

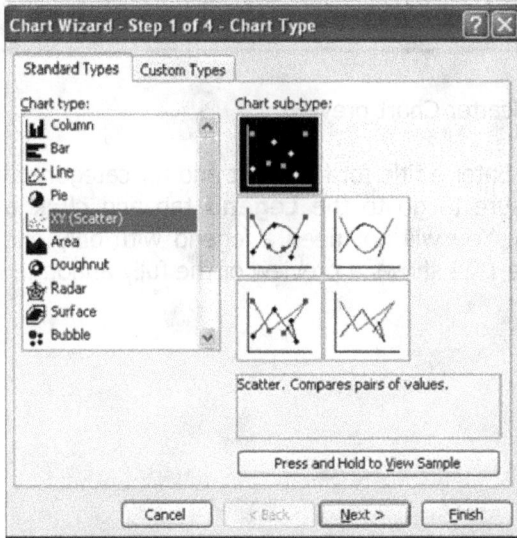

Figure 1.22: XY Scatter diagram options

The Data Range box should reflect the data highlighted in the spread-sheet. The Series option should be set to Columns, which is how the data is organized. This is shown in Figure 1.23.

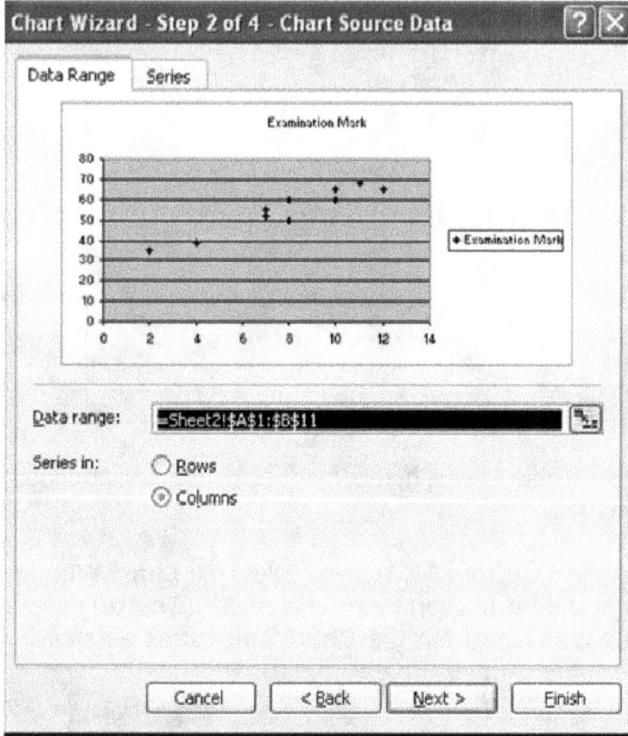

Figure 1.23: Scatter Chart preview

Click **Next** and Enter a title for the chart and for category X and Category Y. Also make sure to go to the **Legend** tab and **click off** the **Show Legend** option. You will not need a legend with only one independent variable[9]. Figure 1.24 shows a preview of the fully annotated chart.

---

[9] The issues of dependent and independent variables will be further explored in Part 2.

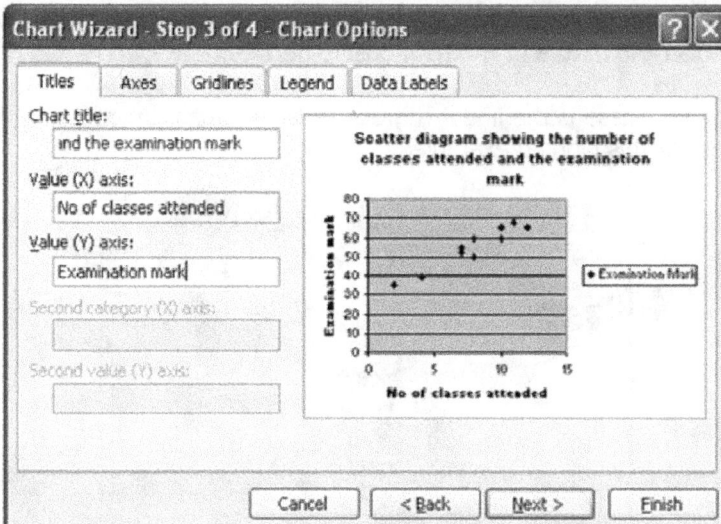

Figure 1.24: Fully annotated scatter chart

Then click **Finish** to insert the chart into the current spreadsheet as shown in Figure 1.25.

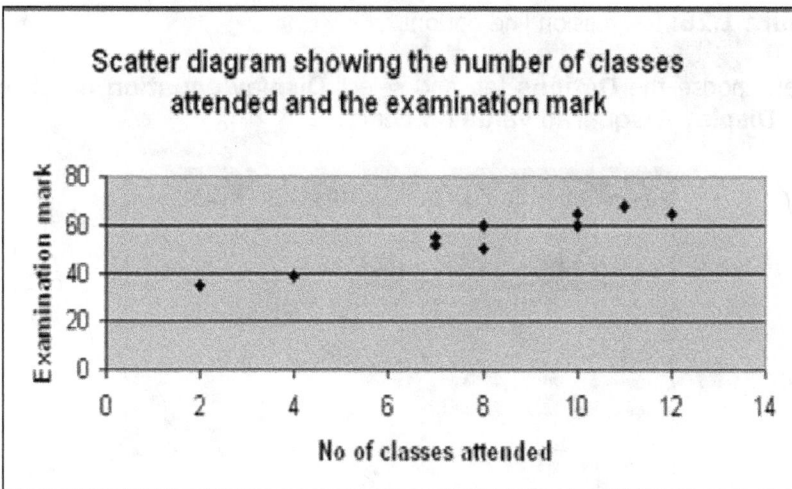

Figure 1.25: Completed scatter diagram

By right clicking the mouse on one of the data points on the chart it is possible to add a trend line to the chart by choosing **Chart** - **Add Trendline.** A dialogue box appears as shown in Figure 1.26 offering six different types of possible models which may fit the data. It is now necessary for the researcher to know which of these particular models would best reflect the nature of the relationship between the X and the Y data.

The simplest case is the linear regression least squared model and this is selected for this worked example.

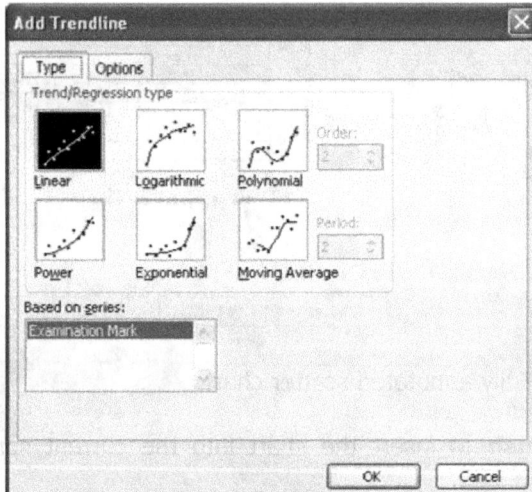

Figure 1.26: Regression line options

Then choose the **Options** tab and select **Display equation on chart** and **Display R-squared value on chart.**

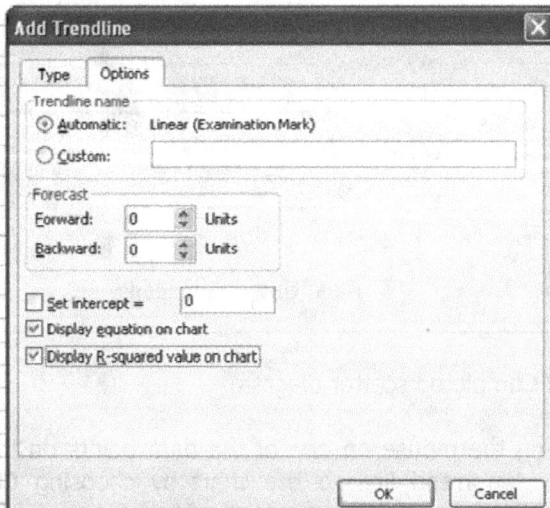

Figure 1.27: Trendline annotation options

Click **OK** to complete the task. The chart now displays the equation for the regression line and R-squared value, as shown in Figure 1.28:

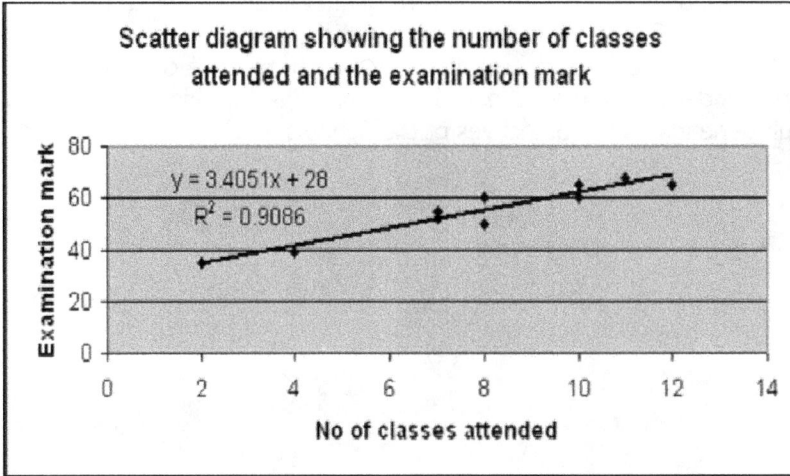

Figure 1.28: Least squared regression line with equation and R^2

The R^2 is often referred to as the coefficient of determination and provides a measure of how well the trend line does at predicting the value of Y for a given X. The R^2 value is always between 0 and 1 and values close to 1 indicate good linear reliability[10]. Note that the value of R^2 above is 0.9086 and this shows a strong positive linear association.

Selecting other trend line options will produce different equations and different R^2 values.

As can be seen from the graph wizard there are many different types of graphs available in Excel and this short introduction is provided to get novices started.

In reporting research findings it is common to use only one type of graph for each set of results. Thus the researcher needs to be aware of which graph type his/her audience will find the most insightful. Of course different types of graphs are frequently used within the one report to show different sets of data.

---

[10] Linear regression is addressed in detail in Part 3 of this book.

1.8 A frequency table

Another descriptive statistical technique is to create a data frequency table which represents the number of times each score for a particular question is given. In Figure 1.29 a frequency table has been created for the last question in the questionnaire which relates to the scores given for the overall performance of the Schools. From this it can be seen that 21 respondents rate the Schools 5 or more. Whether this is a satisfactory result depends on the objectives of the Schools.

	Q	R	S
2	Question 12		
3	O'all Rating		
4	Scores	Frequencies	
5	3	4	
6	4	5	
7	5	5	
8	6	6	
9	7	7	
10	8	3	
11		30	
12			
13			

Figure 1.29: A frequency table using the data in the Overall rating column

In Excel the =frequency(data_array,bins_array) function allows tables as shown in Figure 1.29 to be quickly created.

Using the =frequency() function to produce the above table needs two pieces of data to begin with. The first is the location of all the responses to the question (question 12 above, M4:M33). The second is a list of bin numbers showing the intervals required in the table, Q5:Q10 in Figure 1.29. =frequency() is an array function which means that it is entered in a different way to other functions. The range into which the function is required is first selected (R5:R10). While keeping these cells covered by the extended cursor the following can then be typed into R5.

=frequency(M4:M33,Q5:Q10)

To complete the formula hold down the **<CTRL>** and **<Shift>** keys and then press **Enter**.

As well as knowing the mean or average value of the data it can be useful to know how widely spread the data is and there are a number of different ways of measuring this spread. One approach is to find the largest score for each question and to then subtract the lowest score for each question. The difference between the maximum and the minimum scores is referred to as the range. The Excel functions which are required for this are =Max() and =Min().

	A	Q-01	Q-02	Q-03	Q-04	Q-05	Q-06	Q-07	Q-08	Q-09	Q-10	Q-11	Q-12	School	O'all Rating
61															
62	Maximum	8	9	9	7	8	9	9	9	8	8	9	9		8
63	Minimum	1	1	1	1	2	1	1	2	1	1	1	5		3
64	Range	7	8	8	6	6	8	8	7	7	7	8	4		5
65															

Figure 1.30: The calculation of the Range for the scores for each question.

Looking at Figure 1.30 the following formulae have been entered into cells B62, B63 and B64 respectively. Each formula has then been copied into the range C62:M64 and O62:O64.

=max(B4:B33)
=min(B4:B33)
=B62-B63

Note that a range value of 4 indicates a greater degree of consensus among the informants for question 12 than any other question. There is the same degree of spread (in terms of the range) in respect of the answers to questions 2, 3, 6, 7 and 11 as there is questions 1, 8, 9 and 10 and questions 4 and 5.

This is a first look at the simplest way of assessing the spread of data. More sophisticated and powerful approaches to measuring the spread of data within a sample will be discussed in the next section of this book.

1.9 Standard Deviation and Standard Error

In addition to the mean (a measure of central tendency) it is also useful to consider the standard deviation and the standard error which are both measures of dispersion or spread[11]. The standard deviation is a measure of how dispersed the data is about the mean. The standard error is also a measure of the dispersion. In the case of the standard error the dispersion relates to sample means drawn from the population and this is useful when undertaking hypothesis testing as described in the next Part of this book.

---

[11] Formal definitions of standard deviation and standard error may be found in most statistical texts or on the web.

The formula for the standard deviation[12] that is entered into cell B36 below is:

=stdev(B4:B33)

And the formula for the standard error is the standard deviation of the sample divided by the square root of the sample size. The =count() function has been used in row 37 to provide the data required in the formula below (=count(B4:B33)), and the formula for the standard error in cell B38 is:

=B36/B37^0.5

The results of these functions are shown in Figure 1.31.

	A	B	C	D	E	F	G	H	I	J	K	L	M	N	O	P
34																
35	Mean score	3.47	2.87	5.37	3.48	4.30	3.47	4.67	5.70	4.80	5.61	4.93	8.60		5.53	
36	Standard Deviation	2.05	2.05	2.34	1.79	1.58	2.79	2.34	2.79	2.28	1.97	2.78	1.22		1.59	
37	Count	30	30	30	30	30	30	30	30	30	30	30	30		30	
38	Standard Error	0.37	0.37	0.43	0.33	0.29	0.51	0.43	0.51	0.42	0.36	0.51	0.22		0.29	
39																

Figure 1.31: The mean, standard deviation and standard error

1.10 Other measures of spread

Besides the standard deviation there are other approaches to understanding the spread within a data set which include quartiles.

The mid-point value for the answers to each question is the median value and can be calculated using the median function as follows in cell B40.

=median(B4:B33)

A measure of spread associated with the median is the quartile deviation, or inter-quartile range. The first or lower quartile value is the data point with 25% of the data below it and the third or upper quartile value is the value with 75% of the data below it (the second quartile is, in fact, the median). These points in data distributions are shown in Figure 1.32 below.

---

[12] Note that the square of the standard deviation is called the variance and this function will be used later in this book.

1.11 Standard Deviation and Standard Error

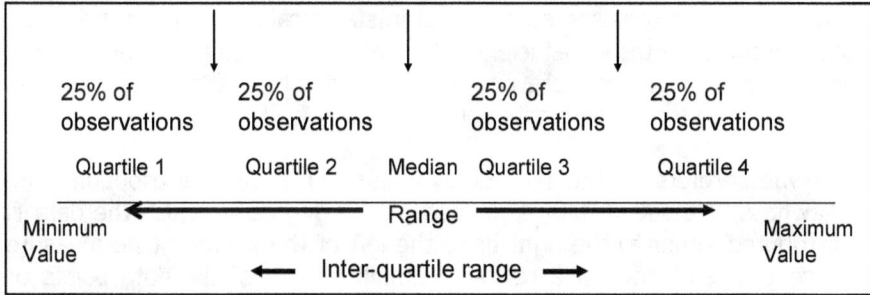

Figure 1.32: Maximum, minimum, range, quartiles and inter-quartile range.

Returning to the spreadsheet the first and third quartiles can be calculated in Excel using the Quartile function as follows:

=quartile(B4:B33,1) ... where 1 represents the 1st quartile value.

=quartile(B4:B33,3) ... where 3 represents the 3rd quartile value

The inter-quartile range is calculated as the range of the middle 50% of the data or in the example B42-B41.

Figure 1.33 shows the results

	A	B	C	D	E	F	G	H	I	J	K	L	M	N	O	P
39																
40	Median	3	2	6	3	5	2	5	7	5	6	6	9		6	
41	Ist Quartile	2	2	3	2	3	1	3	3	3	4	2	9		4	
42	3rd Quartile	5	3	8	4	5	6	7	8	7	7	8	9		7	
43	Inter-Quartile Range	3	1	5	2	2	5	4	5	4	3	6	0		3	
44																

Figure 1.33: Calculation of the other measures of spread including the inter-quartile range

The concept of the semi inter-quartile range[13] is also used and is the inter-quartile range divided by two.

If percentiles are required then use the =percentile() function which operates in the same way as the quartile function.

---

[13] The semi inter-quartile range which is based on ranks rather than absolute values may be seen as an alternative to the standard deviation.

1.12 Measures of shape

Two other measures sometimes used in statistical analysis are the skewness and the kurtosis coefficients of a data set. These are referred to as measures of shape and are typically used to compare the observed distribution with a normal distribution.

Skewness refers to the lack of symmetry in a data distribution. The skewness of a set of data is defined as the degree to which the data is distributed either to the right or to the left of the average (the measure of central tendency). If a relatively small number of the data points or observations tend to the left (toward lower values) the distribution is said to be skewed left or left-skewed or negatively skewed (i.e. the long tail to the left); and distributions with observations reaching far out to the right (toward higher values) are said to be skewed right or right-skewed or positively skewed. If the long tail is to the left then the median will be greater than the mean and if the long tail stretches to the right then the mean will be greater than the median. If the distribution is symmetrical then the mean and the median will have the same value. The calculation of the skewness coefficient is a function of the difference between the mean and the median.

In Excel the skewness of the data set produced by answering question No 1 in the questionnaire is calculated in cell B45 as follows:

=skew(B4:B33)

The formula can be copied across for the other questions.

Looking at the results in Figure 1.35 it can be seen that the skewness for each question does vary. Skewness should be between -1 and +1 otherwise the data is not symmetric. The question is what value of skewness indicates non-symmetry in the distribution. The above heuristic has become an acceptable rule of thumb, although there are more formal tests available.

Diagram	Types
	Positive Skewness

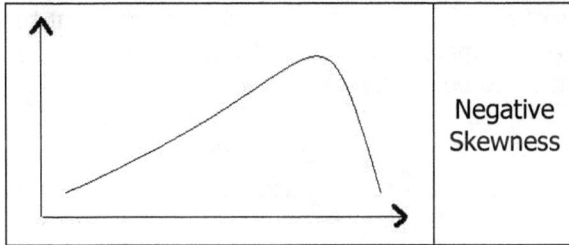

Figure 1.34: Positive and negative skewness

Figure 1.34 shows an example of a distribution with a positive skewness and then an example of a distribution with a negative skewness.

Kurtosis is a measure of the peakedness of the distribution of a data set. Some data sets display a high degree of peakedness while others can be distinctly flat in nature. The kurtosis of this data set is calculated in cell B46 as follows:

=kurt(B4:B33)

And this formula is copied to the range C46:M46. In terms of the accepted heuristic for kurtosis the value of this statistic should be between -1 and +1[14]. If it is greater than 1, it is more peaked than a normal distribution (this means that there are less observations in the tails – fat tailed) and if it is less than -1 it is less peaked than a normal distribution (this means that there are more observations in the tails). Similarly to skewness there are more formal tests available for this statistic.

Looking at the results it can be seen that there is little variation in the kurtosis, with the exception of two data points which relate to questions 2 (see column C) and question 12 (see column M). This analysis suggests that these two issues could be looked at more closely to see if there is any reason why they differ from the others.

	A	B	C	D	E	F	G	H	I	J	K	L	M	N	O	
44																
45	Skewness	0.50	1.666	-0.06	0.43	0.311	0.81	0.069	-0.29	-0.18	-0.44	0.032	-2.81		-0.15	
46	Kurtosis	-0.81	2.503	-1.25	-0.86	-0.33	-0.72	-0.78	-1.74	-0.93	-0.69	-1.33	6.308		-1.11	
47																
48	Skewness - should be between -1 and +1 otherwise not symetric															
49	Kurtosis - should be between -1 and +1 otherwise if >1 more peaked than the normal and if < -1 less peaked															

Figure 1.35: Calculation of the skewness and the kurtosis

---

[14] The kurtosis value in Excel is computer relative to the kurtosis for the normal distribution. The true kurtosis for a normally distributed variable is 3.

The measures of skewness and the kurtosis are important to know if it is intended to perform parametric tests of hypothesis with the data and if modelling is going to be used.

In Figure 1.36 both positive and negative Kurtosis are shown.

Diagram	Types
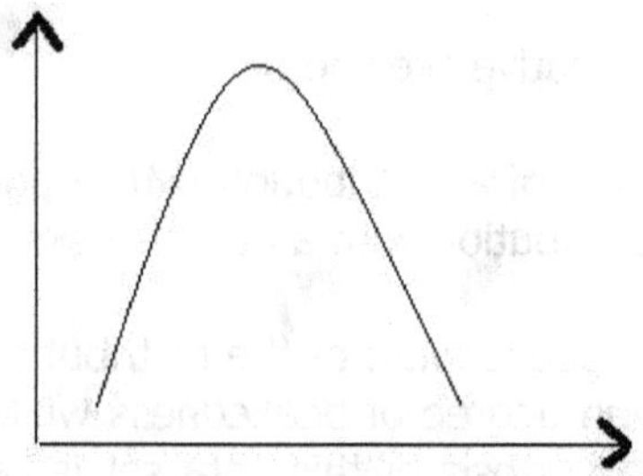	Positive Kurtosis
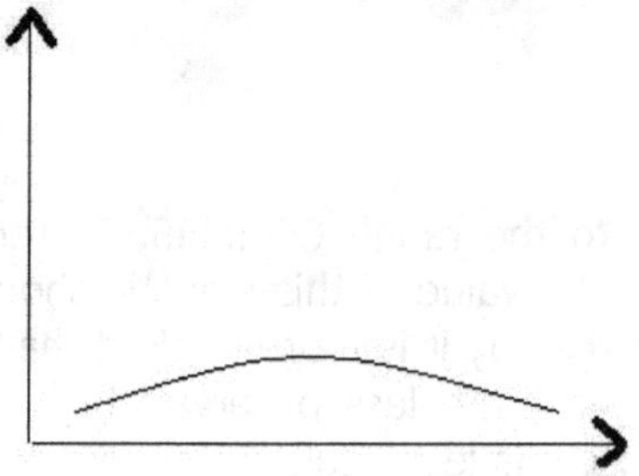	Negative Kurtosis

Figure 1.36: Positive and negative kurtosis

1.13 Outliers

An outlier is an observation or data point that is numerically distant from the rest of the data set. Calculations performed on data sets that include outliers can be misleading. There is a heuristic for identifying outliers. *A data point may be considered to be an outlier if the data point is more than one and a half times the inter-quartile range above the upper quartile, and likewise if the data point is more than one and a half times the inter-quartile range below the lower quartile*[15].

Figure 1.37 shows how outliers would look on a scatter diagram.

---

[15] Sometimes viewing a data point as an outlier may be an important issue. In quality control systems any data point more than two standard deviations from the target value may cause concern and there may be a need for closer consideration. Similarly with regards to medical systems the rules for outliers may be stricter.

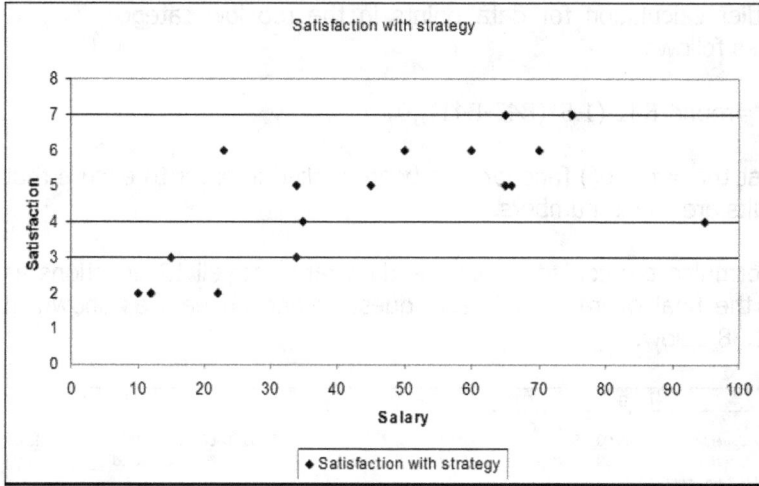

Figure 1.37: The data point on the right hand side may be an outlier

Besides the one relatively obvious outlier in Figure 1.37 there may be another outlier in the scatter diagram above.

Outliers always present a challenge to data analysis. In some cases the outlier represents an error in the measurement of the phenomenon being studied or an error in the transcription of the data. If this is the case then an outlier may be amended or removed from the data set.

Sometimes an outlier is not an error, but rather represents a genuine data point. In this case it should be explained and a decision made as to how to handle the outlier. Sometimes the outlier is retained without change in the data set and some times this data point is adjusted or amended or removed[16].

In this example the outlier calculation for data points in the too high category is performed as follows:

=round(B42+(1.5*(B42-B41)),0)

---

[16] The issue with regards to retaining or removing an outlier is a function of the purpose of the analysis. If the inclusion of the outlier has a direct influence on a decision which should be based on say, average income, and there is/are one or a few individuals who are earning 5 or 10 times the average for the area, then it would probably be perfectly proper to re-move the outlier/s.

The outlier calculation for data points in the too low category is performed as follows:

=round(B41-(1.5*(B42-B41)),0)

Note that the =round() function has been applied in order to ensure that the results are whole numbers.

These formulae are copied across the data range for all 12 questions as well as the final overall satisfaction question and appears as shown in Figure 1.38 below.

A	B	C	D	E	F	G	H	I	J	K	L	M	N	O
50														
51 Outliers - Upper limit	10.00	5.00	15.00	7.00	8.00	12.00	12.00	16.00	12.00	11.00	16.00	9.00		12.00
52 Outliers - Lower limit	-3.00	1.00	-4.00	-1.00	0.00	-6.00	-3.00	-5.00	-2.00	0.00	-7.00	9.00		-1.00
53 Potential outliers upper		*												
54 Potential outliers lower												*		
55														
56	1	1	1	1	2	1	1	2	1	1	1	5		3
57 Max	8	9	9	7	8	9	9	8	8	9	9	9		8
58 Range	7	8	8	6	6	8	8	7	7	7	8	4		5
59														

Figure 1.38: Upper and lower limits and outliers

The upper limit outlier now needs to be compared to the data to see if any of the data points exceed the upper limit outlier. To do this the Excel =max() function has been used in cell B57 as follows:

=max(B4:B33)

(and the formula is copied across for the remaining questions)

Then a test can be performed using the Excel =if() function in cell B53.

=if(B57>B51,"*","")

And an asterisk will be placed into the columns showing a potential outlier at the upper limit.

A similar process is required to ascertain potential outliers at the lower limit, but this time the Excel =min() function is required in cell B56 as follows

=min(B4:B33)

(and the formula is copied across for the remaining questions)

And the test in cell B54 will be:

=if(B56<B52,"*","")

From Figure 1.38 it can be seen that there is a potential for two outliers. The upper limit outlier for question two is 5, and on examination of the data in column C it can be seen that there are data points in excess of 5. Similarly the lower limit outlier for question twelve is 9 and there are data points in column M that are less than 9. As mentioned above the analyst now needs to examine the original questionnaires to see if an error has been made and if so the data point needs to be corrected. If an error has not been made then a decision needs to be taken as to whether the outlier is in fact a representative of the population being studied. If it is believed that the outlier is not, it would have to be adjusted or rejected.

1.14 Grouping variables to form constructs or themes

In this example there are 12 different variables which have been scored by the informants. Although each of these variables reflect a different aspect (indicator or manifest variable) of the student experience it is also possible to say that some of the variables might usefully be grouped to form a supra-variable or construct[17]. A construct is a complex issue or concept which is "constructed" or developed or assembled by studying a number of simpler issues or concepts or variables. Constructs are difficult to evaluate on their own and thus need to be thought about or reviewed through the variables or issues of which they are composed. Constructs are common in social science research as many interesting issues cannot be evaluated directly and the research thus needs to work with the components of these issues. In this example the overall student experience may be considered to consist of three different constructs[18] which are:-

1. The classroom experience;
2. Students' support facilities and;
3. The student living experience[19].

Looking at the 12 variables closely we might like to group them as follows:

---

[17] Another way of thinking about a supra-variable or a construct is a theme and this is very useful as it can help focus the researcher's attention onto a smaller number of important issues.

[18] It is sometimes argued that a more objective way of establishing constructs is to use a multivariate technique called Factor Analysis.

[19] A construct should consist of at least three variables and no more than 7.

The classroom experience comprises issues related to variables 1, 3, 4 and 7.

The student support facilities comprise issues related to variables 2, 5,9,10 and 11.

The student living experience comprises issues related to variables 6, 8 and 12.

Using this approach it may now be said that the student experience is a function of three broad based constructs and it is now possible to assess the relative perceptions of these constructs. To do this we are going to add and average the scores from the questionnaire for the variables concerned. This additive approach is being taken to assess the scores of the constructs. Note there are other ways in which the variables could have been combined and also that the different variables could have been weighted when they are combined. Such methods involve employing some weighting scheme when combining the items.

By grouping the variables as described above and calculating averages as shown in Figure 1.39 we can begin to understand what the informants in the sample thought about these larger issues.

For this part of the book you may wish to use a new worksheet or even a new File in Excel. In doing this you will need to copy the data carefully from the original spreadsheet. If your spreadsheet is now complicated with functions and graphs you can download the original clean data from the web at URL http://www.academic-publishing.org/intro_excel.htm.

	A	B	C	D	E	F	C
1	**Construct Analysis**						
2							
3	**No**	**Construct Name**					
4	1	Classroom experien	1, 3, 4, 7				
5	2	Support facilities	2, 5, 9, 10, 11				
6	3	The Student Living	6, 8, 12				
7							
8							
9	**Construct 1 - The classroom experience**						
10	**C - 01**	**Q - 01**	**Q - 03**	**Q - 04**	**Q - 07**	**C - 01**	
11		3	2	7	5	4.25	
12		1	1	6	1	2.25	
13		2	2	4	3	2.75	
14		8	6	6	7	6.75	
15		1	3	2	9	3.75	
16		3	3	2	8	4.00	
17		6	5	6	1	4.50	
18		2	5	4	1	3.00	
19		7	7	6	1	5.25	
20		1	3	2	9	3.75	
21		3	9	1	6	4.75	
22		4	3	4	7	4.50	
23		1	4	2	4	2.75	
24		3	5	3	5	4.00	
25		4	8	4	3	4.75	
26		5	7	3	7	5.50	
27		6	8	1	5	5.00	
28		2	5	3	5	3.75	
29		6	8	6	3	5.75	
30		2	7	3	2	3.50	
31		1	3	2	3	2.25	
32		2	9	1	6	4.50	
33		4	3	4	7	4.50	
34		1	4	2	4	2.75	
35		3	5	3	5	4.00	
36		4	8	4	3	4.75	
37		5	7	3	7	5.50	
38		6	8	1	5	5.00	
39		2	5	3	5	3.75	
40		6	8	6	3	5.75	

Figure 1.39: The calculation of construct No 1 – The Classroom Experience[20].

---

[20] Note that each variable is given equal weight in this construct.

	H	I	J	K	L	M	N	C
8								
9	**Construct 2 - Students' Support Facilities**							
10	C - 02	Q - 02	Q - 05	Q - 09	Q - 10	Q - 11	C - 02	
11		5	8	6	7	6	6.40	
12		6	7	8	6	2	5.80	
13		2	4	5	7	5	4.60	
14		8	7	3	6	3	5.40	
15		1	3	7	1	7	3.80	
16		3	5	4	4	2	3.60	
17		6	5	4	8	4	5.40	
18		4	3	6	4	6	4.60	
19		9	5	5	3	5	5.40	
20		2	5	8	8	8	6.20	
21		1	5	3	3	2	2.80	
22		1	5	1	8	1	3.20	
23		3	3	6	6	6	4.80	
24		1	3	4	7	9	4.80	
25		2	2	8	5	8	5.00	
26		3	5	5	5	5	4.60	
27		3	2	1	8	1	3.00	
28		2	5	7	6	9	5.80	
29		2	3	4	3	4	3.20	
30		1	6	2	4	2	3.00	
31		2	5	8	8	8	6.20	
32		2	5	3	3	2	3.00	
33		1	5	1	8	1	3.20	
34		3	3	6	6	6	4.80	
35		1	3	4	7	9	4.80	
36		2	2	8	5	8	5.00	
37		3	5	5	5	5	4.60	
38		3	2	1	8	1	3.00	
39		2	5	7	6	9	5.80	
40		2	3	4	3	4	3.20	
41	Average of the averages						4.50	
42								

Figure 1.40: The calculation of construct No 2 – Students' Support Facilities

	P	Q	R	S	T	U	V
8							
9	Construct 3 - The Student Living Experience						
10	C- 03	Q - 06	Q - 08	C - 12	C- 03		
11		9	2	9	6.67		
12		8	3	9	6.67		
13		4	3	9	5.33		
14		9	7	9	8.33		
15		1	4	9	4.67		
16		1	2	9	4.00		
17		6	9	9	8.00		
18		2	6	9	5.67		
19		4	9	9	7.33		
20		8	8	9	8.33		
21		6	8	5	6.33		
22		4	2	5	3.67		
23		1	3	5	3.00		
24		1	9	9	6.33		
25		4	8	9	7.00		
26		1	2	9	4.00		
27		1	6	9	5.33		
28		1	8	9	6.00		
29		2	8	9	6.33		
30		2	2	9	4.33		
31		8	8	9	8.33		
32		6	8	9	7.67		
33		4	2	9	5.00		
34		1	3	9	4.33		
35		1	9	9	6.33		
36		4	8	9	7.00		
37		1	2	9	4.00		
38		1	6	9	5.33		
39		1	8	9	6.00		
40		2	8	9	6.33		
41	Average of the averages			5.92			

Figure 1.41: The calculation of construct No 3 – The Student Living Experience

Looking at the 3 averages calculated it can be seen that the student living experience obtained the highest average score of 5.92. The students' support facilities received the second highest of 4.50 and the class room experience received the third highest average of 4.24.

However there is much more to be said about this analysis which will be addressed later in the book.

1.15 Exploring the construct

When a construct is created conceptually and visually as has been done above it is important to perform a check to see if suitable variables have been chosen to be grouped together to form the construct. The process of this checking requires correlation coefficients to be calculated between each of the variables chosen. A correlation coefficient concerns the relationship between two different variables and is sometimes referred to as a bivariate relationship. A correlation coefficient indicates the strength and direction of the relationship between the variables. Correlation coefficients have values between 1 and − 1. A correlation coefficient of 1 or a value close to 1 indicates a strong positive relationship between the variables concerned. A positive relationship means that as the value of one of the variables increases so the value of the other one increases as well. An example of this would be age and height and weight in primary school boys. A correlation of 0 (zero) means that there is no relationship between the variables and as one variable changes the other variable changes randomly, if at all. A correlation coefficient of -1 (a negative correlation) or a number close to -1 indicates that as the one variable increases the other variable decreases. An example of a negative correlation is or might be the number of pints of beer drunk and the speed at which the drinkers can perform difficult long division sums!

If the correct variables have been grouped together to form a construct then the correlation coefficients between the chosen variables should be positive and their value should be at least 0.3[21].

The next step is to formulate a test to establish the suitability of grouping the variables or indicators in order to create the construct. For the above example it is necessary to calculate the inter item correlations (the word inter item correlations is used as these variables have been grouped to form a construct) between the indicators or manifest variables. For construct 1 this means the calculation of 6 correlation coefficients which are Q1 to Q3, Q1 to Q4, Q1 to Q7, Q3 to Q4, Q3 to Q7 and Q4 to Q7. This is shown on Figure 1.42.

1.16 Inter item correlation coefficients

The term inter item correlation refers to establishing if there is an association between the variables used in the construct. For a construct to be

---

[21] Once again this is simply a heuristic and there are more formal ways of handling this.

useful it is necessary that there should be a material level of correlations between the component parts, i.e. the variables of the construct. Inter item correlation coefficients are calculated in the same way as correlation coefficients.

The Excel formulae for the inter item correlations required here are in Figure 1.42 as follows:

=correl(B11:B40,C11:C40)

and

=correl(B11:B40,D11:D40)

and

=correl(B11:B40,E11:E40)

and

=correl(C11:C40,D11:D40)

and

=correl(C11:C40,E11:E40)

and

=correl(D11:D40,E11:E40)

	A	B	C	D	E	F	G	H	I
42	Inter item correlation Coefficients - Construct 1								
43	Q1 to Q3		0.54						
44	Q1 to Q4		0.41						
45	Q1 to Q7		-0.07						
46	Q3 to Q4		-0.08						
47	Q3 to Q7		-0.25						
48	Q4 to Q7		-0.45						

Figure 1.42: Testing the suitability of Construct No 1

The rule of thumb regarding the indicator or manifest variables being appropriate is that all the correlations should be positive. Furthermore they should not be less than 0.3[22]. From the above analysis it may be seen that the indicator or manifest variables used in Construct 1 cannot be regarded as suitable. Although two of the correlations of the indicator or manifest variables are greater then 0.3 the principal objection raised by this analysis is that 4 of the inter item correlations are negative[23].

Having obtained this result it might be possible to change or exchange some of the indicators or manifest variables in the construct and then to

---

[22] A more formal test requires the use of the Cronbach's Alpha which will be addressed later.
[23] Note it is always a necessary but not a sufficient condition that all the indicator variables of the construct have positive correlation with each other.

re-calculate the correlation coefficients to see if the new construct complies with the requirements.

In Construct 2 the indicator or manifest variables used are Q2, Q5, Q9, Q10, Q11 and the inter item correlations are all too small and three of them are negative.

The Excel formulae for the inter item correlations in Figure 1.43 are:

=correl(J11:I40,J11:J40)

and

=correl(J11:J40,K11:K40)

and

=correl(J11:I40,L11:L40)

and

=correl(J11:I40,M11:M40)

and

etc

	A	B	C	D	E	F	G	H	I
52	Inter item correlation Coefficients - Construct 2								
53	Q2 to Q5		0.41						
54	Q2 to Q9		0.09						
55	Q2 to Q10		0.00						
56	Q2 to Q11		-0.16						
57	Q5 to Q9		0.02						
58	Q5 to Q10		0.08						
59	Q5 to Q11		-0.22						
60	Q9 to Q10		-0.13						
61	Q9 to Q11		0.75						
62	Q10 to Q11		0.03						

Figure 1.43: Testing the suitability of Construct No 2

In this example both Construct No 1 and Construct No 2 failed the correlations test. Construct No 3 could be tested in the same way as the other two.

The result of this is that it would not be regarded as appropriate to group these two sets of indicators or manifest variables. It is of course possible that these variables might be effectively grouped with other variables in the questionnaire to form supra-variables or constructs and the analyst may wish to explore different combinations. It may also be appropriate to leave the development of constructs until a more advanced technique called Factor Analysis[24] is performed on the data.

1.17 Examining the Numbers

Before concluding this section an analyst may wish to know how the ratings for the School of Business (coded in the spreadsheet as 1) compare to the ratings for the School of Accounting (coded in the spreadsheet as 2). There are several ways of achieving this. The approach used here is to first of all sort the data in the column containing the code for the school.

The procedure for sorting in ascending order in Excel is to first highlight the data to be sorted with the cursor and then chose **Data, Sort, Ascending**. It is important to select the full data range A101:O131 before selecting Data Sort as if only column N were selected the numbers would no longer relate to the rest of the data.

Figure 1.44 shows the data after it is sorted ascending on column N.

A	B	C	D	E	F	G	H	I	J	K	L	M	N	O
A primary statistical overview --------------- adjusted with corrections														
100 Scores given to the individual questions ···>														
101	Q-01	Q-02	Q-03	Q-04	Q-05	Q-06	Q-07	Q-08	Q-09	Q-10	Q-11	Q-12	School	O'all Rating
102 Respondent 2	1	6	1	6	7	8	1	3	8	6	2	9	1	6
103 Respondent 4	8	8	6	6	7	9	7	7	3	6	3	9	1	6
104 Respondent 5	1	1	3	2	3	1	9	4	7	1	7	9	1	3
105 Respondent 6	3	3	3	2	5	1	8	2	4	4	2	9	1	4
106 Respondent 7	6	6	5	6	5	5	1	9	4	0	4	9	1	4
107 Respondent 9	7	9	7	6	5	4	1	9	5	3	5	9	1	8
108 Respondent 11	3	1	9	1	5	6	8	8	3	3	2	5	1	3
109 Respondent 12	4	1	3	4	4	4	7	2	1	8	1	5	1	7
110 Respondent 13	1	3	4	2	3	1	4	3	6	6	6	5	1	7
111 Respondent 17	6	3	8	1	2	1	5	6	1	8	1	9	1	6
112 Respondent 20	2	1	7	3	6	2	2	2	2	4	2	9	1	5
113 Respondent 22	2	2	9	1	5	6	8	9	3	3	2	9	1	4
114 Respondent 23	4	1	3	4	5	4	7	2	1	0	1	9	1	7
115 Respondent 24	1	3	4	2	3	1	4	3	6	6	6	9	1	7
116 Respondent 28	6	3	8	1	2	1	5	6	1	8	1	9	1	6
117 Respondent 1	3	5	7	7	8	9	5	7	6	7	5	9	2	6
118 Respondent 3	2	2	2	4	4	4	3	3	5	7	6	9	2	6
119 Respondent 8	2	4	5	4	3	2	1	6	6	4	6	9	2	5
120 Respondent 10	1	2	3	2	5	8	9	8	8	8	8	9	2	8
121 Respondent 14	3	1	5	3	3	1	5	9	4	7	8	9	2	4
122 Respondent 15	4	2	0	4	2	4	1	0	5	0	9	2	5	
123 Respondent 16	5	3	7	3	5	1	7	2	6	5	5	9	2	6
124 Respondent 18	2	2	5	3	5	1	5	8	7	6	9	9	2	3
125 Respondent 19	5	2	8	5	3	2	4	8	4	3	4	9	2	7
126 Respondent 21	1	2	3	2	5	8	3	8	8	8	8	9	2	8
127 Respondent 25	3	1	5	3	3	1	5	9	4	7	9	9	2	4
128 Respondent 26	4	2	8	4	2	4	3	8	8	5	8	9	2	5
129 Respondent 27	5	3	7	3	5	1	7	2	5	5	5	9	2	6
130 Respondent 29	7	7	5	3	5	1	5	8	7	5	9	9	2	3
131 Respondent 30	6	2	8	6	3	2	3	8	4	3	4	9	2	7
132														

Figure 1.44: Data sorted by School

---

[24] Factor Analysis is an advanced multivariate technique for which a specialized statistical package is required. The market leader is called SPSS. Factor analysis allows the researcher to group variables to create supra-variables which may be used in a way similar to the constructs described here.

Once the data is sorted then it is possible using a simple function to average the scores for the School of Business and the School of Accounting for comparative purposes.

This is shown in Figure 1.45.

	Q - 01	Q - 02	Q - 03	Q - 04	Q - 05	Q - 06	Q - 07	Q - 08	Q - 09	Q - 10	Q - 11	Q - 12	School	O'all Rating
99 *A primary statistical overview ---------------- adjusted with corrections*														
100														
101 *Scores given to the individual questions --->*														
102 Respondent 2	1	6	1	6	7	8	1	3	8	6	2	9	1	6
103 Respondent 4	8	8	6	6	7	9	7	7	3	6	3	9	1	6
104 Respondent 5	1	1	3	2	3	1	9	4	7	1	7	9	1	3
105 Respondent 6	3	3	3	2	5	1	8	2	4	4	2	9	1	4
106 Respondent 7	6	6	5	6	5	6	1	9	4	8	4	9	1	4
107 Respondent 9	7	9	7	6	5	4	1	9	5	3	5	9	1	8
108 Respondent 11	3	1	9	1	5	6	6	8	3	3	2	5	1	3
109 Respondent 12	4	1	3	4	5	4	7	2	1	8	1	5	1	7
110 Respondent 13	1	3	4	2	3	1	4	3	6	6	6	5	1	7
111 Respondent 17	6	3	8	1	2	1	5	6	1	8	1	9	1	6
112 Respondent 20	2	1	7	3	6	2	2	2	2	4	2	9	1	5
113 Respondent 22	2	2	9	1	5	6	6	8	3	3	2	9	1	4
114 Respondent 23	4	1	3	4	5	4	7	2	1	8	1	9	1	7
115 Respondent 24	1	3	4	2	3	1	4	3	6	6	6	9	1	7
116 Respondent 28	6	3	8	1	2	1	5	6	1	8	1	9	1	6
Average for Business														
117 School	3.67	3.40	5.33	3.13	4.53	3.67	4.87	4.93	3.67	5.47	3.00	8.20		5.53
118 Respondent 1	3	5	2	7	8	9	5	2	6	7	6	9	2	7
119 Respondent 3	2	2	2	4	4	4	3	3	5	7	5	9	2	5
120 Respondent 8	2	4	5	4	3	2	1	6	6	4	6	9	2	5
121 Respondent 10	1	2	3	2	5	8	9	8	8	8	8	9	2	8
122 Respondent 14	3	1	5	3	3	1	5	9	4	7	9	9	2	4
123 Respondent 15	4	2	8	4	2	4	3	8	8	5	8	9	2	5
124 Respondent 16	5	3	7	3	5	1	7	2	5	5	5	9	2	6
125 Respondent 18	2	2	5	3	5	1	5	8	7	6	9	9	2	3
126 Respondent 19	6	2	8	6	3	2	3	8	4	3	4	9	2	7
127 Respondent 21	1	2	3	2	5	8	3	8	8	8	8	9	2	8
128 Respondent 25	3	1	5	3	3	1	5	9	4	7	9	9	2	4
129 Respondent 26	4	2	8	4	2	4	3	8	8	5	8	9	2	5
130 Respondent 27	5	3	7	3	5	1	7	2	5	5	5	9	2	6
131 Respondent 29	2	2	5	3	5	1	5	8	7	6	9	9	2	3
132 Respondent 30	6	2	8	6	3	2	3	8	4	3	4	9	2	7
Average for School of														
133 Accounting	3.27	2.33	5.40	3.80	4.07	3.27	4.47	6.47	5.93	5.73	6.87	9.00		5.53
134														
B School less														
135 A School	0.40	1.07	-0.07	-0.67	0.47	0.40	0.40	-1.53	-2.27	-0.27	-3.87	-0.80		

Figure 1.45: Comparing the scores obtained for the Business School with the scores obtained for the School of Accounting.

Although the overall scores are the same there are a number of differences in Figure 1.45 which are worthy of comment.

One of the ways of considering the differences between these scores is to subtract one from the other. This will indicate the variables which were scored better or worse.

Row 135 in Figure 1.45 shows the Business School scores less the Accounting School scores.

It is then useful to display these as a line graph as is shown in Figure 1.46.

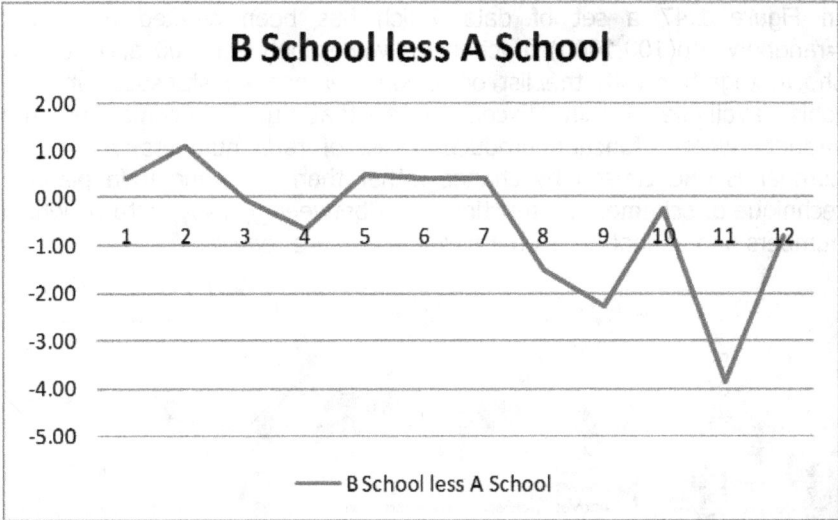

Figure 1.46: Graph of differences between School of Business scores less the School of Accounting scores

Figure 1.46 shows that on 5 issues the School of Business has outperformed the School of Accounting. This may be compared to the fact that the School of Accounting has outperformed the School of Business on 7 issues.

1.18 A quick set of summary statistics

In addition to the functions and commands which have been mentioned above, Excel has a short cut which allows a set of summary statistics to be quickly produced. This short cut requires the use of the **Tools - Data Analysis** command.

In order to illustrate the use of the summary statistics facility in Excel a new set of data has been used because the data in the original questionnaire has already been used for similar purposes. Also the new set of data has been produced using a new Excel function which readers may find interesting and useful. The new function is =randbetween(). The argument[25] for this function is the smallest number and the largest number required.

In Figure 1.47 a set of data which has been created using the =randbetween(100,1000) function for values between 100 and 1000 is shown together with the list of optional embedded statistical analysis tools available within Excel. Note that the outcome of the =randbetween() function produces a list of rand numbers. A random number is one chosen by chance rather than according to a planned technique or scheme. The function =randbetween() always returns whole numbers and cannot be used if non-integers are required.

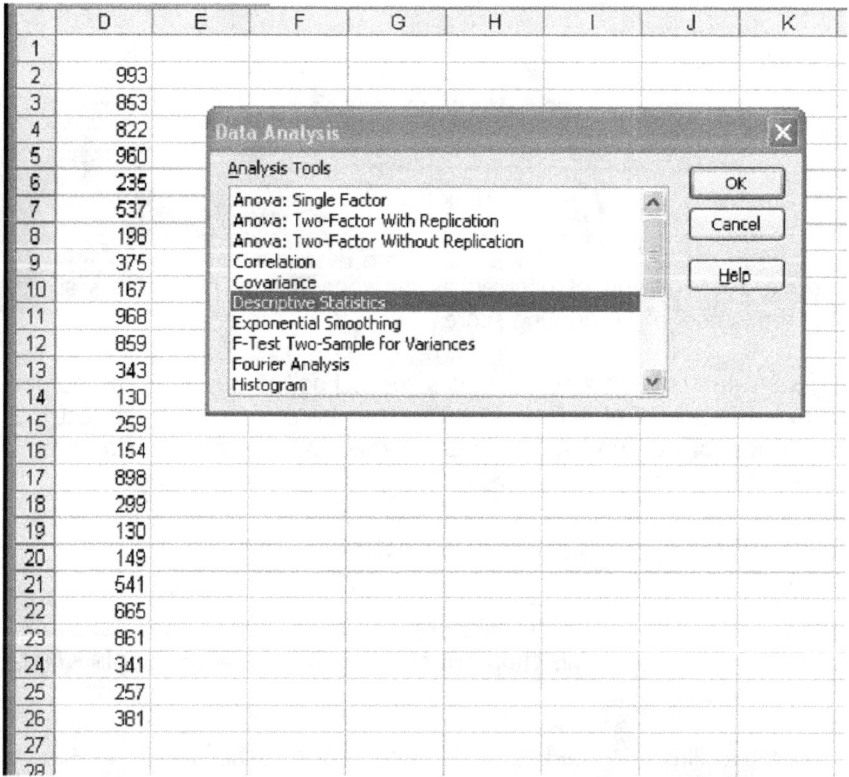

	D	E	F	G	H	I	J	K
1								
2	993							
3	853							
4	822							
5	960							
6	235							
7	537							
8	198							
9	375							
10	167							
11	968							
12	859							
13	343							
14	130							
15	259							
16	154							
17	898							
18	299							
19	130							
20	149							
21	541							
22	665							
23	861							
24	341							
25	257							
26	381							
27								
28								

Data Analysis

Analysis Tools

Anova: Single Factor
Anova: Two-Factor With Replication
Anova: Two-Factor Without Replication
Correlation
Covariance
Descriptive Statistics
Exponential Smoothing
F-Test Two-Sample for Variances
Fourier Analysis
Histogram

OK
Cancel
Help

Figure 1.47: Randomly created data and some of the options within the Data Analysis command.

---

[25] In Excel a function is said to have an argument which defines how the function will operate or/and on which cells it will perform its calculations. In technical terms this is called the syntax of the function.

Once the Descriptive Statistics option is chosen a report is placed on the spreadsheet at the cursor position as shown in Figure 1.48.

	D	E	F	G
1				
2	993			
3	853			
4	822		Column1	
5	960			
6	235		Mean	495
7	537		Standard Error	62.92196
8	198		Median	375
9	375		Mode	130
10	167		Standard Deviation	314.6098
11	968		Sample Variance	98979.33
12	859		Kurtosis	-1.52781
13	343		Skewness	0.402282
14	130		Range	863
15	259		Minimum	130
16	154		Maximum	993
17	898		Sum	12375
18	299		Count	25
19	130		Largest(1)	993
20	149		Smallest(1)	130
21	541		Confidence Level(95.0%)	129.8645
22	665			
23	861			
24	341			
25	257			
26	381			

Figure 1.48: Summary Descriptive statistics offered by Excel

Although the above approach may be useful and it certainly provides an instant result, it is a black box approach. This implies that the research may be overloaded with statistics which are unnecessary. Also it may not be clear to the researcher exactly how some of these statistics were actually calculated or what they mean.

1.19 A spreadsheet for quantitative analysis

A wide variety of different techniques have been described in this part of the book. Most of these activities, but perhaps not all of them, will be required in order to be able to write an insightful report on the data collected. Because many different types of data analysis are involved it is important to plan the use of the spreadsheet in advance. Excel allows the use of multiple worksheets within one file and time should be taken to decide which tasks should be performed in which worksheets.

Once this has been done then it is useful to conceptualize when the data and the calculations will be performed in the different worksheets. It is important to keep a separate note of these decisions in order to be able to easily find where in the spreadsheet different aspects of the analysis have been performed. A map of the File and each worksheet may be helpful when returning to do further work.

Always print out the completed data entry, calculations and graphs as you go along. Always make back up copies as you complete each separate phase of your analysis. These activities are sometimes referred to as housekeeping. Taking care with housekeeping will ensure that you maximize the effectiveness of the use of the spreadsheet.

1.20 Summary-Part 1

This section of the book has addressed concepts, techniques and issues relating to the use of descriptive statistics, which can be seen as the first step in coming to terms with the use of statistical techniques in research.

There is a wealth of descriptive statistical approaches available to the researcher through the use of a spreadsheet tool such as Excel. The above section has focused on a small number of Excel functions and commands to illustrate how they may be used to describe the phenomenon being studied. For researchers wishing to go further and deeper into the interpretation of a data set there are many other Excel functions to explore.

The worked examples have demonstrated that there is a pre-requisite of having a general skill of understanding data before using the Excel functions. It also shows that the results obtained by the Excel functions need to be carefully examined before any interpretations are made. In fact the greater skill required from an academic research point of view lies in the interpretation of the results obtained through the analysis.

Finally it is important to point out that dedicated statistical packages such as SPSS/SAS/Minitab provide much more statistical power than any spreadsheet. These software products will with a few points and clicks provide a full range of statistics required by the academic researcher. However newcomers to research may find the task of learning to understand statistics as well as a statistical package daunting. It is for this reason that this book, using a well known personal productivity tool, has been written.

Self test 1

No.	Question	Answer
1	What is a data set?	
2	What are the different types of data and why is it important to be aware of these?	
3	Distinguish between a population and a sample.	
4	What is a central tendency and describe how we calculate the three different statistics we use for central tendencies.	
5	How do changes in values of our data or the addition of a new large data point affect our different measures of central tendency?	
6	What do we mean by spread in the context of a data set?	
7	What are our main measures of spread?	
8	What is an interquartile range?	

No.	Question	Answer
9	What is an outlier and what is one rule of thumb for establishing whether a data point might be considered to be an outlier?	
10	What are measures of shape and why are they important?	
11	Distinguish between kurtosis and skewness	
12	What is a construct?	
13	How do you establish the suitability of a construct?	
14	What is the primary value of descriptive statistics?	

List of Excel Functions used in this Part of the book.

Function	Result
=round()	rounds a number to the specified number of decimal places.
=average()	calculates the arithmetic mean for the numbers in the argument.
=if()	delivers a specified value in the cell depending on the result of the test in the argument.
=max()	returns the maximum value in the argument.
=min()	returns the minimum value in the argument.
=stdev()	calculates the standard deviation of the values provided in the argument.
=count()	counts the number of cells that contain numbers, and counts numbers within the list of arguments.
=median()	returns the medium value of the data in the argument.
=mode()	returns the most frequently occurring value in the argument.
=quartile()	returns quartile values of a data set. .
=skew()	returns a value indicating the degree of skewness of a distribution.
=kurt()	returns a value indicating the degree of kurtosis of a distribution.
=correl()	calculates the correlation coefficient between two variables.
=frequency()	calculates how often values occur within a range of numbers.

Function	Result
=rand()	randomly selects and returns a number between 0 and 1.
=randbetween()	returns a number between the two values specified as top and bottom.

More details of these functions are provided in the Help command within the spreadsheet.

Assignment No 1

Using the data and the statistics calculated in the example of the School of Business and the School of Accounting write a report, not more than 1500 words long (4 to 5 pages), on the student attitudinal differences in the two different Schools. Please use graphs and data frequency tables which you may create from your data file.

Additional exercises – Part 1

All the data supplied below can be downloaded from the web at URL http://www.academic-publishing.org/intro_excel.htm. Each data set used in these exercises has been uploaded as a separate Excel file.

1. What are the first activities which the research analyst needs to undertake in order to ensure that the data analysis will be useful?

2. Using the data supplied below calculate some measures of central tendency and some measures of data dispersion.

83	55	47	81	65	87	14	89	60	20	94	27	39
27	92	21	11	31	2	61	7	20	3	30	46	95
29	56	31	3	86	36	63	54	86	2	5	4	77
28	3	94	39	97	40	28	56	41	2	67	55	71
78	20	86	62	83	59	77	12	99	73	57	80	20

3. Give examples where the different measures of central tendency are more effective than the others.

4. Using the data supplied below which shows the results of six informants to a ten question questionnaire, display the measures of central tendency as a line chart, a bar chart and as a histogram.

	Q1	Q2	Q3	Q4	Q5	Q6	Q7	Q8	Q9	Q10
Informant 1	3	4	6	3	3	5	7	7	3	3
Informant 2	6	7	5	5	5	5	2	5	4	2
Informant 3	8	5	5	4	7	6	4	3	6	6
Informant 4	5	6	9	9	8	9	8	6	7	7
Informant 5	8	3	9	1	5	7	1	2	3	9
Informant 6	5	4	4	5	7	6	7	6	6	4

5. Using the data supplied below calculate the median and the quartiles. Using these statistics comment on the likelihood of there being any outliers in the data.

27	62	25	36	63	66	26	42	70	53	73	25
36	70	57	41	48	25	28	75	75	33	31	51
51	3	58	71	49	71	46	50	48	54	70	29
39	26	60	28	54	62	75	29	48	74	57	51
51	51	72	69	52	56	48	49	51	45	62	45
47	35	34	68	58	72	56	25	57	72	44	45
36	28	65	39	46	62	59	44	75	55	66	25
36	70	35	44	69	70	29	67	50	75	99	44
47	31	36	40	72	35	64	43	42	62	56	59

6. If you believe that there is an outlier in this data set (in Question 5) remove it and recalculate the statistics and explain the differences which you observe.

7. Calculate the kurtosis and the skewness coefficients of the data supplied below. Explain what these mean and how they may be used in research.

59	53	58	54	54	52	54	60	57	55	60	60
60	53	53	53	55	58	50	55	56	58	52	51
50	56	57	59	60	57	59	54	54	59	58	59
58	50	53	54	59	53	54	51	56	55	52	53

8. The answers to three questions from a questionnaire are supplied below. Combine these three questions into one construct. Using an appropriate statistical test the construct to see if it is likely to be valid.

	Q1	Q2	Q3
Informant 1	3	4	6
Informant 2	6	7	5
Informant 3	8	5	5
Informant 4	5	6	9
Informant 5	8	4	9
Informant 6	5	4	6
Informant 7	8	4	8
Informant 8	3	7	9
Informant 9	5	7	9
Informant 10	8	7	9
Informant 11	3	5	8
Informant 12	5	4	7

9. What are the key characteristics which make data useful to a researcher?

10. Explain the reasons why a data trail, version control and backup copies are important.

Part 2

Data Frequency Tables, Distributions, Estimation, and Hypothesis Testing

The challenge of the language of statistics

There is nothing particularly difficult or mysterious about statistics and its use. This is especially true if the learner takes one step at a time and makes sure that he or she has a good understanding of a topic before going on to the next one. It is important to note that there are few people who will fully understand the implications of statistical language and the concepts **the first time they hear them**. However understanding grows with exposure and as learners struggle with this language so their ability to use statistics in research will grow and develop. It is important to persevere at this and not be panicked by the novelty of the subject.

There are many new words and phrases to learn and each of these have specific meanings. Often the words sound familiar and sometimes the colloquial meaning of these words is not exactly the same when they are used in the context of statistics. Knowing the meaning of the words is the first step in learning how to use the concepts of statistics.

Because this is an introductory book we have used a set of Z-tables and t–tables in this Part to introduce hypothesis testing. Using Excel will remove the need for tables but looking up the values in this old way does give the reader a feel for where the numbers Excel generates come from. The tables are based on formulae which represent the probability distributions and these formulae are not provided in the book as they can distract readers who only want to know how to use these techniques.

Appropriate tables are supplied in the Appendices.

The material presented in this Part 2 of the book assumes that the reader is familiar with topics discussed in Part 1.

Mark Twain is reputed to have asserted that *"He uses statistics like a drunk uses a lamppost: for support rather than illumination."* Clearly this is not a recommended way of making use of these powerful techniques.

Glossary of Terms

1-tailed test	A test in which the alternative hypothesis is directional e.g. $\mu > 3.47$ (the critical region is in the right hand tail of the distribution) or $\mu < 3.47$ (the critical region is in the left hand tail of the distribution).
2-tailed test	A test in which the alternative hypothesis is non-directional e.g. $\mu \neq 3.47$ (the critical region includes both the right hand tail of the left hand tail of the distribution).
Bell shaped curve	One of the descriptors of a normal distribution. The bell shaped curve has a unique maximum value and is symmetrical around the mean of the distribution.
Confidence interval	The range within which the true value of a parameter lies with a specified level of confidence.
Critical region	Critical region is the set of values of the test statistic for which we reject the Null Hypothesis.
Data frequency table	This is an approach to summarizing data so that patterns within the data may be observed. Typically the number of times an observation occurs is counted and a table is created where observations are listed together with the number of their occurrences. For variables which have a large number of observations it is customary to group the outcomes into intervals and then to count the number of times an observation occurs within the interval.

Degrees of freedom (df or dof)	Estimates of statistical parameters can be based upon different quantities of data. The number of independent pieces of information or data points that go into the estimate of a parameter is called the degrees of freedom (df). Sometimes dof (degrees of freedom) is used in place of df. The letter v is often used to denote degrees of freedom. In calculating the t-statistics in this part of the book the df is equal to the sample size minus K, where k ≥ 1. The value of k depends on the test being performed.
Dependent samples	Dependent samples will usually consist of paired sets of observations such as may be found when a researcher tests and retests a situation before and after an intervention.
Estimation	There are point estimates and interval estimates. A *point estimate* occurs when a single point value is offered as the best estimate of a true value or parameter of the population from which the sample is drawn. An *interval estimate* provides a range within which a true value lies with a specified level of confidence.
Hypothesis	A hypothesis is a proposition, a suggestion or a claim about the consequence/s of a held belief. It is also sometimes more pejoratively spoken of as a guess.
Hypothesis testing	The process of setting up and testing a suggestion or claim in order to try to reject it and thus "accept" the alternative hypothesis.

H_0	Null Hypothesis which is to be tested with the view of being rejected (e.g. *The 'true' average* (μ) *is equal to 3.47*). The Null Hypothesis is usually stated as a claim that some proposition is true. The Null Hypothesis cannot ever be said to have been proved but if it is not rejected then it is "accepted" pro-tem. Formally the language is that the Null Hypothesis is either rejected or not rejected.
H_1	The Hypothesis that is accepted (i.e. the alternative hypothesis) if the Null Hypothesis is rejected. This is called the alternative hypothesis i.e. *The true average* (μ) *is not equal to 3.47.*
Independent samples	Samples are independent when the data elements in one of the samples does not influence the selection of the data elements for the other sample.
Inferential statistics	When statisticians use data from a sample — a subset of the population — to make statements about a population, they are performing statistical inference. This involves estimating values accompanied by a statement concerning the uncertainty associated with it.
Level of significance (denoted by α alpha)	The probability of erroneously rejecting the Null Hypothesis under the assumption that the Null Hypothesis is true e.g. if the significance is 5% this implies that the researcher is prepared to wrongly reject the Null Hypotheses in favour of the Alternative Hypothesis 5 in 100 times.
Linear interpolation	This is a method for the estimation of a value between 2 known points or coordinates. It assumes that there is a straight line relationship in the variable between the known points.
Normal distribution	The normal distribution is a continuous probability distribution which describes the theoretical probability of different observations occurring if a distribution is normal.

P-Value	Under the assumption that the Null Hypothesis is true, the P-value is the probability of erroneously rejecting the Null Hypothesis. The smaller the P-value the less likely the Null Hypothesis is supported by the data. It is usual to compare the P-value to a given level of significance (denoted by α) usually 0.05 or 0.01
	If the P-value is 0.31, from the sample evidence, you should not reject the Null Hypothesis, as you will make the wrong decision 31 times per 100 trials.
Parameters	Characteristics of a population such as the mean and the standard deviation are referred to as parameters. They are numerical values which summarise the actual distribution to which they refer.
Probability distribution	A probability distribution describes the range of possible values of a variable.
Sampling frame	The sampling frame is the actual set of units from which a sample will be drawn.
Standard error of the mean	The standard deviation of a sampling distribution of means for samples of a given size n. The standard error is given by $\sigma / \sqrt{n}$, where σ is the population standard deviation for the variable and n is the sample size.
Statistical Significance α	Statistical significance occurs if the result cannot be ascribed to sampling error. This means that the result was not random and thus there is something systematic in the relationship. In some research situations even a non-significant result may be interesting. If the significant level is 5% then this means that the result obtained would not occur more than 5% of the time by chance alone. This refers to the reliability of the research. Traditionally 5% is the level used in the social sciences.

Test statistic	The test-statistic is based on a hypothesized parameter value. The number for the test statistic which is calculated from the sample values is called the calculated value of the test statistic. It is a number calculated under the assumption of the Null Hypothesis and then compared to theoretical (probability) tables.
t-Distribution	A probability density function which has many of the properties of a normal distribution but which produces better results with small samples. A t-distribution will have more values in the tails than the normal distribution. Many statisticians point out that the t-test was initially called the Student's t-test because it was developed by a man working at the Guinness Breweries in Dublin who was not allowed, by his employer, to publish his work in his own name. His name was William Gosset.
t-test	The **t-test** is based on a test statistic where the sample is drawn from a normal distribution of known mean mu but where the standard deviation sigma is not known and is estimated by the sample standard deviation. The critical values for this test depend on the sample size. The t-distribution satisfactorily approximates the normal distribution for sample sizes of 30 or more.
The t-test for Paired Difference	An example of when to use a paired t-test is when we have a sample which is chosen randomly from a population and is tested say for their weight and then they are asked to follow a diet for one month. A month later these same people are tested again to see if they have lost weight. Each individual would have a pair of related observations or data points i.e. one reading before and one reading after the diet. The Null Hypothesis would then be that on average the difference between their weight before and after is zero. The t-test itself is applied in the normal way.

μ	The Greek letter μ (mu) is used as a symbol to represent the true value of the mean of a population. μ is a parameter of a probability distribution.
σ	The lower case Greek letter σ (sigma) is used as a symbol to represent the true standard deviation of a population. σ is a parameter of a probability density distribution.
Σ	The upper case Greek letter Σ (sigma) is used as a symbol to represent the sum of a series.
s	This is normally used to indicate the standard deviation of the sample data.
$\bar{X}$	The symbol $\bar{X}$ is used to represent the calculated average of a sample. It is referred to as X-bar.
X-score	The X-score is a term which is sometimes used interchangeably with the terms data point, observation.
Z-test	A Z-test is a test based on a test statistic for where the distribution is assumed to be normal with mean=zero and variance = 1. The underlying assumption is that the observations for the variable being tested come from a normal distribution with known mean mu and known standard deviation sigma.

Understanding statistical techniques

2.1 Introduction

Part 1 addressed the issues of descriptive statistics. Means, medians, standard deviations, correlation coefficients and other statistical measures have been used to describe a sample of data which we have obtained. It will have been noticed that most of the exercises in Part 1 were based on data obtained by the use of a simple questionnaire.

In Part 2 new ideas and new techniques are introduced and in so doing, the learner will move **beyond the world of descriptive statistics** into what is referred to as **inferential statistics**. The difference between descriptive and inferential statistics is that with descriptive statistics it is only possible to make statements about the sample. In inferential statistics it is possible to use data from the sample to make statements about the whole population. Specifically, if we have a suitable sample it is possible to know quite a lot about the whole population from which the sample came. It is important for researchers to always keep in mind the difference between the population (the total set of all possible elements from which a sample is drawn.) and the sample (a part of something larger such as a subset of a population. This sample is usually drawn using a sampling frame).

Before commencing the discussion of inferential statistics it is necessary to introduce learners to a few other concepts and the first issue we address is the shape of the data through data frequency tables.

2.2 Data Frequency Tables

Data frequency tables have been considered before in Part 1 but they are addressed here again because much of what follows is based on the idea that if we know what a particular data frequency table or data frequency distribution looks like, then we really know quite a lot about the variable which this table or distribution represents. Remember we discussed some of the issues about a data distribution when we addressed skewness (left or right) and kurtosis (peaked or not peaked) in Part 1. Shortly we will look at a data distribution which is not skewed and where the kurtosis is neither over or under peaked.

Remember the data frequency table refers to a way of presenting a summary of the data in such a manner that it facilitates the possibility of seeing patterns or relationships in the data. A data frequency table shows how many times each data point (observation or outcome) occurs in a given data set. Distributions may take different shapes and this section of the book will consider data which is typical of that obtained from the questionnaire concerning the background of students registered at a School of Business and a School of Accounting used in Part 1. The issue or variable which will be considered here is the length (in months) of working experience which students obtained before registering for their post-experience degree.

In this example we have obtained 30 completed and usable question-naires from students from the School of Business and another 30 com-pleted and usable questionnaires from students from the School of Ac-counting. We have 60 data points in all.

A usable questionnaire is one which has been sufficiently completed that it may be included in the data set obtained. Researchers sometimes ex-clude questionnaires where more than a few questions have not been completed or answered by the respondent. When this happens it is usu-ally believed that the questionnaire was poorly designed. In the same way as discussed in Part 1 a small number of missing data points or ele-ments may be estimated. Sometimes there can be a very large number of non-respondents i.e. questionnaires not being returned at all, and this can damage the credibility of the survey.

The 30 respondents from the School of Business supplied the following number of months working experience:

Table 2.1: School of Business, number of months working experience

23	28	29	34	34	39	43	44	45	45	48	48	49	54	54
54	55	56	56	65	65	65	67	73	76	76	77	78	87	92

Respondents from the School of Accounting replied with the following data:

Table 2.2: School of Accounting, number of months working experience

10	12	12	16	19	20	22	23	23	23	26	28	29	32	33
34	34	41	43	43	44	45	45	54	56	56	56	65	67	76

These two data sets have been reproduced in this section across columns to conserve page length in this book. These data would normally be en-tered in a spreadsheet in one column.

It is possible to create a data frequency table by just counting the num-ber of times each data point occurs. However, it is often the case that it is better to group data into intervals such as 10-19, 20-29 etc. This occurs with data for quantitative variables such as age, weight, income etc, where there are likely to be many different outcomes.

The first step in producing a Frequency Table is to establish the range of the data. The technique for doing this has been described in Part 1. The range for the School of Business is 69 and the range for the School of Accounting is 66.

The second step is to decide the number of groups/intervals into which the data should be divided. A heuristic for this is that the data may be grouped into the number of intervals represented by the square root of the sample size. As the sample size is 30 five or six groups would be appropriate in this exercise[26]. It is useful to keep the width of the intervals constant except perhaps for the first and final groups. In this exercise we have used interval markers of under 25, 36, 48, 60, 72 and greater than 72. These numbers need to be entered I6 to I11.

Excel has a function which allows data frequency tables to be constructed which is called =frequency().

The =frequency() function is an array function which means that it is entered in a different way to other functions. The function needs two pieces of information:-

1. the full range of data from which the frequency distribution is required
2. the intervals which are to be used in the data frequency table. This is called the bin range.

Considering Figure 2.1, the required data distribution in intervals has been entered into the range I6 through I11. The =frequency() function can now be used in the adjacent column to calculate the frequencies. As =frequency() is an array function the range J6 through J11 is first selected and then to produce a frequency table for the responses from the School of Business, the following formula is entered in J6.

=frequency(C3:C32,I6:I11) [CTRL + Shift + Enter]

---

[26] There is in general agreement that the number of intervals should not be less than 5 and not more than 20.

	A	B	C	D	E	F	G	H	I	J
1			Raw data							
2			Months SoB	Months SoA						
3		1	29	10						
4		2	76	23					Data	
5		3	77	32					Distribution	Frequency
6		4	56	26					25	1
7		5	45	28					36	4
8		6	54	56					48	7
9		7	56	43					60	7
10		8	34	44					72	4
11		9	54	56					>72	7
12		10	65	20						
13		11	48	41						
14		12	76	29						
15		13	44	45						
16		14	34	56						
17		15	43	34						
18		16	48	76						
19		17	49	65						
20		18	54	45						
21		19	23	22						
22		20	28	12						
23		21	55	33						
24		22	39	43						
25		23	65	54						
26		24	67	23						
27		25	73	12						
28		26	45	16						
29		27	92	19						
30		28	78	34						
31		29	87	23						
32		30	65	67						

Figure 2.1: The data and the =Frequency() function

In the case of an array function it is necessary to hold down the **CTRL key and the Shift Key and to then press Enter**. The result is that the frequency is calculated for each interval or bin in the range and are placed in cells J6 to J11.

To calculate the frequencies of the School of Accounting, select the range K6:K11 and enter the formula

=frequency(D3:D32,I6:I11) [CTRL + Shift + Enter]

The frequency table which is produced by Excel is shown in the right hand corner of Figure 2.1 in the range I4 to J10.

The results of the =frequency() function are now reproduced in Table 2.3.

Table 2.3: School of Business Frequency Table of the number of students and the number of months working experience.

Months Experience	No of Students
Under 25	1
26-36	4
37-48	7
49-60	7
61-72	4
above 72	7
Total	30

Having established the frequency of the individual groups or classes, the relative frequency can be calculated as a percentage of each group relative to the total. The cumulative relative frequency is then the percentage across the range shown in Tables 2.4 and 2.5.

Table 2.4: School of Business Frequency Table with relative frequency

Months Experience	No of Students	Relative frequency
Under 25	1	0.03
26-36	4	0.13
37-48	7	0.23
49-60	7	0.23
61-72	4	0.13
above 72	7	0.13
Total	30	1.00

Table 2.5: School of Business Frequency Table with relative frequency and **cumulative relative frequency**

Months Experience	No of Students	Relative frequency	Cumulative Relative frequency
Under 25	10	0.33	0.33
26-36	7	0.23	0.57
37-48	6	0.20	0.77
49-60	4	0.13	0.90
61-72	2	0.07	0.97
Above 72	1	0.03	1.00
Total	30	1.00	

These frequency tables may be plotted as histograms. Figure 2.2 shows the results for the School of Business and. Figure 2.3 shows the results for the School of Accounting.

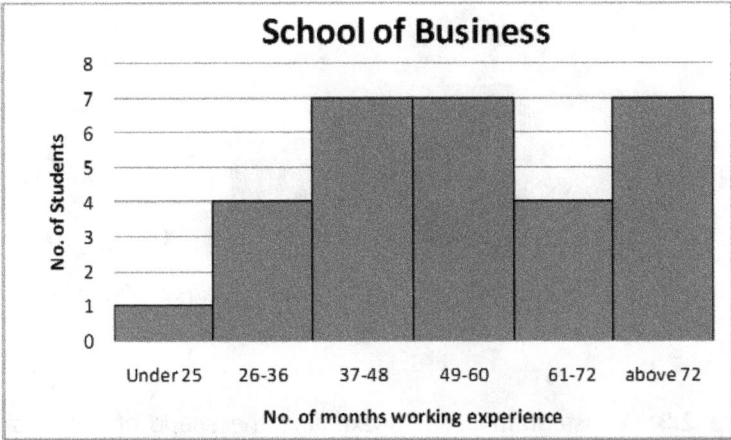

Figure 2.2: A histogram used to examine the shape of the data frequency table for the School of Business

Excel does not directly produce a histogram with the bars touching each other as shown in Figure 2.2. To obtain this effect a normal bar chart is first drawn. Then the cursor is placed on one of the bars and the right mouse button clicked. Choose Format Data Series and then Options. This will allow the Gap Width to be specified as Zero and the histogram effect is achieved.

Note that this chart using the given intervals is tri-modal. This example shows one of the difficulties with using the mode as it is not unique. It may also be the case that this data actually contains more than one distinct sub-group

In Figure 2.3 there is a distinct trend for degree candidates to register for the post-graduate degree soon after their first degree and thus without a larger number of years working experience.

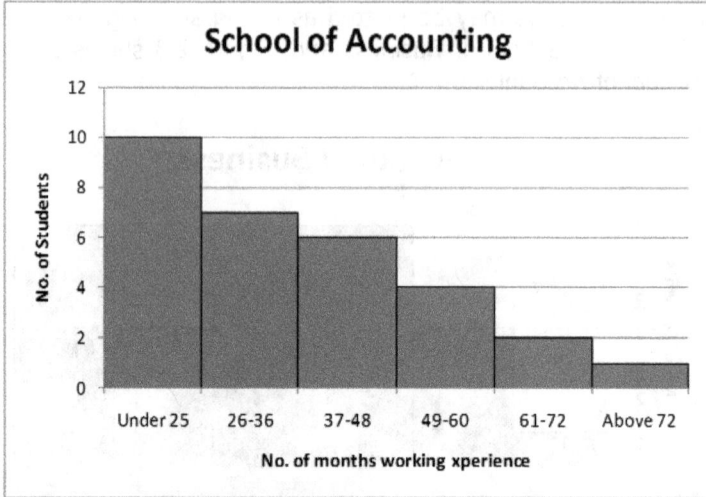

Figure 2.3: A histogram used to examine the shape of the data frequency table for the School of Accounting

No further analysis is required to recognise that the distribution of work experience had by the degree candidates in the School of Business and the School of Accounting is different. These two data sets can be plotted on the same axis using a line graph shown in Figure 2.4.

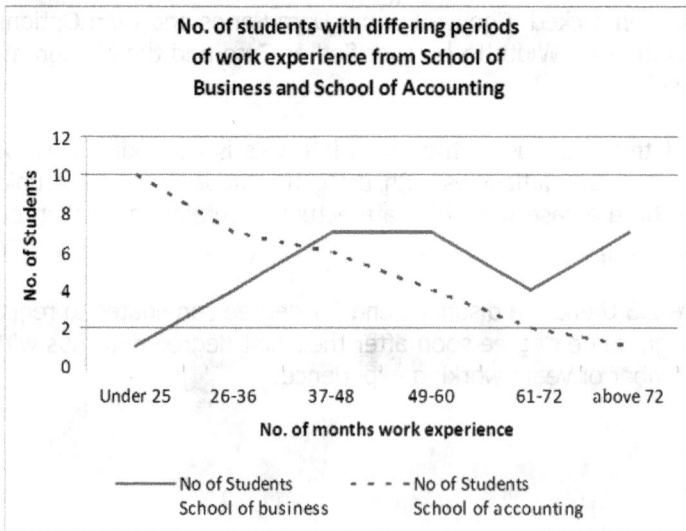

Figure 2.4: The School of Business and the School of Accounting data as traces on one graph

The line graphs as shown in Figure 2.4 are sometimes called a trace or frequency polygon as they show the line which joins the mid-points of the tops of the rectangles in the histograms.

It may be seen from both the tables and the graphs that there are differences between these two distributions. The School of Business has more mature students (more working experience) and these are spread across the work experience range with three modal points, which are the most work experienced groups. In the case of the School of Accounting there are fewer students with more working experience and the mode is the least work experienced group.

As mentioned above the data frequency table describes the pattern in the data and this is one way in which a distribution may be represented.

In addition a distribution may be described using the mean and the standard deviation. It is also possible to use a mathematical formula to describe a distribution. However, it should be noted that the data distributions described above are not probability distributions. Probability distributions are described below.

2.3 Normal Distribution

In Figures 2.2 and 2.3 above a practical data frequency distribution was created using the =frequency() function, and in this case graphed, from the sample data we obtained using a questionnaire. This way of presenting the data showed that there was a particular shape to the data obtained and this represented a pattern in the opinions which were offered. In other instances the shape of the data would represent how events took place. There are many different types of shapes which will appear when data is graphed. One of the most frequently encountered is bell shaped and thus suggests that the sample and population come from what is called a normal distribution. The normal distribution is of great importance in statistical analysis. The normal distribution is referred to as a probability distribution. The notion of probability is central to the idea of the normal distribution and we will refer to this many times in the balance of this Part of the book. The normal distribution is sometimes called a Gaussian distribution. Carl Friedrich Gauss was a famous German mathematician working in the 19th century.

A probability distribution is sometimes thought of as a theoretical data frequency distribution which states how outcomes or observations are expected to behave. As with the data frequency distributions already de-

85

scribed above it may be represented by tables or diagrams or a mathematical formula.

The graph of a normal distribution is bell shaped which is symmetrical around the mean value in the middle of the graph, and it has a number of particular properties. Figure 2.5 shows the shape of a typical Normal distribution curve produced in Excel and the distribution table of values is shown in Figure 2.8, which will be referred to in detail later.

By convention the total area under a normal shaped curve is always 1. Thus the bell shaped curve consists of two sides each of which is 0.5 in area. The probabilities are represented by the area under the curve. By definition this means that we cannot talk about the probability of a single value occurring. We talk about the probability of values being greater than or equal to some observed or specified value. We can also talk about the probability of values being between certain limits. Because the area under the curve is equal to 1 the probabilities mentioned above may be understood as being the fraction of the population that lies above or below or within the specified values. It is important to recall that the probability of an event which will certainly occur such as the fact that we will all die is 1 and the probability of an event which is impossible such as we will all fly to the moon is 0 (zero).

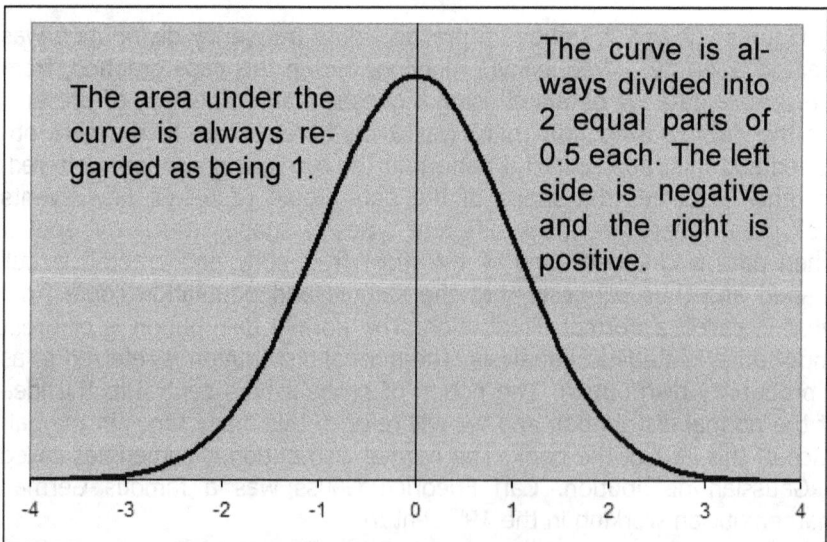

The area under the curve is always regarded as being 1.

The curve is always divided into 2 equal parts of 0.5 each. The left side is negative and the right is positive.

-4   -3   -2   -1   0   1   2   3   4

Figure 2.5: The bell shape of a standardised normal distribution curve or graph

The Normal distribution is a continuous probability distribution which describes the frequency of the outcomes of the random variable. The actual shape of the normal distribution curve is a function of the mean value and standard deviation[27] of the distribution. The mean and the standard deviation of the distribution are referred to as the parameters of the distribution.

All the following distributions are normally distributed.

Different means and different standard deviations lead to different bell shaped curves as may be seen in Figure 2.6.

Distribution	Mean	Std dev
Distribution 1 The number of work permits issued each year in the country	12,500	750

Normal Distribution

| Distribution 2
The number of children vaccinated against flu each year in the country | 17,500 | 5000 |

Normal Distribution

---

[27] The mean and the standard deviation were discussed in Part 1 where it was shown how to calculate them using Excel functions.

Distribution	Mean	Std dev
Distribution 3 The number of microchips manufactured in China each day	187,000	50,000

Normal Distribution

Distribution	Mean	Std dev
Distribution 4 The number of burgers sold in the fast-food restaurants in Dublin airport each month.	3,500	400

Normal Distribution

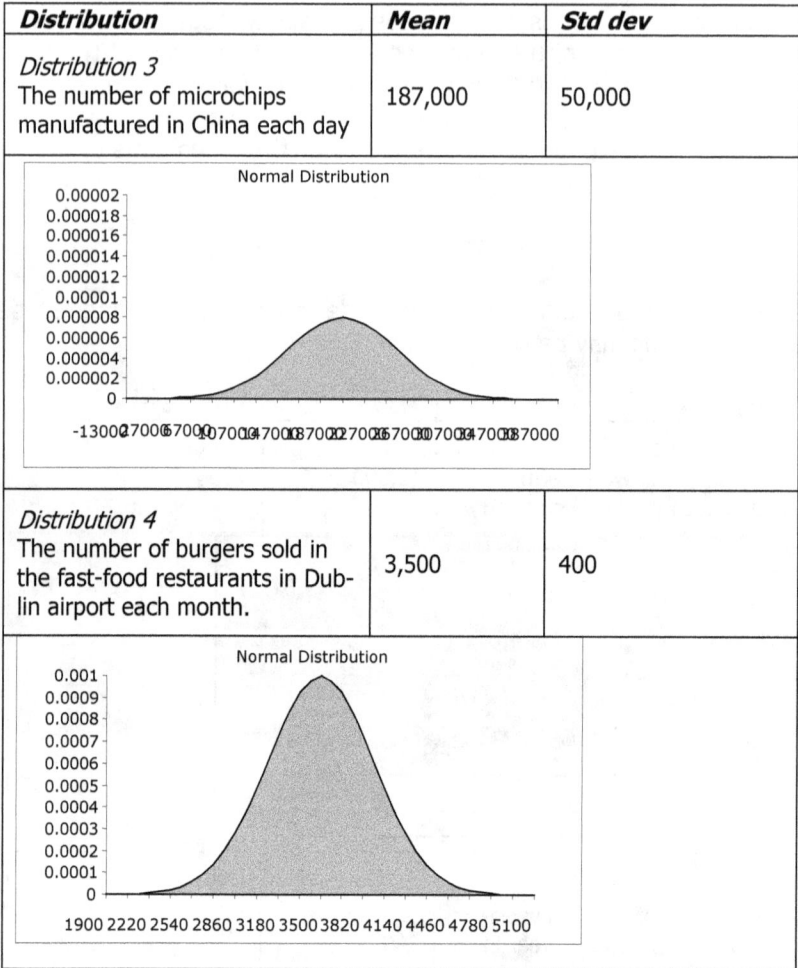

Figure 2.6: Different data sets which display the characteristics of a normal distribution.

The theoretical distributions in Figure 2.6 have different means and different standard deviations, but it is also possible for there to be many distributions with the same mean, but with **different standard deviations** as is shown in Figure 2.7. Note the smaller the standard deviation the "tighter" the graph, and the larger the standard deviation the "flatter" the graph. Tight graphs, i.e. ones with small standard deviations, suggest that there will be less variability in the sample and flat graphs i.e. ones with large standard deviations, suggest that there will be a high degree of variability. This higher standard deviation can mean more risk than a lower degree of variability.

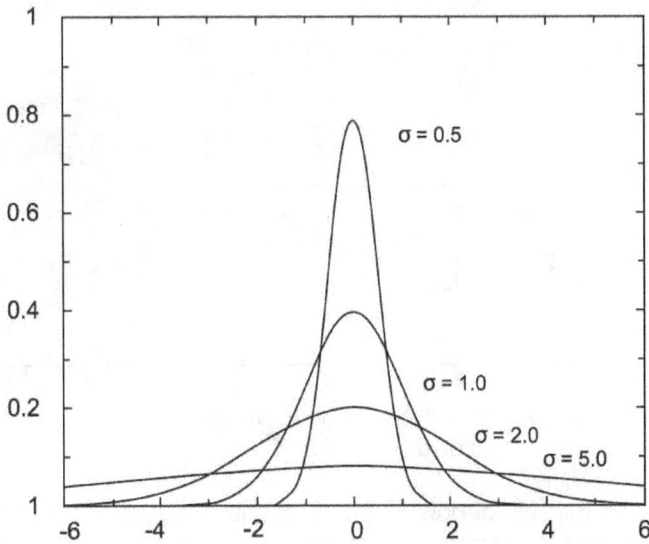

Figure 2.7: Four data distributions with the same mean but with 4 different standard deviations.

In Figure 2.7 the σ is used to denote the standard deviation.

One of the more important attributes of the normal distribution curve is the specific way in which the outcomes of the variable are spread about its mean. If a distribution is normal then by definition 68% of the population outcomes/values lies within *plus or minus one standard deviation* from the mean and 95% of the population outcomes/values lies within *plus or minus two standard deviations* (actual value is 1.96 but this is usually expressed or rounded to 2) from the mean. And finally 99% of population outcomes/values lies within *plus or minus three standard deviations* (rounded up from 2.58 to the nearest integer) from the mean. This is illustrated in Figure 2.8.

Note, in theory the tails of the graph in Figure 2.8 do not touch the x-axis. They are said to extend to infinity. As a result it is possible to occasionally find very large or very low values which are actually data points within the distribution[28].

---

[28] Recall the issue of outliers which was discussed in Part 1 of the book. Some outliers will be perfectly respectable members of a data set whose values are to be found deep in the tails of the distribution.

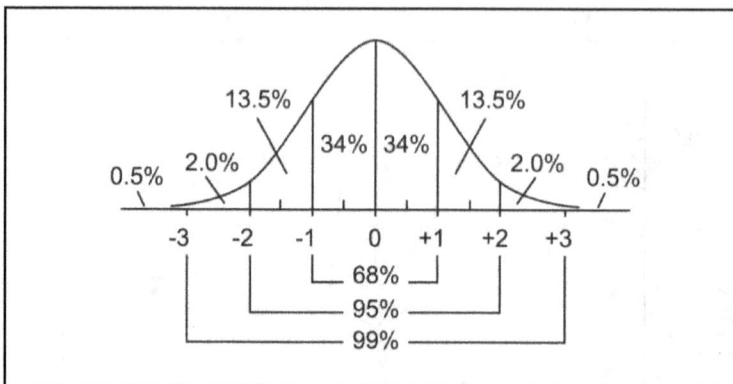

Figure 2.8: The percentage of the data within 1, 2 and 3 standard deviations[29] under a normal distribution.

Remembering the rule of how data is distributed in a normal distribution[30] and using these characteristics we can interpret research results in a meaningful manner. For a normal distribution where the mean is 25 and the standard deviation is 4, we can say that approximately 99% of the population values lie between 25 + (3 * 4) which equals 37 and 25 − (3 * 4) which equals 13. This means that we can say that we expect with 99% confidence that an observation drawn from this distribution will take a value of between 13 and 37. Note that it is assumed that the observation has been *randomly taken from the population* and it is important to remember that the two tails of the normal curve *theoretically stretch to infinity.* So it is possible to obtain a very small value and a very large value, which although highly unlikely, are valid observations or values in the normal distribution[31].

An application of this is to use the normal distribution to establish the relative position of an observed value to others in a population. For example, suppose an individual drawn at random from the above example (mean = 25 and standard deviation = 4) exhibits a value of 33 then it may be said that the individual is two standard deviations above the mean and is therefore in the top 2.5% of the population.

It should be noted in Figure 2.8 that there are three divisions of the curve on either side of the mean i.e. 3 standard deviations. If the data

---

[29] It is important to recall that although 1, 2 and 3 standard deviations are frequently used to describe the distribution of data under the normal curve these numbers are only approximations. The actual numbers are 0.84, 1.96 and 2.5.

[30] This is sometimes referred to as the 68-95-99 Rule.

[31] It is possible that invalid observations occur i.e. errors and if this is the case they need to be adjusted or omitted from the data.

distribution is taken as a whole there are six possible divisions between what would be, for practical purposes, the maximum and the minimum values of the distribution. Therefore if the range of a data set i.e. the difference between the maximum and the minimum values, are taken and divided by 6 then this resultant number may be used as a heuristic for the standard deviation. Clearly the actual calculation of the standard deviation is better and with a spreadsheet this is easy to do. But sometimes this heuristic is useful.

2.4 The standard normal curve

Any variable a researcher is working with will have its own mean and standard deviation. All these means and standard deviations could be different and if every time we wanted to study a situation we had to work (i.e. make our calculations) with different means and standard deviations we would be faced with arithmetical challenges. However we are able to minimise this arithmetic work by *standardising* any variable to have a mean of zero and a variance or standard deviation equal to 1.

Returning to Figure 2.8 the normal distribution shown here is called the *standard normal curve* because the mean is zero and the standard deviation is 1. It is unusual for any normal distribution to have a mean of zero and a standard deviation of 1. However, any normal distribution variable can be standardised or transformed so that it may be considered to have a mean 0 and standard deviation 1. When this is done the resulting standardised variable is called the Z variable and the probability associated with the Z variable is shown in the Standard Normal Distribution Tables in Figure 2.10 (on page 86).

Now to explore the idea of probability.

Example 1
Recall that having processed the results of the questionnaire in Part 1 we found the response to Question 1 to have a normal distribution[32] of mean 3.47 and a standard deviation of 2.05.

We find an additional questionnaire (apparently a late submission) with a response rating of 8 to question 1.

The quality of the lectures is excellent								
Strongly Disagree							*Strongly Agree*	
1. ☐	2. ☐	3. ☐	4. ☐	5. ☐	6. ☐	7. ☐	8. ☒	9. ☐

---

[32] In order to be able to use this type of logic it is necessary to make an assumption about how the data was distributed.

We wish to establish the probability of a score of 8 or more coming from such a distribution (i.e. the distribution we found when we first analysed the data we obtained in Part 1). If traditional tables are to be used like those in Figure 2.10 then the first step is to standardize the score 8 in terms of the number of standard deviations it is from the mean. This is done by using the formula[33]:

$$Z = \frac{X - \mu}{\sigma}$$

Where, X is any given data point (we sometimes call this number the X-score) in the sample, in this case 8, μ is the mean of the population, in this case 3.47 and σ is the standard deviation of the population in this case 2.05.

Therefore

$$Z = \frac{8 - 3.47}{2.05}$$

= 2.21 Standard Deviation units above the mean.

The 2.21 is sometimes called the **standardised value** of 8 in terms of a data distribution where the mean is 3.47 and the standard deviation is 2.05.

The location of the Z = 2.21 which is the number of standard deviations the new data point, 8, is from the mean, may be viewed in Figure 2.9.

2.5   Normal curve and probability

In Figure 2.9 the area under the curve to the left of the Z-score (2.21) represents the probability that a value could be 8 or less, i.e. there is a high probability here. The area under the curve to the right of the Z-score (2.21) represents the probability that a value could be 8 or more, i.e. there is a low probability here. Note that we cannot use this technique to say what is the probability of a score being 8 as for a continuous variable any single X-score has a probability of zero.

---

[33] The Greek symbols μ (this character is pronounced mu) and σ (this character is pronounced sigma) are used by statisticians to represent the mean of the population and the standard deviation of the population. This will be discussed further later in this book.

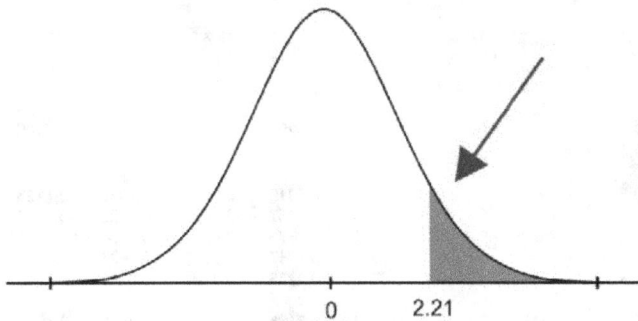

Figure 2.9: Using the normal curve to show the area of the curve representing the probability of a Z-score greater than 2.21

The Z-table which will be used here to find the corresponding probability is in Figure 2.10 below.

To use the Z-tables look down the first column in the table on the extreme left until 2.2 is found. The column next to the right shows the value of the Z-score for 2.20. If you move one column further to the right the value is that required for a Z-score of 2.21. Note if a Z-score of 2.22 had been required it would have been necessary to move another step to the right.

The table value for 2.21 is actually 0.9864 which represents the probability for a Z-score being less than 2.21 standard deviations above the mean. Therefore the probability of getting a value of 8 or more is equal to one minus 0.9864 which is 0.0136 or 1.36%[34]. Note that we subtract the 0.9864 from 1 because the total area under the curve is 1. A probability of 1.35% is very low and it would be wise to question the validity of the late arriving questionnaire with a score of 8.
Fhypothisis

---

[34] The area in the table is the area under the Standard Normal Curve to the left of the computed value of Z. In this case we are interested in the area under the curve to the right of the calculated value of Z.

z	0.00	0.01	0.02	0.03	0.04	0.05	0.06	0.07
0.0	0.5000	0.5040	0.5080	0.5120	0.5160	0.5199	0.5239	0.5279
0.1	0.5390	0.5438	0.5478	0.5517	0.5557	0.5596	0.5636	0.5675
0.2	0.5793	0.5832	0.5871	0.5910	0.5948	0.5987	0.6026	0.6064
0.3	0.6179	0.6217	0.6255	0.6293	0.6331	0.6368	0.6406	0.6443
0.4	0.6554	0.6591	0.6628	0.6664	0.6700	0.6736	0.6772	0.6808
0.5	0.6915	0.6950	0.6985	0.7019	0.7054	0.7088	0.7123	0.7157
0.6	0.7257	0.7291	0.7324	0.7357	0.7389	0.7422	0.7454	0.7486
0.7	0.7580	0.7611	0.7642	0.7673	0.7704	0.7734	0.7764	0.7794
0.8	0.7881	0.7910	0.7939	0.7967	0.7995	0.8023	0.8051	0.8078
0.9	0.8159	0.8186	0.8212	0.8238	0.8264	0.8289	0.8315	0.8340
1.0	0.8413	0.8438	0.8461	0.8485	0.8508	0.8531	0.8554	0.8577
1.1	0.8643	0.8665	0.8686	0.8708	0.8729	0.8749	0.8770	0.8790
1.2	0.8849	0.8869	0.8888	0.8907	0.8925	0.8944	0.8962	0.8980
1.3	0.9032	0.9049	0.9066	0.9082	0.9099	0.9115	0.9131	0.9147
1.4	0.9192	0.9207	0.9222	0.9236	0.9251	0.9265	0.9279	0.9292
1.5	0.9332	0.9345	0.9357	0.9370	0.9382	0.9394	0.9406	0.9418
1.6	0.9452	0.9463	0.9474	0.9484	0.9495	0.9505	0.9515	0.9525
1.7	0.9554	0.9564	0.9573	0.9582	0.9591	0.9599	0.9608	0.9616
1.8	0.9641	0.9649	0.9656	0.9664	0.9671	0.9678	0.9686	0.9693
1.9	0.9713	0.9719	0.9726	0.9732	0.9738	0.9744	0.9750	0.9756
2.0	0.9772	0.9778	0.9783	0.9788	0.9793	0.9798	0.9803	0.9808
2.1	0.9821	0.9826	0.9830	0.9834	0.9838	0.9842	0.9846	0.9850
2.2	0.9861	0.9864	0.9868	0.9871	0.9875	0.9878	0.9881	0.9884
2.3	0.9893	0.9896	0.9898	0.9901	0.9904	0.9906	0.9909	0.9911
2.4	0.9918	0.9920	0.9922	0.9925	0.9927	0.9929	0.9931	0.9932
2.5	0.9938	0.9940	0.9941	0.9943	0.9945	0.9946	0.9948	0.9949
2.6	0.9953	0.9955	0.9956	0.9957	0.9959	0.9960	0.9961	0.9962
2.7	0.9965	0.9966	0.9967	0.9968	0.9969	0.9970	0.9971	0.9972
2.8	0.9974	0.9975	0.9976	0.9977	0.9977	0.9978	0.9979	0.9979
2.9	0.9981	0.9982	0.9982	0.9983	0.9984	0.9984	0.9985	0.9985

Figure 2.10: A set of published Standard Normal Distribution Tables (Z-tables) showing probabilities for less than a given Z-score

The table shown in Figure 2.10 gives the probability of obtaining a Z-score from the specified value (in this case 8) back to the extreme left end (tail) of the curve. As in this example we wanted to calculate the probability of 8 or more occurring, it was necessary to find the area of the curve to the right of the z-score.

Subtracting the table value from one (unity) in order to determine the probability can sometimes present difficulties to the newcomer to this technique. In Figure 2.11 the normal curve is shown as comprising the section having a probability of 0.9864 and the section having a probability of 0.014. The area under the curve to the left of the Z-score is what is tabulated. Thus when we are interested in the area to the right of the Z-score we need to subtract the tabulated area from 1. Figure 2.11 shows the two parts of the area under the curve.

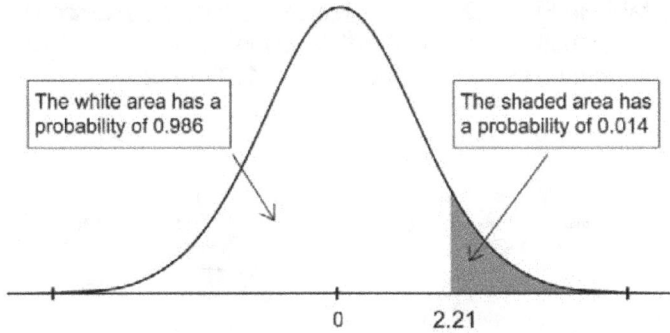

The white area has a probability of 0.986

The shaded area has a probability of 0.014

0   2.21

Figure 2.11: The sum of the two areas (blank and shaded) is equal to 1

Example 2

Another example to illustrate the above technique considers the probability of a value of 7 or more being returned for the question.

The quality of the lectures is excellent								
Strongly Disagree								*Strongly Agree*
1. ☐	2. ☐	3. ☐	4. ☐	5. ☐	6. ☐	7. ☒	8. ☐	9. ☐

The first step is to standardise the X-score using the same formula as before.

$$Z = \frac{7 - 3.47}{2.05}$$

$$= 1.72 \text{ Standard Deviation units}$$

The location of the Z-score (1.72) is shown in Figure 2.12 below and the required area to the right has been shaded. Remember that the area to the left of the Z-score is the probability of a score of 7 or less.

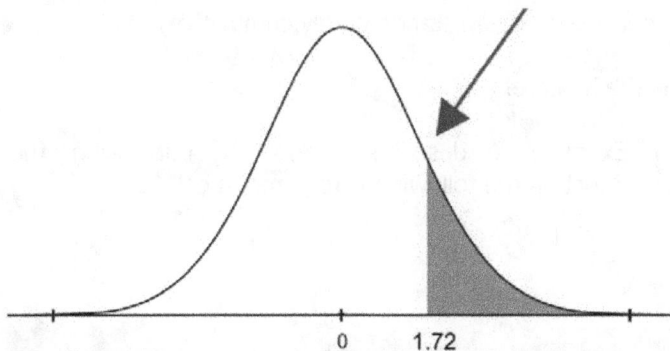

0   1.72

Figure 2.12: Using the normal curve to find the probability of the Z-score being greater than or equal to 7 or more.

Using the table in Figure 2.13, the area to the left of the Z-score (1.72) is 0.9573. Therefore the probability of obtaining a value of 7 or more is equal to one minus 0.9573 which equals 0.0427 or 4.27%.

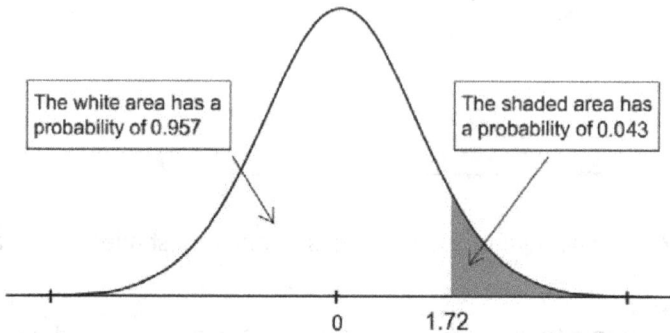

Figure 2.13:- The areas of the normal distribution and the probabilities associated there with.

With the use of Excel we do not have to resort to Z-score tables. Excel will calculate the numbers required and it will do so more speedily and also to a greater degree of accuracy.

2.6 The =normdist() function

Instead of using tables to look up Z-scores with which to compare a calculated test statistic to a theoretical statistic, a researcher can use Excel. Excel offers a function to calculate the probability of an observation being a member of a population with a given mean and a given standard deviation. This is the =normdist() function.

The form of this function in Excel is:

=normdist(x,mean,standard_dev,cumulative)

where x is the X-score.

Repeating Example 2 described previously but using the Excel =normdist() function the following is required in cell C6.

	A	B	C	[
1	**Normal Distribution**			
2	Observation		7	
3	Mean		3.47	
4	Standard Deviation		2.05	
5	Cumulative		TRUE	
6	Probability		0.957461	

Figure 2.14: The Excel spreadsheet used to calculate the probability of an X-score for normal distributions

In Figure 2.14 the formula in cell C6 is

=normdist(C2,C3,C4,C5)
      where   C2 = X-score (observed Value)
                           C3 = Mean to be tested against,
                           C4 = Standard deviation
                           C5 = Indicator point to use the probability density function. TRUE indicates the area under curve and FALSE indicates the ordinate[35].

The result shows a probability of the X-score being less than 7 to be 0.957461. Therefore, as before, to calculate the probability of the X-score being greater than 7 it is necessary to subtract the answer from one i.e. 1 - 0.957461=0.0427 or 4.27%.

Example 3
To look at another example, if we have a population with a mean of 40 and a standard deviation of 5, and we want to know the probability that an observation or outcome obtained from this population could be 30 or more we can use Excel as follows.

Figure 2.15 shows the result f using of the =normdist() function in cell B6.

---

[35] The FALSE indicator for this Excel function has not been used in this book. See the Excel Help function for more information about this option.

	A	B	C
1	**Normal Distribution**		
2	Observation	30	
3	Mean	40	
4	Standard deviation	5	
5	Cumulative	TRUE	
6	Probability	0.02275	

Figure 2.15: The calculation of the probability of the observation occurring from the probability distribution curve.

Once again in Figure 2.15 the formula in cell B6 is

    =normdist(B2,B3,B4,B5)
        where   B2 = Observed Value,
                     B3 = Mean to be tested against,
                     B4 = Standard Deviation
                     B5 = Indicator point to use the probability density function. TRUE indicates the area under curve and FALSE indicates the ordinate.

The result shows a probability of the X-score being less than 30 to be 0.02275. Therefore, as before, to calculate the probability of the X-score being greater than 30 it is necessary to subtract the answer from one. i.e. 1 - 0.02275 = 0.97 or 97%.

Example 4
In another example we consider the same mean 40 and the same standard deviation of 5 but this time we want to know the probability that an observation or outcome obtained from this population could be 36 or more. We proceed as follows:

	A	B	C
13	**Normal Distribution**		
14	Observation	36	
15	Mean	40	
16	Standard deviation	5	
17	Cumulative	TRUE	
18	Probability	0.211855	

Figure 2.16: The calculation of the probability of the observation occurring from the probability distribution curve.

In Figure 2.16 the formula in cell B18 is

=normdist(B14,B15,B16,B17)
=0.211855

The Excel spreadsheet shows a probability of 0.0211855. As before to calculate the probability of the X-score being greater than 36, it is necessary to subtract the value returned by Excel from 1. This calculates to 78.8% (i.e. 1 - 0. 0211855 = 0.788).
= 79% (rounded up)

Example 5

In this example, we consider the distribution of year end exam results that follow a normal distribution with a mean of 55 and a standard deviation of 10. If the results followed this distribution in the next examination what mark would you expect to divide the class into two groups, one of which consisted of 95% of the pupils and the other 5% of the pupils.

The Z-value for 95% (or .95) of the curve is in the right hand tail and by consulting the tables it will be found to occur at 1.645 and this is represented in Figure 2.17.

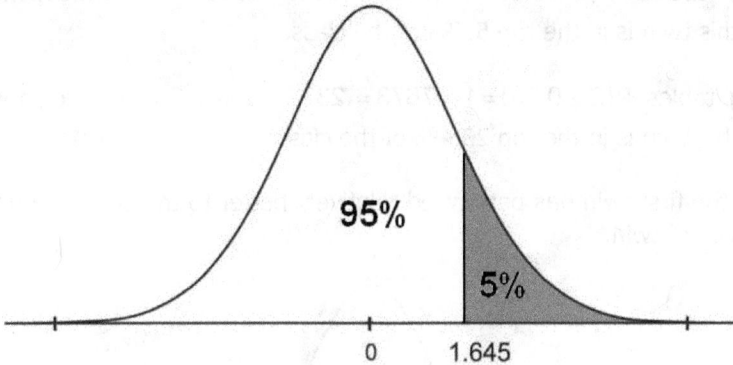

Figure 2.17: Z-value of 1.645 splits the total area into 95% and 5%.

The standardised value of the marks (X) is equal to $\dfrac{X-55}{10}$ which is set to equal 1.645 in this example.

This is represented by

$$\frac{X-55}{10} = 1.645$$

Multiplying both sides of this equation by 10 and rearranging to solve for X we find:

$$X = 55 + 1.645 * 10$$
$$X = 71.45$$

Example 6

The Jones twins are highly competitive. The first twin is in a group for mathematics which has been given a test for which the results are distributed normally with a mean of 65 and a standard deviation of 5. The first twin's score is 73. The second twin is in a different group which does a totally different type of mathematics test and whose results are distributed normally with a mean of 35 and a standard deviation of 11. The second twin scores 43. Which twin has done relatively better in their test?

First twin: Z-score $= \dfrac{73-65}{5} = 1.6$ standard deviations

Second twin: Z-score $= \dfrac{43-35}{11} = 0.73$ standard deviations

Using tables $P(Z \geq 1.6) = 1 - .9452 = .0548 = .055 = 5.5\%$ which means that this twin is in the top 5.5% of the class.

Using tables $P(Z \geq 0.73) = 1 - .7673 = .2327 = .234 = 23.4\%$ which means that this twin is in the top 23.4% of the class

Thus the first twin has performed relatively better to the peer group than the second twin.

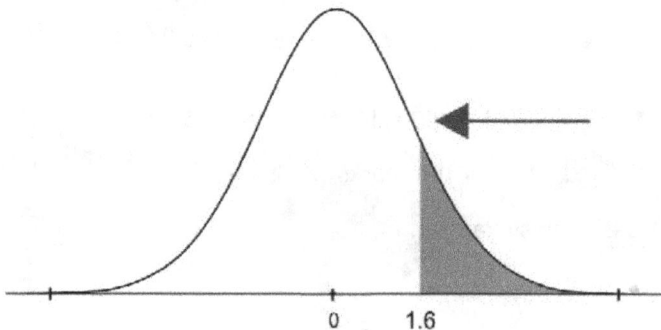

Figure 2.18: The shaded part of the curve shows the probability of first twin with a score of 73.

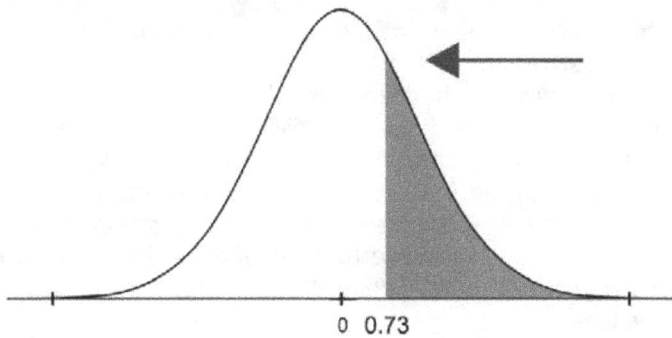

Figure 2.19: Shows the probability for the second twin with a score of 43.

2.7   Estimation and confidence interval

In the context of this book, estimation is the process of establishing the likely value of a variable. The most direct form of estimation is to establish a single-point value. As has been addressed in Part 1 of this book, the mean, the median or the mode may be used as single-point estimates. However, the use of these single statistics does not always contain enough information and the alternative, which is an interval estimate, may be required.

For example, looking at the results of Question 1 from the questionnaire in Part 1 of this book the question was:

The quality of the lectures is excellent								
Strongly Disagree								*Strongly Agree*
1. ☐	2. ☐	3. ☐	4. ☐	5. ☐	6. ☐	7. ☐	8. ☐	9. ☐

With a sample size of 30, the mean score for this question was 3.47 and the standard deviation was 2.05.

If a single point estimate of the true mean score (μ) for Question 1 is required then the average score $\overline{X}$ of 3.47 can be used. This is the "best" estimate using a single-point value. However, it is possible that more information about the estimate of the mean is required. Here an interval estimate can be calculated and in this case the single number is accompanied by confidence limits.

Recall that the average score for Question 1 of the sample of the 30 questionnaires returned is $\overline{X}$ = 3.47 with a standard deviation s=2.05. Because we are dealing with a sample mean the confidence interval which we require will use the standard error as described in Part 1. This is calculated as the standard deviation divided by the square root of the size of the sample. In this case the estimate of the standard error for Q1 is 0.374. To establish the 95% confidence limits we need to add 2 standard errors[36] to the calculated mean and subtract 2 standard errors from the calculated mean. In this case the results are 4.21 and 2.73 respectively. Thus we conclude with 95% confidence that the true lies between these two values.

We might also be interested in knowing what the position is at a confidence level of 99%. In this case we add 3 standard errors to the calculated mean and subtract 3 standard errors from the calculated mean, which produces results of 4.59 and 2.35 respectively. This technique of estimating the interval value of the responses can be used for all questions in the questionnaire in Part 1 if required.

2.8   Standard Error of the Mean

As indicated above the Standard Error (SE) was first mentioned in Part 1 of this book in the same section as the standard deviation, but its use was not described. Whereas the standard deviation applies to a whole population the standard error only applies to the sampling distribution of the means drawn from a population.

Many different samples of the same size may be drawn from a population. The number of samples can be very large if the values comprising the sample are allowed to be taken more than once from the population. If this is the case we refer to the samples as having been taken with replacement.

In Figure 2.20 below the samples are of the same size.

---

[36] Remember that the actual number is 1.96 but this is frequently rounded to 2.

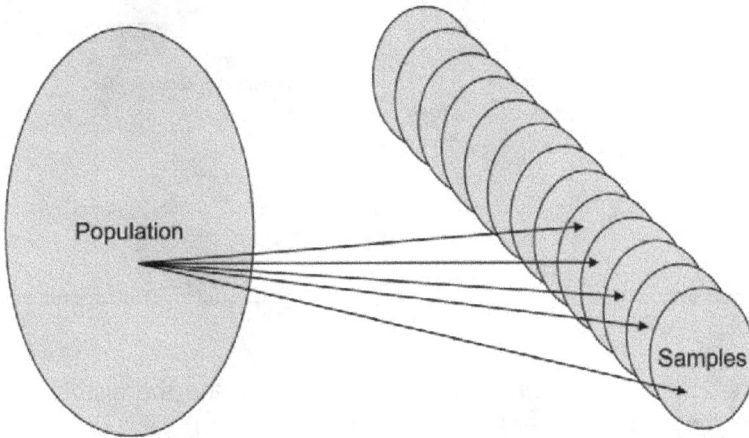

Figure 2.20: A large number of samples may be taken from a population especially if the sample elements are taken another time.

Since the samples are drawn from the same population the population standard deviation for each sample is σ sigma. Thus the population standard error $SE_{(P)}$ for samples of size n is

$$SE_{(P)} = \frac{\sigma}{\sqrt{n}}$$

In practice the value of σ is not known and thus is estimated from the observations from a single sample for which the inferences are to be based. The SE is calculated by dividing the standard deviation of the single sample on which inferences are to be made by the square root of the sample size (n) i.e.

$$SE = \frac{\text{Sample Standard Deviation}}{\sqrt{\text{Number of Observations}}}$$

$$SE = \frac{SD}{\sqrt{n}}$$

The SE will always be smaller than the standard deviation of the population (for n $\geq$ 2).

Furthermore, in Figure 2.21 we show that the distribution of sample means will be closer to the mean of the population than the data points in the original population as the standard deviation of the sample means is smaller.

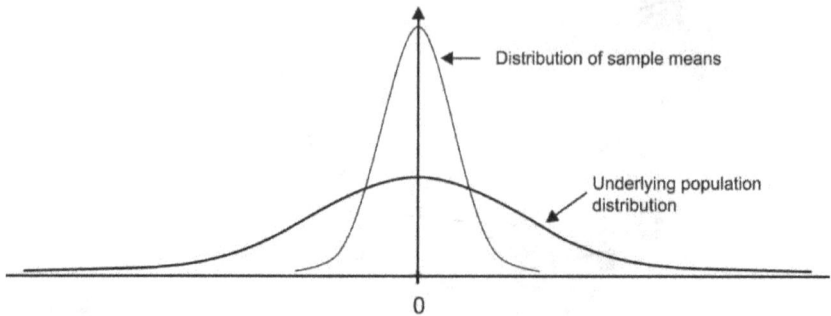

Figure 2.21: The distribution of the population and the distribution of sample means within that population

The sampling distribution of the mean of a sample of size N≥30 from a population with mean μ and standard deviation σ will be approximately normally distributed with mean μ and standard error $= \dfrac{\sigma}{\sqrt{n}}$. This follows from one of the most important principles in statistics which is referred to as the central limit theorem[37].

As a consequence the Z-score will be $Z = \dfrac{\left(\overline{X} - \mu\right)}{\left(\dfrac{\sigma}{\sqrt{n}}\right)}$ for sample means and will follow a standard normal distribution.

The standard error is used for interval estimation of the true mean μ and for carrying out tests of hypotheses concerning the true mean μ of a distribution.

In practice we usually do not know the value of σ and estimate it with the sample standard deviation referred to as s. At that point the Z-score (normal distribution) is not used, but instead a t (the so-called Student t) distribution is used.

The equivalent of the Z-score equation then becomes

---

[37] The central limit theorem states that with a large population the means of the samples taken will be normally distributed and that the mean of the means of the samples will be the mean of the population and the standard deviation of the distribution of the means will be standard deviation of the population from which the population was drawn divided by the square root of the sample size. For the central limit theorem to apply the sample should be greater than 30 and it should be small relative to the population.

$$t_{n-1} = \frac{(\overline{X} - \mu)}{\frac{s}{\sqrt{n}}}, \qquad v = n - 1 \text{ (where v=degrees of freedom)}$$

which follows a t-distribution with (n-1) degrees of freedom.

The use of the t-distribution[38], when the sample size is less than 30, actually depends on knowing that the random variable being studied follows a normal distribution. However, since the t-distribution or t-statistic is known to be robust with respect to the normal distribution assumption, we tend to use it without paying too much attention to this issue.

In general when we work with means of samples we use the standard error, but when we work with individual data points we use the standard deviation.

The larger the sample sizes in use the smaller the standard error.

2.9 Hypothesis testing

Hypothesis testing is a central concept in statistical reasoning and thinking and when this technique is mastered it will provide the researcher with a number of useful tools.

Hypothesis testing is an important way in which we can increase our confidence in the findings of our research and a number of examples will now be used to illustrate this. A hypothesis test which is often performed tests a claim concerning the "true" mean (or some other parameter) of the population.

In carrying out such a test one needs to specify the Null Hypothesis, the Alternative Hypothesis and the level of significance.

Before the test can be performed the researcher needs to draw a sample of acceptable or perhaps "credible"[39] size from the population and then compute the mean and the standard deviation of the sample.

---

[38]There are actually two assumptions necessary for the t-test (1) that the values in your sample should be independent of each other (2) the selection of any values from the population should not affect the selection of another and random sampling with replacement is regarded as the most appropriate way of doing this. The second assumption is that your population should be normally distributed. The t-test is preferred because it may be used in many situations where the population variability is not known.

[39] The "credible" size will depend on the hypothesis being tested and will vary considerably.

Then the appropriate test statistic needs to be computed. This is given by

$$t_{n-1} = \frac{\left(\overline{X} - \mu_0\right)}{\dfrac{s}{\sqrt{n}}}$$

where μ_0 is the value of the mean specified under the Null Hypothesis and (n-1) is a parameter of the t-distribution[40] which is referred to as the degrees of freedom. Increasingly the t-test is used in these circum-stances as it provides usable results with both small and large samples.

For example, assuming that as a result of the original study the man-agement of the Faculty sets a bench mark of 3.47 for the student quality evaluation. At a later point in time a new sample of 20 students are asked to complete the same questionnaire as before.

We are interested in the reply to Question 1. In this case the average for this new sample is 4.2 and the standard deviation is 2.0.

The research question is: *Does this new data set support **the claim** that the true average for the population is statistically significantly greater than 3.47 at the 5% level of significance?*

Note the hypothesis is always a claim which we then try to refute i.e. reject. A hypothesis is not proven, and it is technically not correct to say that a hypothesis is accepted. A hypothesis is either rejected or not re-jected.

There are 5 steps in this type of hypothesis testing which are:-

Step 1: State the Null Hypothesis and the Alternative Hypothesis as:

The Null Hypothesis	H_0:	$\mu_0 = 3.47$
The Alternative[41] Hypothesis	H_1:	$\mu_1 > 3.47$

Note that this is a one-tailed test. We are only interested in the right side of the distribution probability function and this is because the Alternative Hypothesis H_1 is $\mu_1 > 3.47$. This test is sometimes referred to as direc-

---

[40] Statistical packages such as SPSS always compute the t-statistic and its associated prob-ability as the t-distribution which accommodates all sample sizes. For large sample sizes the t-distribution and the normal distribution can be considered identical.

[41] The Alternative Hypothesis is sometimes called the Research Hypothesis. Some research-ers refer to the Null as the "Ho" and the Alternative as the "Ha".

tional. If the Alternative Hypothesis H_1 is $\mu \neq 3.47$ then we would have to use a two-tailed test. The Alternative Hypothesis H_1 is $\mu_1 > 3.47$ or $\mu_1 < 3.47$.

The difference between the use of hypotheses with regards to one and two-tailed tests will be discussed in some detail later.

Step 2: Establish the level of significance of α = 5%. This is the traditional level of significance used in social science. Other levels of significance are used in other branches of science.

Step 3: Decide on the test statistic, the level of significance and determine whether it is a one-tailed or two-tailed test.

The t-statistic is chosen because the sample size is less than 30 and the value of σ is unknown. This is a one-tailed test as we are interested in an alternative hypothesis that $\mu_1 > 3.47$ which indicates a bias in one direction.

Level of significance α = 0.05 or 5%

Step 4: The test statistic is calculated using the formula previously described.

> Sample mean = 4.2
> μ (the hypothesis mean) = 3.47
> Sample standard deviation = 2
> Sample size (n) = 20
> Degrees of freedom (n-1) = 19

$$t_{19} = \frac{(4.2 - 3.47)}{\left(\dfrac{2}{\sqrt{20}} \right)}$$

$$t_{19} = 1.63$$

$$\text{Calc-}t_{19} = 1.63$$

Using the t-tables on page 101 the theoretical value is 1.73 (Table-t). This needs to be compared to the Calc-t.

Note that different authors and teachers of statistics use different language to describe the calculated t and the t which is obtained from the tables. Here we use Calc-t when the number is produced by using the formula and we use Table-t when the number is produced by looking at tables. This number from the tables is also referred to as the theoretical value of t and also as the critical value of t. In general, this statistic will be referred to as Critical-t in this book.

One of the benefits of using Excel is to avoid the use of the t-Tables. Excel will produce the number required faster and more accurately. When the Excel generated t value is used we have referred to it as the critical t.

Step 5: Compare the test statistic Calc-t = 1.63 to the Critical-t = 1.73.

The rule is that if the absolute value of Calc-t >Critical-t[42] then reject the Null Hypothesis, otherwise do not reject the hypothesis.

A table of t-values is provided in Figure 2.22. These are sometimes referred to as theoretical values.

x	0.1	0.05	0.025	0.01	0.005	0.0025	0.001	x
1	3.077685	6.313749	12.70615	31.82096	63.6559	127.3211	318.2888	1
2	1.885619	2.919987	4.302656	6.964547	9.924988	14.08916	22.32846	2
3	1.637745	2.353363	3.182449	4.540707	5.840848	7.4532	10.21428	3
4	1.533206	2.131846	2.776451	3.746936	4.60408	5.59754	7.17293	4
5	1.475885	2.015049	2.570578	3.36493	4.032117	4.773319	5.893526	5
6	1.439755	1.943181	2.446914	3.142668	3.707428	4.316826	5.207548	6
7	1.414924	1.894578	2.364623	2.997949	3.499481	4.029353	4.785252	7
8	1.396816	1.859548	2.306006	2.896468	3.355381	3.832538	4.500762	8
9	1.383029	1.833114	2.262159	2.821434	3.249843	3.689638	4.29689	9
10	1.372184	1.812462	2.228139	2.763772	3.169262	3.581372	4.143658	10
11	1.36343	1.795884	2.200986	2.718079	3.105815	3.496607	4.024769	11
12	1.356218	1.782287	2.178813	2.68099	3.054538	3.428451	3.929599	12
13	1.350172	1.770932	2.160368	2.650304	3.012283	3.372479	3.852037	13
14	1.345031	1.761309	2.144789	2.624492	2.976849	3.325695	3.787427	14
15	1.340605	1.753051	2.131451	2.602483	2.946726	3.286041	3.732857	15
16	1.336757	1.745884	2.119905	2.583492	2.920788	3.251989	3.686146	16
17	1.333379	1.739606	2.109819	2.56694	2.898232	3.222449	3.645764	17
18	1.330391	1.734063	2.100924	2.552379	2.878442	3.196583	3.610476	18
19	1.327728	1.729131	2.093025	2.539482	2.860943	3.1737	3.579335	19
20	1.325341	1.724718	2.085962	2.527977	2.845336	3.1534	3.551831	20
21	1.323187	1.720744	2.079614	2.517645	2.831366	3.13521	3.527093	21
22	1.321237	1.717144	2.073875	2.508323	2.818761	3.118839	3.504974	22

Figure 2.22: A published table of one-tailed t-values for specified levels of significance and degrees of freedom

---

[42] The value of Table-t which is here extracted from a set of t-tables is also obtainable by using the appropriate function in Excel and it is sometimes referred to as the critical value of t.

Note that this table requires the use of degrees of freedom (dof or df or v) which are calculated as the sample size minus 1. The degrees of freedom are shown in Figure 2.22 in the first column to the left (v) and the level of significance is the first row in the same figure. The level of significance equates to the area under the curve and hence the letter A is used in the first row in Figure 2.22.

2.10 The =tinv() function

To calculate the Critical-t value used in the hypothesis testing example above the Excel function =tinv() is used.

=tinv() is used to find the t-value as a function of the probability and the degrees of freedom.

The format of the function is =tinv(probability, df)
Where

probability=the probability associated with the two-tailed t test by default.
df = the degrees of freedom which is equal to n-1

The formula in cell B11 in Figure 2.23 uses =tinv()

We can determine the theoretical (Critical-t) value at a specified level of significance, e.g. for a significance level of 5% the theoretical Critical-t value for the above example is 1.73. This was produced by entering =tinv(2*B5,B3-1). As the Calc-t value 1.63 is less than the Critical-t value 1.73 the Null Hypothesis **cannot** be rejected.

The rule is....**if the absolute value of Calc-t >Critical-t then reject.**

Note that the t-statistic has been typically used for small samples i.e. samples containing less than 30 data points. However, for large samples (i.e. with 30 or more data points) the t-distribution and the normal distribution are almost identical. Thus the t-distribution is sometimes used across the whole range of values.

	A	B	C	D	E	F	G
1	Population mean	3.47					
2	Sample mean	4.2					
3	Count	20					
4	Standard dev.	2					
5	Significance level	5%					
6							
7	t calculated	1.632					
8	t critical value	1.729					
9	Decision	Do not reject null hypothesis					
10							
11	B7 = ABS(B2-B1)/(B4/SQRT(B3))						
12	B8=TINV(2*B5,B3-1)						
13	B9=IF(B7<B8,"Do not reject null hypothesis","Reject null hypothesis")						
14							
15	As Excel produces two-tailed t-critical values by default,						
16	a one-tailed t-critical value can be returned by replacing						
17	the probability with 2*probability.						
18							

Figure 2.23: Using =tinv()

2.11 More examples using the t-statistic

Example 7

To further illustrate these principles some additional examples are now provided.

Surveys over previous years have revealed that satisfaction with working conditions at the University was normally distributed with a value of 4.1 on a scale of 1 to 7.

As a result the University has introduced several new initiatives regarding pay and benefits over the past 2 years.

A new survey of 36 faculty members has been performed and the current average satisfaction score for the faculty was 4.5. The standard deviation for this sample is 1.9.

Does the new survey suggest that there is a significant increase in the level of satisfaction? You want to work at a level of confidence of 95% which is the reciprocal of a level of significance of 5%.

110

Steps in the Solution

Step 1: State the Null Hypothesis and the Alternative Hypothesis

The Null Hypothesis H_0: $\mu=4.1$
The Alternative H_1: $\mu>4.1$

Step 2: Decide on the test statistic, the level of significance and determine whether it is a one-tailed or two-tailed test.

The t-statistic is chosen although the sample size is greater than 30 but the value of σ is unknown. This is a one-tailed test as we are interested in an alternative hypothesis that μ>4.1 which indicates a bias in one direction.

Level of significance α = 0.05 or 5%

Step 3: Calculate the value of t.

$$t_{n-1} = \frac{\left(\overline{X} - \mu_0\right)}{\dfrac{s}{\sqrt{n}}}$$

$$t_{35} = \frac{(4.5 - 4.1)}{\dfrac{1.9}{\sqrt{36}}}$$

$$t_{35} = \frac{0.4}{0.32}$$

$$\text{Calc-} t_{35} = 1.25$$

Step 4: Use the test statistic (remember the degrees of freedom is the sample size (36) minus 1).

The rule is....**if the absolute value of Calc-t >Critical-t then reject.**

From t-tables (see Appendix 2) or from Excel we see that t_{35} (α = 0.05) = 1.69. As our calculated t=1.25 the Null Hypothesis cannot be rejected at the 5% level of significance. Therefore, there does not seem to have been any improvement in the faculty's perception of working conditions.

Excel can be used to perform the calculations in this example, as shown in Figure 2.24. In this spreadsheet the data supplied in this example are entered in column B from row 1 to 5. These are the population mean of 4.1, the sample mean of 4.5, the sample size (which is called the count in Excel) of 36, the standard deviation of 1.9 and the reciprocal of the level of significance (called the confidence level) which is 95%.

	A	B	C	D	E	F	G
1	Population mean	4.1					
2	Sample mean	4.5					
3	Count	36					
4	Standard dev.	1.9					
5	Significance level	5%					
6							
7	t calculated	1.263					
8	t critical value	1.69					
9	Decision	Do not reject null hypothesis					
10							
11	B7 = ABS(B2-B1)/(B4/SQRT(B3))						
12	B8=TINV(2*B5,B3-1)						
13	B9=IF(B7<B8,"Do not reject null hypothesis","Reject null hypothesis")						
14							

Figure 2.24: Excel spreadsheet for *Example 7* designed to perform a t-test at the 5% level of significance.

The calculated t-value is shown in cell B7 and is 1.263.

The rule now becomes.... if the absolute value of Calc-t >Critical-t then reject.

Note the term probability in Excel is synonymous with the term level of confidence, which in turn is related to the level of significance. Also note that the **=tinv() performs a 2-tailed test** and therefore it is necessary to multiply the probability by 2 before it works in a 1-tailed environment. The t-critical value is shown in cell B8 and is 1.690.

In cell B9 the =if() function is used to interpret the results of the calculation and the table value. Note the format of the =if() in excel is

=if(logical_test,value_if_true,value_if_false)

It is useful to now consider whether the Null Hypothesis could be rejected at the 10% level. From the tables or from the computer we see

112

that t_{35} ($\alpha=0.10$) = 1.306. Therefore the Null Hypothesis cannot be rejected at the 10% level of significance either.

The Excel calculations are shown in Figure 2.25:

	A	B	C	D	E	F	G
1	Population mean	4.1					
2	Sample mean	4.5					
3	Count	36					
4	Standard dev.	1.9					
5	Significance level	10%					
6							
7	t calculated	1.263					
8	t critical value	1.306					
9	Decision	Do not reject null hypothesis					
10							
11	B7 = ABS(B2-B1)/(B4/SQRT(B3))						
12	B8=TINV(2*B5,B3-1)						
13	B9=IF(B7<B8,"Do not reject null hypothesis","Reject null hypothesis")						
14							

Figure 2.25: Excel spreadsheet for example number 7 designed to perform a t-test at the 10% level of significance.

Example 8

Surveys over previous years have revealed that the mean satisfaction with working conditions at the University was 4.1 on a scale of 1 to 7.

As a result the University has introduced several new initiatives regarding pay and benefits over the past 2 years.

A new survey of 36 faculty members has been performed and the current average satisfaction score for the faculty was 5.5. The standard deviation for this sample is 1.9.

Does the new survey reveal that there is a significant increase in the level of satisfaction? You want to work at a significance level of 5%.

Steps in the Solution

Step 1: State the Null Hypothesis and the Alternative Hypothesis

Null Hypothesis H_0: $\mu=4.1$ and
Alternative Hypothesis H_1: $\mu>4.1$

113

Step 2: Decide on the test statistic, the level of significance and determine whether it is a one-tailed or two-tailed test.

The t-statistic is chosen as the sample size is greater than 30 but the value of σ is unknown. This is a one-tailed test as we are interested in an alternative hypothesis that μ>4.1 which indicates a bias in one direction.

Level of significance α = 0.05 or 5%

Step 3: Calculate the t.

$$t_{n-1} = \frac{(\overline{X} - \mu_0)}{\dfrac{s}{\sqrt{n}}}$$

$$t_{35} = \frac{(5.5 - 4.1)}{\dfrac{1.9}{\sqrt{36}}}$$

$$t_{35} = \frac{1.4}{0.32}$$

$$\text{Calc - } t_{35} = 4.4$$

Step 4: Use the test statistic (remember the degrees of freedom is the sample size 36-1=35).

The rule is....**if the absolute value of Calc-t >Critical-t then reject**.

From t-tables (page 100) or from the computer we see that t_{35} (α=0.10) = 1.690. As our Calc-t = 4.4 the Null Hypothesis can be rejected. Therefore there seems to have been an improvement in the faculty's perception of working conditions.

Figure 2.26 shows how this example would be calculated using Excel.

	A	B
1	Population mean	4.1
2	Sample mean	5.5
3	Count	36
4	Standard dev.	1.9
5	Significance level	5%
6		
7	t calculated	4.421
8	t critical value	1.690
9	Decision	Reject null hypothesis
10		
11	B7 = ABS(B2-B1)/(B4/SQRT(B3)	
12	B8 = TINV(2*B5,B3-1)	
13	B9 = IF(B7<B8,"Do not reject null	
14	hypothesis","Reject null hypothesis")	
15		

Figure 2.26: Excel spreadsheet for *Example 8*

2.12 Paired samples t-test to compare means

The paired samples t-test is used to compare the values of means from two related samples. One of the most important applications of this is the 'before and after' scenario. In such cases the difference between the means of the samples is not likely to be equal to zero as there will be sampling variation. The Hypothesis test will answer the question "Is the observed difference sufficiently large to reject the Null Hypothesis?"

In Figure 2.27 below the examination scores for 10 candidates have been recorded before and after the candidates participated in a revision course. The scores are shown in Rows 3 and 4 of the spreadsheet. It is important to note that under these circumstances the data is not considered independent.

Does this evidence suggest that the revision course had an effect on the performance of the candidates?

Note that in this case we are looking at the same sample before and after an intervention.

Steps in the Solution

Step 1 – Pair the data: Subtract the scores before and after the intervention (revision course). Average the differences and calculate their standard deviation. This is shown as the Difference in Figure 2.27 below.

115

	A	B	C	D	E	F	G	H	I	J	K	L
1	Candidates	1	2	3	4	5	6	7	8	9	10	
2	Score before	38	41	52	27	18	19	14	50	38	40	
3	Score after	40	45	49	30	24	24	19	49	36	39	
4	Difference	2	4	-3	3	6	5	5	-1	-2	-1	
5												

Figure 2.27: The data is paired

d is defined as the "score after" minus the "score before".
i.e. $d = X_{before} - X_{after}$

$\bar{d} = 1.8$ where $\bar{d}$ = mean of the values of d
$s_d = 3.293$ where s_d = standard deviation of the values of d

Step 2: State the Null Hypothesis and the Alternative Hypothesis

The Null Hypothesis   H$_0$: $\mu_d = 0.0$
The Alternative Hypothesis   H$_1$: $\mu_d > 0.0$

Step 3: Decide on the test statistic, the level of significance and determine whether it is a one-tailed or two-tailed test.

The t-statistic is chosen because the sample size <30. This is a one-tailed test as we are interested in an alternative hypothesis that $\mu_d > 0.0$ which indicates a bias in one direction.

Level of significance $\alpha = 0.05$ or 5%

Step 4: Calculate the t-statistic.

$$t_{n-1} = \frac{(\bar{X} - \mu_0)}{\dfrac{s}{n}}$$

$$t_{n-1} = \frac{(1.8 - 0)}{\dfrac{3.293}{\sqrt{10}}}$$

Calc - t$_9$ = 1.73

Step 5: Use the test statistic (remember the degrees of freedom is the sample size (10) minus 1)).

116

The rule is**....if the absolute value of Calc-t >Critical-t then reject**.

From Excel (or from the tables on P101) we see that Critical-t_9=1.833. As our calc-t = 1.73 the Null Hypothesis cannot be rejected. Therefore it seems that there is insufficient evidence to suggest that the revision course was effective.

The Excel calculations are shown in Figure 2.28.

	A	B	C	D	E	F	G	H	I	J	K	L
1	Candidates	1	2	3	4	5	6	7	8	9	10	
2	Score before	38	41	52	27	18	19	14	50	38	40	
3	Score after	40	45	49	30	24	24	19	49	36	39	
4	Difference	2	4	-3	3	6	5	5	-1	-2	-1	
5												
6	Average difference	1.8										
7	Standard dev.	3.293										
8	Count	10										
9	Significance level	5%										
10												
11	t calculated	1.728										
12	t critical value	1.833										
13	Decision	Do not reject null hypothesis										
14												
15	B6=AVERAGE(B4:K4)											
16	B7=STDEV(B4:K4)											
17	B11 = ABS(B6-0)/(B7/SQRT(B8))											
18	B12=TINV(2*B9,B8-1)											
19	B13=IF(B7<B8,"Do not reject null hypothesis","Reject null hypothesis")											
20												

Figure 2.28: Excel spreadsheet showing hypothesis testing for a paired t-test

2.13 The t-test for independent samples

In most cases, samples will be independent rather than paired, and if we want to test the significance of the difference between their means, we must use a different method to the one presented above.

For example, the senior management of University A claim that on average their reward package is better than the reward package offered by their competitor University B. A random sample of 20 employees from University A and a random sample of 30 employees from University B were asked to score on several dimensions the reward scheme offered to them and the following scores were recorded as shown in Figure 2.29.

University A scores		University B scores		
121	125	125	122	135
120	120	125	130	130
119	125	140	130	130
100	140	90	135	135
128	120	140	150	130
122	120	100	130	150
119	87	90	145	89
115	93	100	125	140
125	126	110	128	130
125	120	135	128	80

Figure 2.29: Independent data which is not paired i.e. two different samples of different sizes[43].

Does this evidence substantiate University A's claim? You should work at a significance level of 5%[44].

Steps in the Solution

Step 1: Calculate the mean, the standard deviation and the variance (the standard deviation squared i.e. S^2) for each sample.

$$\overline{X}_1 = 118.5 \qquad S_1 = 12.15 \qquad S_1^2 = 147.63$$
$$\overline{X}_2 = 124.23 \qquad S_2 = 17.71 \qquad S_2^2 = 350.19$$

Step 2: State the Null Hypothesis and the Alternative Hypothesis.

We will test the Null Hypothesis that there is no difference between the mean scores of the reward packages offered, against the alternative hypothesis that University A's reward package is better than University B's reward package:

Null hypothesis $\qquad$ H₀: $\qquad \mu_1 = \mu_2$
Alternative hypothesis $\quad$ H₁: $\qquad \mu_1 > \mu_2$

---

[43] For two samples to be independent they do not have to be of different sizes.
[44] This test using independent samples relies on an assumption of equal variances and these need to be tested for in advance by means of the F-test. If both samples have more than 30 data elements this is unnecessary.

As we are in fact assuming that both samples have been drawn from the same population, the estimated variance of this population (or pooled variance) is:

$$\hat{S}^2_{pooled} = \frac{(n_1 - 1) * s_1^2 + (n_2 - 1) * s_2^2}{n_1 + n_2 - 2}$$

$$\hat{S}^2_{pooled} = \frac{(20 - 1) * 147.63 + (30 - 1) * 350.19}{20 + 30 - 2}$$

$$\hat{S}^2_{pooled} = 270.01$$

Step 3: Decide on the test statistic, the level of significance and determine whether it is a one-tailed or two-tailed test.

The t-statistic is chosen as the value of α is not known and S is used as an estimate. This is a one-tailed test as we are interested in an alternative hypothesis that $\mu_1 > \mu_2$ which indicates a bias in one direction.

Level of significance $\alpha = 0.05$ or 5%
Here the df is $(n_1 + n_2 - 2)$.

Step 4: Calculate the t.

$$t_{(n_1 + n_2 - 2)} = \frac{\bar{X}_1 - \bar{X}_2}{\sqrt{\hat{S}^2_{pooled}\left(\frac{1}{n_1} + \frac{1}{n_2}\right)}}$$

$$t_{(20+30-2)} = \frac{118.5 - 124.23}{\sqrt{270.01\left(\frac{1}{20} + \frac{1}{30}\right)}}$$

Calc-t_{48} = - 1.209

Step 5: Use the test statistic (remember the degrees of freedom).

The rule is….**if the absolute value of Calc-t >Critical-t then reject**.

From t-tables on Page 101 or from the computer we see that Critical-t_{48} (α=0.05) = 1.677. As our calc-t = 1.209 the test statistic is not significant and the Null Hypothesis cannot be rejected. Therefore there is insufficient evidence to suggest that the University A's reward package is better. The calculations in Excel are shown in Figure 2.30 below.

	A	B	C	D	E	F	G
1		A	B		A	B	
2	Mean	118.50	124.23		121	125	
3	Standard dev.	12.15	18.71		120	125	
4	Significance level	5%			119	140	
5	t-test: Two samples assuming equal variances				100	90	
6		A	B		128	140	
7	Observations	20	30		122	100	
8	Variance	147.63	350.19		119	90	
9	Pooled variance	270.01			115	100	
10	Hypothesized mean difference	0			125	110	
11	df	48			125	135	
12	t calculated	1.209			125	135	
13	t critical value	1.677			120	130	
14	P(T<=t) one-tail	0.116			125	130	
15					140	135	
16	Decision	Do not reject null hypothesis			120	130	
17					120	150	
18	B7=COUNT(E2:E31)				87	89	
19	B8=VAR(E2:E21)				93	140	
20	B9=((B7-1)*B3^2+(C7-1)*C3^2)/((B7-1)+(C7-1))				126	130	
21	B11=B7+C7-2				120	80	
22	B12=ABS(B2-C2)/SQRT((B9*(1/B7+1/C7)))					122	
23	B13=TINV(2*B4,B11)					130	
24	B14=TDIST(B12,B11,1)					130	
25						135	
26	Notice that the two samplemean values (variance)are					150	
27	118.5(147.63 and 130.33(261.95). The one-tailed calculated					130	
28	t-statistic is 1.209 and the highlighted p-value for this test is					145	
29	P=0.116. Since the p-value is higher than 0.05, this does					125	
30	not provide evidence to reject the null hypothesis of equal					128	
31	means at the 5% level of significance.					128	
32							

Figure 2.30: Excel spreadsheet with hypothesis testing for independent samples.

2.14 Right-tailed and Left-tailed hypothesis tests

All the examples above used only one-tailed t tests. These tests took the form of Null Hypothesis H_0: $\mu1 = \mu2$ and Alternative Hypothesis H_1: $\mu1 > \mu2$. These tests are referred to as right-tailed tests. If the tests had the form of Null Hypothesis H_0: $\mu1 = \mu2$ and Alternative Hypothesis H_1: $\mu1 < \mu2$ then the tests are referred to as left-tailed tests.

Figure 2.31 shows a graph of a right-tailed test and Figure 2.32 shows a graph of a left-tailed test.

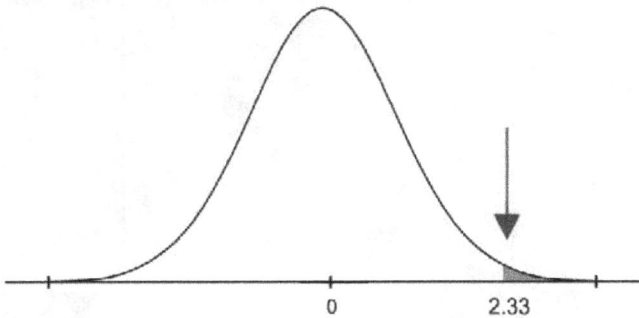

Figure 2.31: A right-tailed test

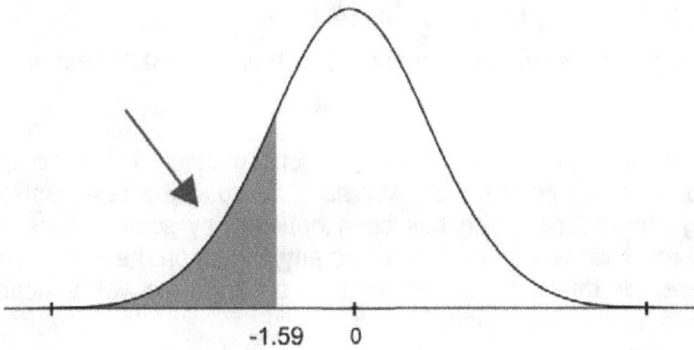

Figure 2.32: A left-tailed test

2.15 Two-tailed Hypothesis tests

A two-tailed test is carried out when the researcher is looking for any change from an expected result, not specifically an increase or a decrease.

These tests take the form of a Null Hypothesis H_0: $\mu1 = \mu2$ and the Alternative Hypothesis H_1: $\mu1 \neq \mu2$. These tests are referred to as two-tailed tests.

If the significance level is α %, then the critical region is in two parts, half in the lower tail and half in the upper tail.

Figure 2.33 shows that the calculated statistic could be either larger or smaller than the table/Excel statistic.

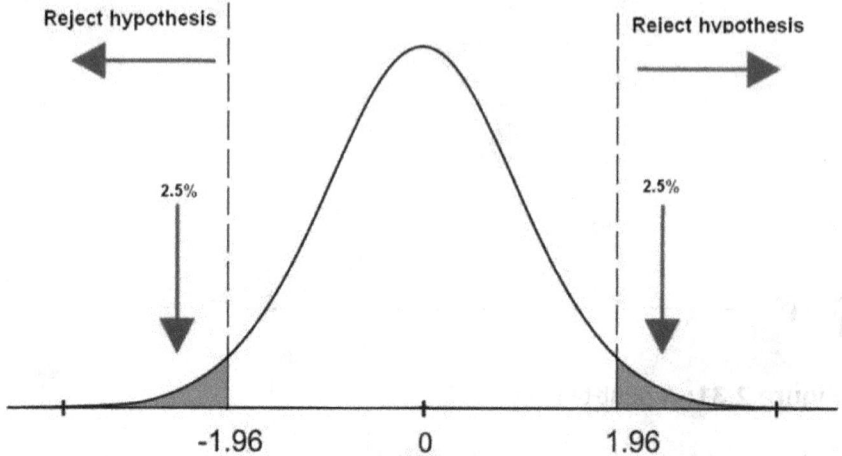

Figure 2.33: A two-tailed test where Z-values 1.96 and -1.96 define the critical regions (shaded in grey above) with an α of 0.05 that is 0.025 in each tail.

As an example, in the past the mean performance score for employees was 60 on a 100 point scale[45]. We have introduced a new controversial training programme which has been opposed by some unions and we wish to establish whether this has had any impact on the employees' performance. We take a single sample of 25 observations with a mean score of 55 and a standard deviation of 15.

We want to test to see if the new mean is significantly different from the original at the 5% level of significance.

Steps in the solution

Step 1: Research question is....*Is the new mean significantly different to the old mean?*

State the Null Hypothesis and the Alternative Hypothesis

Null Hypothesis H_0: $\mu = 60$ and
Alternative Hypothesis H_1: $\mu \neq 60$

Step 2: Decide on the test statistic, the level of significance and determine whether it is a one-tailed or two-tailed test.

---

[45] We are assuming that the true standard deviation, i.e. the population standard deviation is not known.

The t-statistic is chosen as the sample size is less than 30 and the value of σ is unknown. This is a two-tailed test as we are interested in an alternative hypothesis where $\mu \neq 60$.

Level of significance $\alpha = 0.05$ or 5%.

Step 3: Calculate the t-statistic.

$$t_{n-1} = \frac{\left(\overline{X} - \mu_0\right)}{\dfrac{s}{\sqrt{n}}}$$

$$t_{24} = \frac{(55 - 60)}{\dfrac{15}{\sqrt{25}}}$$

$$Absolute \quad Calc - t_{24} = -1.67$$

When consulting Critical-t we can see that it only provides the area in the right hand tail of the distribution. Thus as we are using a two-tailed test with a 5% significance, we need to look for 2.5% in either tail. This means that we consult the t-tables for df=24 and 2.5%. This returns a value of 2.06.

Thus use the rule ... **If the absolute value of Calc-t>Critical-t then reject.**

Step 4: Since the absolute value of -1.67 is < Critical-t, we do not reject the Null Hypothesis. This is translated into the fact that the new controversial training programme does not appear to have had any significant impact on performance.

Figure 2.34 shows the above example in Excel.

	A	B
1	Sample mean	55
2	New mean	60
3	Count	25
4	Standard dev.	15
5	Significance level	5%
6		
7	t calculated	1.667
8	t critical value	2.064
9	Decision	Do not reject null hypothesis
10		
11	B7 = ABS(B2-B1)/(B4/SQRT(B3))	
12	B8 = TINV(B5,B3-1)	
13	B9 = IF(B7<B8,"Do not reject null	
14	hypothesis","Reject null hypothesis")	
15		

Figure 2.34: Two-tailed test

Note that the formula in cell B8 does not require the probability to be multiplied by 2 as Excel defaults to a two-tailed test.

2.16 The use of P-values

The P-value, which is increasingly supplied as an integral part of computer reports is effectively a short cut for hypothesis testing. The P-value is a probability value and thus it has to be between 0 and 1.

The P-value associated with a test is the probability that we obtain the observed value of the test statistic or a value greater in the direction of the alternative hypothesis calculated when the Null Hypothesis is true (has not been rejected).

The P-value is an estimate of erroneously rejecting the Null Hypothesis on the basis of the sample data. This applies to both one and two-tailed tests.

In the case of a one-tailed test we determine the area under the t-distribution in the appropriate direction. To do this we determine the value from the tables.

For the previous example involving a two-tailed test we can now determine the P-value as follows.

Steps in the solution

The required P-value is the area $A_1 + A_2$ under the curve as shown in Figure 2.35. This includes the area to the left of the calculated t-value - 1.67, but also the area to the right of 1.67 as the test is two-tailed.

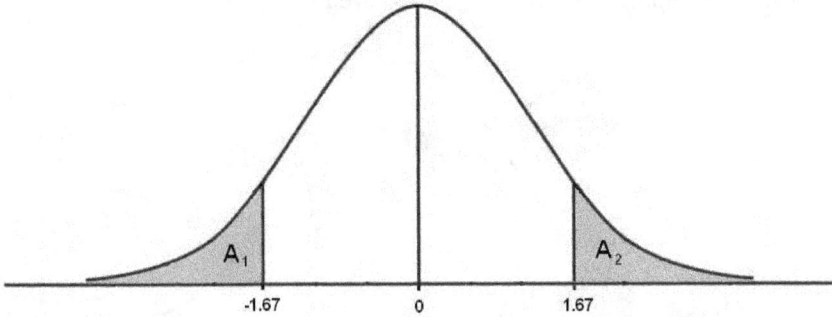

Figure 2.35: Required area for the two-tailed test when t-calc = ± 1.67.

As the graph is symmetrical, the required area $A_1 + A_2 = 2* A_2$. We now calculate the area A_2 as follows using linear interpolation.

Step 1: From the t-tables on p.101, it is noted that it is not possible to find an exact area for the number 1.67 with 24 degrees of freedom.

Step 2: Linear interpolation

1.67 lies between 1.3278 (representing an area of 10%) and 1.7109 (representing an area of 5%) as shown in Figure 2.36.

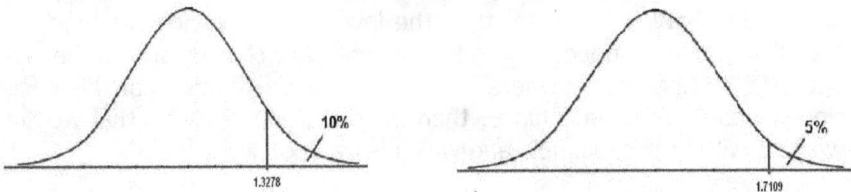

Figure 2.36: Areas under the curve representing 10% and 5%

The difference between these areas = 10% - 5% = 5%

Step 3: The area between 1.3278 and 1.67 is now calculated as a fraction of 5% (.05).

125

$$Area = \frac{1.67 - 1.3178}{1.7109 - 1.3178} * .05$$

$$= .04479$$

$$= 4.479\%$$

This value is represented by the shaded area in Figure 2.37.

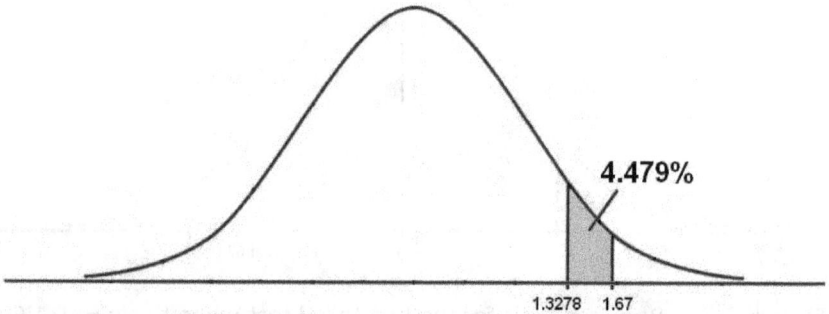

Figure 2.37: Area under the curve between 1.378 and 1.67.

Step 4: Finally, the required area A_2 (to the right of 1.67) is now obtained by subtracting 4.479% from 10% (area to the right of 1.3278).

$$A_2 = 10.00 - 4.479 = 5.521\%$$

This corresponds to a P-value of 0.05521

Step 5: As we have a two-tailed test, the associated P-value will be 2* A_2 = 2 * .05521 = .1104 or 11.04%.

Step 6: Comparing the P-value with the level of significance 0.05 (5%) and as the P-value is greater than the level of significance we conclude that there is not support for rejecting the Null Hypothesis. If the hypothesis is rejected then there is a one in eleven chance that this decision is incorrect, which is higher than the one in 20 (P=0.05) that we are working with in this example and which is traditionally used.

The P-value is another way of thinking about statistical significance. The P-value gives us the level of confidence with which we can reject the Null Hypothesis. If we were to reject the Null Hypothesis in this example we would expect to find that 11 times out of 100 we would be in error. One way of recalling the application of the P-value is to remember *If the P-value is low then the hypothesis must go!*

P-values have only been in regular use in recent years. The reason for this is that it was formerly believed that the significance level should be decided for a test before the data analysis was performed. The reason for this was that the result of the test should be decided exclusively on the pre-chosen significance level. It was believed that if the P-value was known and the results of the test were marginal, researchers might change the significance level to suit their objectives and comply with the data.

2.17 A test for the normal distribution

In this book we have referred to data being normally distributed which is an assumption we need to make in order to be able to use the Z-test and the t-test. However we have not yet addressed the issue of how one might know if it is reasonable to assume that a given data set is normally distributed. We will use two different approaches to consider this matter. The first is the shape of the graph of the data and the second is the value of a series of statistics including the coefficient of skewness and kurtosis.

Data distributions which are skewed would not be considered normally distributed. Two examples of skewed data distributions are given in Figure 2.38 and Figure 2.39.

In Figure 2.38 the data distribution is skewed negatively which means that the mean is to the left of the median.

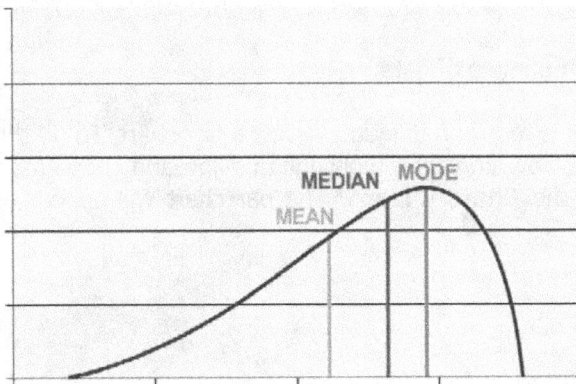

Figure 2.38: A negatively skewed distribution.

In Figure 2.39 the data distribution is skewed positively which means that the mean is to the right of the median.

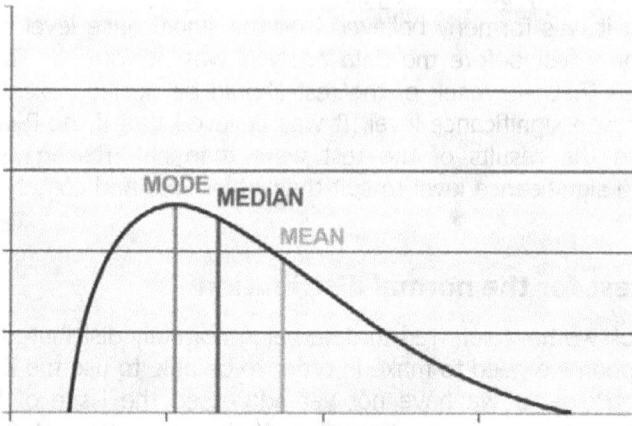

Figure 2.39: A positively skewed distribution.

The data as represented by these graphs could not be treated as normally distributed.

Consider the following set of 30 data points or elements.

	A	B	C	D	E	F	G	H	I	J
4	1	1	2	2	3	3	4	4	4	5
5	5	5	6	6	6	6	6	5	5	5
6	5	4	4	3	3	2	1	1	1	4

Figure 2.40: Sample of data

The first task is to graph this data set as a bar chart. To do this move the data into one row and then highlight this line and chose the **Bar Chart** option from the **Chart Wizard**. The bar chart will appear as shown in Figure 2.41.

128

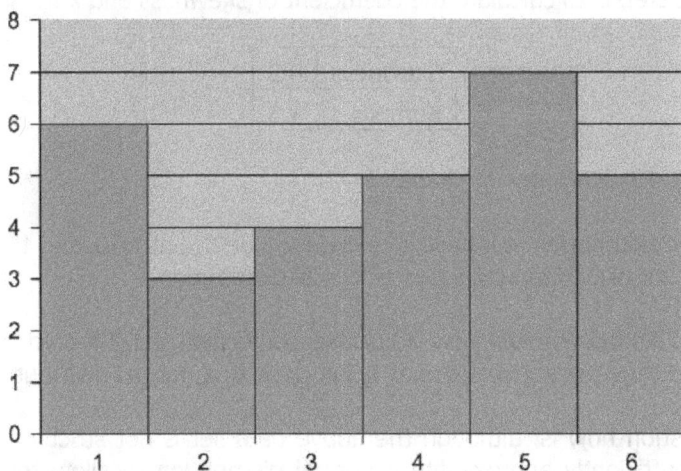

Figure 2.41: A bar chart of the data

One of the main characteristics of a normal distribution is that the data is distributed under a bell shaped curve which is symmetrical i.e. it will give an equal number of data points on each side of a central point which is determined by the mean. From Figure 2.41 it may be seen that the data is approximately bell shaped. There is no one central data point in this data and there are more data points to the right of the centre of the data than there are to the left.

By eyeballing the bar chart we can see that the distribution of the data is not perfectly normal. However, the bar chart is approximately normal and therefore we should look at some of the other indicators of a normal distribution.

The first statistics we consider are the mean, median and the mode.

Mean	3.9
Median	4
Mode	5

Figure 2.42: Measures of average

If a data distribution is normal then the mean, the median and the mode should be equal. Clearly this is not the case. However there is not a great difference between the values of these three statistics.

The next step is to calculate the coefficient of skewness and kurtosis.

Skewness	0.3
Kurtosis	1.3

Figure 2.43: Measures of shape

A normal distribution will have a skewness coefficient of 0 and thus the above score of 0.3 approximates a normal distribution.

A normal distribution will have a kurtosis coefficient of 1.3 if calculated in Excel and thus the above score of 1.3 is close to a normal distribution.

The question now is, although the above data set is not strictly normal, does it sufficiently approximate a normal distribution to allow the techniques that assume the normal distribution to be used?

In general the normal distribution techniques are often sufficiently robust to be usable with the above data. If it were decided that a more formal test for normality was required other techniques could be used.

In the social sciences, many scales and measures have scores that are positively or negatively skewed. This could reflect the underlying construct being measured as might be the case when respondents record their scores on life satisfaction questionnaire items giving rise to a negative skew for the distribution, with the majority of the respondents being reasonably happy with their situation in life. The incomes of salary earners are generally positively skewed with most earners at the lower end of the scale.

There are more formal ways of deciding if a data set is normally distributed. One of these includes the use of the chi-square test and this is beyond the scope of the book.

2.18 Summary-Part 2

This Part moves the learner from relatively simple statistical concepts towards the more powerful ideas and techniques. The material here introduces the learner to inferential statistics. This has been done by addressing data distributions and then moving on to the probability distribution which is most frequently used i.e. the normal distribution and the use of the Z score. Estimation, both point and interval, has also been addressed. The use of the t-distribution has been demonstrated.

The central concept of hypothesis testing is then examined and applied to paired t-tests and t-tests on independent samples.

The earlier section of this Part only addresses one-tailed tests and so towards the end, two-tailed tests are introduced as are the P-value and a test to establish if a data set is normally distributed.

This Part of the book relies on the use of a material number of worked examples as this is the way that learners will acquire the skills needed to be proficient with these techniques.

Readers are reminded to save their workings in Excel and to make paper copies or printouts where they require further backup.

List of Excel functions used for the first time in this Part of the book.

Function	Result
=frequency()	This is an array function which calculates how often values occur for a specified range of values.
=normdist()	Calculates the P-values for the Normal Distribution. This is a one-tailed probability.
=tdist()	Calculates the P-values for the t Distribution
=tinv()	Calculated the theoretical or table values from the t-Distribution. This is two-tailed.
=abs()	Returns the absolute or positive value of a calculation irrespective of the result of the calculation.

More details of these functions are provided in the Help command within the spreadsheet.

Self test 2

No.	Question	Answer
1	What is a data frequency table?	
2	What is a useful heuristic for calculating the width of a data interval for a frequency table?	
3	Give 4 characteristics of a normal distribution.	
4	What do we mean by a standardized normal distribution?	
5	Define the Z-score?	
6	What are normal distribution tables?	
7	Define the term test statistic.	
8	What is the Null Hypothesis?	
9	When can we say we have proved the Null Hypothesis?	
10	Explain the meaning of μ	

No.	Question	Answer
11	Explain the meaning of σ	
12	Explain the meaning of $\overline{X}$	
13	When is the t-test preferable to a Z-test?	
14	What is meant by paired t-tests?	
15	When is a t-test said to be in-dependent?	
16	What does it mean to say that the hypothesis is always a claim?	
17	What does the theoretical value of t mean?	
18	What does a P-value of 0.05 mean?	
19	When is it necessary to use a two-tailed test?	
20	In what ways are normal distri-bution and the t-distribution similar and in what way do they differ?	

Assignment No 2

1. What is the difference between sample statistics and population parameters?
2. What do you understand by point estimation and interval estimation?
3. How do you interpret the confidence levels associated with interval estimation?
4. What do you understand by the term "level of significance"?
5. What is the difference between statistical significance and practical significance?
6. Given that a new process does not appear to have an adequate level of output how would you formulate and express a Null Hypothesis and an Alternative Hypothesis? How would you design such a study?
7. Explain the difference between a one-tailed and a two-tailed test.
8. A new approach to instructing students is adopted by the Institute. You are asked to design a test to establish if it has had an impact on the performance of the students. Is this going to be a one-tailed or a two-tailed hypothesis test?

Additional exercises

1. Display the data below as a frequency distribution and draw an appropriate graph of the frequency distribution.

	A	B	C	D	E	F	G	H	I	J
1	4	29	113	121	168	106	56	33	190	58
2	56	63	113	170	89	138	117	47	77	170
3	52	195	29	106	118	70	116	97	149	135
4	180	33	78	151	86	42	7	175	91	182
5	56	44	98	124	72	150	193	128	103	39
6	109	111	145	103	173	192	107	156	172	1
7	134	157	78	160	43	85	138	161	91	138
8	183	193	51	79	130	189	88	52	113	109
9	155	111	165	132	37	184	75	20	29	150
10	10	150	61	97	77	97	174	60	68	11
11	18	27	150	191	194	146	37	39	94	46
12	31	73	1	145	96	60	152	8	194	155
13	46	193	36	103	80	28	110	50	17	5
14	188	14	86	159	149	150	41	151	24	134
15	149	165	91	117	4	35	119	115	92	33
16										

2. What heuristic have you used to establish the width of the intervals you have used? Produce a second frequency distribution and graph using this data and comment on the difference between them.

3. Using the data supplied below comment on whether you would consider this data set to be normally distributed. Explain your answer.

1	2	3	4	5	6	6	6	7	7
7	8	8	8	8	7	7	7	7	6
6	6	5	4	3	2	2	2	2	

4. The number of pupils completing their secondary education in the county each year is normally distributed with mean 14000 and standard deviation 750. What is the probability that 16000 will complete their secondary education this year?

5. Sean is in a large school where the scores for mathematics are normally distributed with a mean (μ) of 55 and a standard deviation (σ) of 10. Sean has passed his mathematics exam with a score of 80. Carole is from a similar school where the scores for mathematics are normally distributed but they take a different examination which has a mean of 30 and a standard deviation of 5. Carole's score is 42. Who has done better in the mathematics exams?

6. Explain the meaning of the Null Hypothesis (H_0) and the Alternative Hypothesis (H_1).

7. The Widget Company Limited has been making widgets for many years and its output is normally distributed. Historical records show that the mean weight of widgets is 350 and the standard deviation is 50. A new widget is produced with a weight of 450. With a significance level of 5% is there support to claim that the 450 widget belongs to the same group as the others?

8. A group of 10 students is asked to rate the quality of the food in the student refectory on a scale of 1 to 10 where 1 is very poor and 10 is excellent. The replies of the students are shown below. A new supervisor is appointed in the student refectory and he introduces a new menu as well as a more friendly attitude towards the students. The opinions of the same group of students are canvassed again and the results of the second set of interviews are also shown below. Is there evidence to support the hypothe-

sis that the new supervisor has improved the students' rating of the refectory? Work at a significance level of 5%.

	S1	S2	S3	S4	S5	S6	S7	S8	S9	S10
Test before intervention	4	5	3	6	5	4	3	4	3	3
Test after interverntion	4	3	6	6	7	6	5	6	4	4

9. The IQ of physics graduates is recorded at two different universities. At the first university there are 20 physics graduates and at the second university there are 25 physics graduates this year. Using the data supplied below examine the hypothesis that the graduates from the first university have scored better in their IQ tests. Work at a significance level of 5%.

University A	123	170	130	160	173	170	142	126	148	143
	144	166	166	152	167	147	144	162	139	148
University B	152	169	156	175	169	136	173	158	135	139
	155	149	174	167	146	172	159	139	136	142
	155	146	169	172	172					

10. Explain why some researchers or statisticians believe that using the t-test for hypothesis testing is better than using the Z-score.

11. A factory produces widgets with a mean diameter of 160 mm and a standard deviation of 11mm. New technology has been introduced and is supposed to improve the accuracy of our process. We take a sample of 25 widgets with a mean of 155 and a standard deviation of 15. Has our process been improved? Work at a significance level of 5%.

12. Under what set of circumstances may a researcher say that he/she has proved his/her hypothesis?

13. Explain the importance of the P-value.

14. Formulate a Null Hypothesis and Alternative Hypothesis which will require a two-tailed test.

15. How might a researcher test a data set in order to establish if it is normally distributed?

A Note on Excel Functions

There are approximately 365 functions in Excel which are divided into 11 categories. In addition it is possible to purchase more in the form of add-ins which extend the power of the spreadsheet.

Excel provides some help in choosing the right function by using the Insert Function commands but to employ functions effectively you need to be acquainted with the mathematics behind the function.

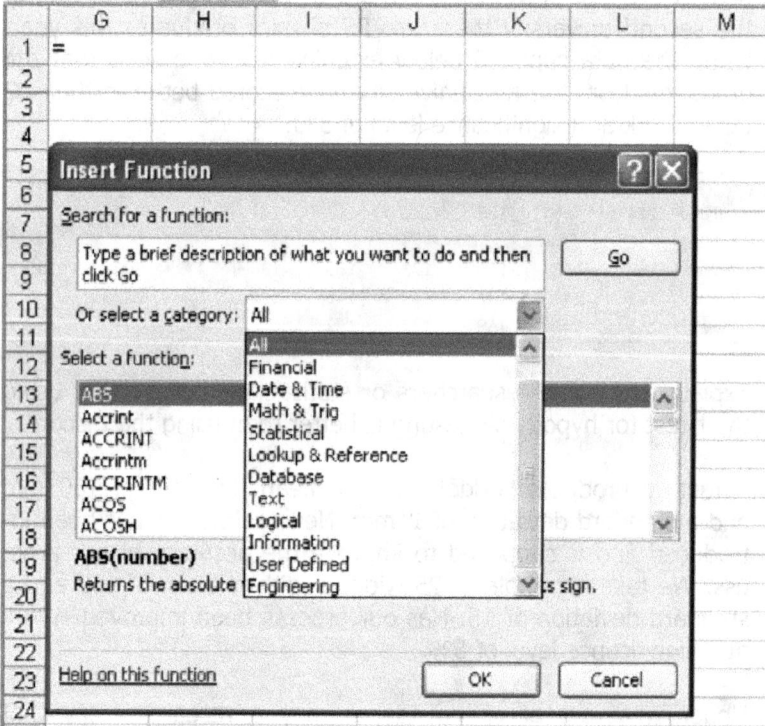

The form of an Excel function is always **=FunctionName(Argument)** where the Argument may be a cell, a group of cells or other forms of data.

Part 3

Linear Regression, $\chi 2$(Chi-square) and ANOVA (Analysis of Variance)

Some interesting techniques

This Part of the book explores how to create a regression model, a chi-square test and ANOVA tests and it supplies some comment on how to interpret the results.

Like the previous Parts of this book this Part requires some small knowledge of Excel. If you don't understand basic Excel you will need help with this.

This book is accompanied by a computer file in which the data has already been entered.

Statistics is a subject in which there is one dominant learning issue. For most people statistics will only be understood through the process of doing. Concepts and the ability to conceptualise are of course important but skill in this field of study will only materialise out of the hard work of application of the techniques. And applying these techniques once or twice is generally insufficient. Repetition will reinforce understanding and develop skills.

Glossary of Terms

y=βx+c+e **or** **y=a+bx** **or** **y=mx+c**	The standard formula for simple linear regression. This equation is sometimes accompanied by the letter "e". The "e" represents the error or unexplained (random) variation which is always present in such models.
y=β_1x$_1$+β_2x$_2$+.....+β_kx$_k$+c$_k$+e	Formula for multiple linear regression.
ANOVA (Analysis of Variance)	A statistical test of whether the means of several independent groups are all equal. This technique is normally used with three or more groups of data.
ANOVA Single factor or One-way	Used when working with 2 or more groups and their mean scores are to be compared on a continuous variable.
ANOVA Two factor	This is used when two or more variables are being studied and the researcher is interested in the impact of two independent variables on one dependent variable.
Bivariate analysis	This refers to the analysis of the relationship between two variables.
Contingency table	Contingency tables are normally used with nominal data and used to record and analyse the relationship between two or more variables.
$\chi2^{\cdot}$ (Chi-square)	A theoretical probability distribution in inferential statistics used to compare actual observations to expected observations and defined as: $$\chi^2 = \sum \frac{(O-E)^2}{E}$$ Only nominal or qualitative data is normally used.

Expected frequency	The observed frequencies agree with the expected frequencies.
Eyeballing the data	The visual inspection of the data to see if there are any obvious trends.
F-statistic	The F-statistic in the ANOVA table provides a test for the predictive ability for the model. It is a function of the R^2 and should it be found to be significant then it may be concluded that the model has significant predictive ability.
Goodness of fit test	A statistical model which compares an observed set of data to an expected distribution.
Method of least squares	The method of drawing a line representing the best fit for a data set.
Multicollinearity	In regression analysis multicollinearity concerns the correlations between the predictor variables (inter item correlations). It is undesirable for the predictors to be too highly correlated. It is recommended that the intercorrelations not exceed 0.70. Should the intercorrelations exceed 0.70 then the predictors are said to exhibit undesirable levels of multicollinearity. Similarly if the correlation between variables is less that 0.30 it is generally considered that there is an inadequate correlation between the variables.
One-way classification	The basis for the simplest case of the analysis of variance in which a set of observations are categorized according to values of one variable or one characteristic.

Outlier	An outlier is an observation or data point that is numerically distant from the rest of the data set of which it forms part.
Residuals	The difference between the calculated and observed data points.
r	r is a measure of the extent to which two variables are linearly associated. It is also known as the co-efficient of correlation. The value of r lies between -1 and +1. The value of +1 indicated the strongest positive linear association. The value of -1 indicates the strongest negative association. The value 0 indicates little or no linear association between the variables but there may be a relationship of a non-linear kind. The r is sometimes referred to as Pearson's product moment co-efficient of correlation.
r^2	r^2 is called the co-efficient of determination and is a measure of the amount of variance shared (common) between two variables. It measures what proportion of the variation in Y which may be attributed to the variation in the value of X.
R	R is referred to as the coefficient of multiple determination and in linear regression modelling applications indicates the correlation between a single dependent variable and a set of independent (predictor) variables.
Regression	Fitting a mathematical model which links a dependent variable to one or more independent variables. The researcher specifies the nature of the relationship between the dependent and the independent variables i.e.

| | which variable is the independent (predictor) variable and which is the dependent variable.

Regression analysis shows an association between the variables concerned but it does not imply any cause and effect. |
|---|---|
| **Sample size** | The number of data points used in the calculations. Different statistical techniques require different sample sizes and it's important to know the sample size required before you commence your data collection. |
| **Scatter diagram or plot or graph** | Normally reserved for 2 dimensional graphs consisting of X and Y-axis. A diagram showing the location of data points on an axis without any joining lines. |
| **t-statistics** | In regression the t statistic provides a test for significance of the individual predictors. Should the t value be found to be significant then the corresponding regression parameter is said to be significantly different from zero and its associated variable is said to be a significant predictor of the dependent variable. |
| **2X2 table** | A matrix with 2 rows and 2 columns |

Regression Analysis

3.1   Correlation and regression

Before embarking on a study of regression analysis it is useful to understand the concept of correlation. In correlation analysis the focus is on
whether an association exists between two variables, sometimes referred
to as bivariate analysis. The correlation co-efficient provides an indication
of the nature and the strength of the association. In correlation analysis
there is no cause-effect relationship assumed. You may recall that in Part
1 inter-item correlation coefficients were used to help validate the constructs. In that case we were exploring whether the variables which were
combined to form the construct were adequately associated with one
another.

Regression analysis allows the modelling of relationships between a single output variable (dependent) and one or more input variables (independent). Modelling allows us to combine the input variables so as to
predict and explain the output variable. This requires the researcher to
specify the outcome variable and the predictor variables. In order for a
researcher to be able to claim the predictor variable/s to be the cause
and the outcome variable to be an effect it is necessary for the model to
be grounded in adequate theory. There is no formal statistical test available to establish cause and efect relationships. Variables may be deemed
to be in a cause and effect relationship if they are logically and tempo-
rally connected and if there is an adequate theoretical explanation for
this relationship. In asserting cause and effect it is important to be aware
of confounding variables. A confounding variable is a variable that the
researcher failed to control or eliminate and which led to an incorrect
interpretation of the test. A typical situation where a confounding variable is active is when the independent and dependent variable appear to
be in a cause and effect relationship but actually they only have a relationship with the third or confounding variable.

3.2   Different correlation coefficients

As has already been discussed a correlation coefficient can range between -1 and +1. If a correlation coefficient is large i.e. close to +1 then
it is said that the variables are strongly positive correlated. This is shown
in the first section of Figure 3.1A. Here it may be seen that as the class
attendance increases so do the marks which the students obtain. Class

attendance is the independent[46] variable and the marks obtained by the students is the dependent variable.

It is likely that the correlation between these two variables will be close to 1.

In the second section of Figure 3.1A we have an example of a strongly negative correlation. In this example the speed at which the vehicle is driven and the time taken for a journey are correlated. The speed of the vehicle is the independent variable and the time taken is the dependent variable. It is likely that the correlation coefficient between these variables will be close to -1.

In the final example provided in Figure 3.1A the number of stats visible at night is correlated with the number of ice cream cones sold in the market place. There is no correlation between these variables and the correlation coefficient will be close to zero.

Scatter Diagram	Types of Correlation	Example
Marks / Class attendance	Positive	Scatter diagram showing a positive correlation be-tween class atten-dance and the marks students achieved in their summer examina-tion
Time to destination / Speed	Negative	Scatter diagram showing a nega-tive correlation between the speed of a vehicle and the time to destination.

[46]The independent variable is sometimes called the predictor variable and the dependent variable is also called the outcome variable or the response variable.

Scatter Diagram	Types of Correlation	Example
 Ilo of stars ... Ice-cream sales	None	Scatter diagram showing no correlation between the number of starts and sales of ice-cream.

Figure 3.1A: Positive, negative and zero correlations

3.3 From research question to questionnaire to data

This section concerns an organisation in which the top management has come to believe that there maybe concerns among the managers about the organisation's strategy. As there are a considerable number of managers it was decided that their opinions of this topic could be accessed by way of a self completion questionnaire.

The research question here asks *Is there any connection between the management's indicated satisfaction with the organisation's strategy and their salary level or their length of service or both?* This section of the book only considers the replies received from three of the questions in the questionnaire or measuring instrument. Managers were invited to rate their satisfaction with the organisation's strategy on a scale of 1 to 7 where '1' indicated the lowest level of satisfaction and '7' indicated the highest level[47].

In addition the managers were invited to provide information about themselves in terms of their salary, their length of service to the organisation and their age next birthday[48]. The salary was rounded to the nearest thousand and the length of service to the nearest year. The age next birthday is also provided. Figure 3.1 shows these variables after they have been entered into the spreadsheet and checked to ensure that no errors were made during the data entry process.

---

[47] In regression analysis the dependent variable has to be a quantitative variable. In this example the scores on satisfaction will be treated as though they were quantitative (i.e. as measured on an interval scale). For categorical dependent variables purpose built modelling techniques such as Discriminant Analysis and logistic regression analysis may be used.

[48] These variables will be regarded as the independent or predictor variables.

Seventeen questionnaires were returned but this is considered an adequate sized sample for the technique of regression analysis.

	A	B	C	D	
1	**Regression analysis**				
2	Salary	Length of service	Age next birthday	Satisfaction with strategy	
3	10	3	50	2	
4	12	2	22	2	
5	15	4	65	3	
6	22	3	32	2	
7	23	1	43	6	
8	34	1	34	5	
9	34	4	64	3	
10	35	5	62	4	
11	45	4	34	5	
12	50	7	33	6	
13	60	6	62	6	
14	65	6	45	5	
15	65	3	55	7	
16	66	8	65	5	
17	70	5	32	6	
18	75	4	35	7	
19	95	9	65	4	

Figure 3.1: Original Data as entered from the questionnaire

3.4   Simple linear regression

The researcher or analyst is interested in the first instance in establishing if there is a relationship between the informants' views[49] of the organisation's strategy and the level of their income. It is suggested that the level of income would be the independent (or predictor) variable while the view of the strategy is the dependent variable.

In applying regression analysis there is a need to use a sample size which gives credibility to the results. There are a number of rules of thumb relating to the sample size to be used. The minimum sample size should be 5 observations per independent variable in the regression model. It is, however, suggested that in designing a regression study 10 observations per independent variable should be aimed at as there will always be unusable questionnaires returned to the research co-ordinator. Here 17 ob-

---

[49]This study used only one variable to represent the satisfaction of the employees with the organisation's strategy. This has been for the purposes of illustration of the use of regression analysis. In practice a more comprehensive approach often involving multiple variables/items would be taken for the measurement/assessment of satisfaction with any aspect of an organisation.

servations have been returned which exceeds the 5 per independent variable.

There are a number of ways to start the process leading up to regression analysis. One of the ways is to "eyeball" the data. In simple terms this means to visually scrutinise the data, which may be done with the numbers in tabular form or they may be presented graphically by making use of what is referred to as a scatter plot. In general it is thought that a graphical representation of the data is a useful way to see if there are any obvious trends. With regards to eye-balling the data if there is no apparent pattern in the data then it may not be worth while to proceed with regression analysis. On the other hand eyeballing the data might reveal a pattern which is non-linear and thus some other approach might be more useful.

The first step is thus to produce a scatter plot or graph showing the independent and the dependent variable. The approach taken here is that the two variables are extracted from the original location in the spreadsheet and are located together in two adjacent columns. Then in order to draw a meaningful graph the data first needs to be sorted by the independent variable. This is shown in Figure 3.2.

	E	F
1		
2	Salary	Satisfaction with strategy
3	10	2
4	12	2
5	15	3
6	22	2
7	23	6
8	34	5
9	34	3
10	35	4
11	45	5
12	50	6
13	60	6
14	65	5
15	65	7
16	66	5
17	70	6
18	75	7
19	95	4

Figure 3.2: The original data sorted by Salary

From simply looking at the two columns it does appear that as the independent variable increases the dependent variable also increases and thus there may be some statistically significant relationship between these two variables.

Then these columns are produced as a scatter diagram in Figure 3.3 and they appear as follows.

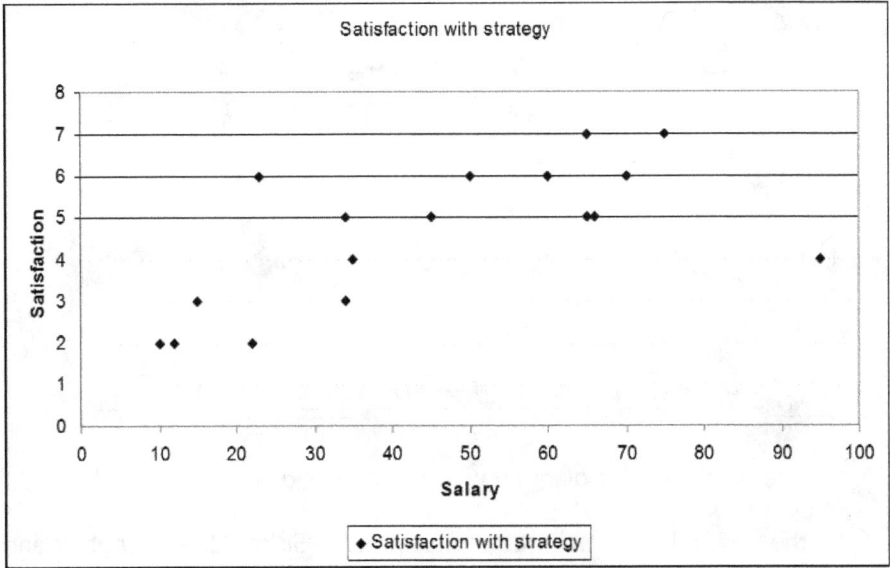

Figure 3.3: A Scatter diagram showing Satisfaction by Salary

From the above graph it can be seen perhaps a little more clearly that in general as the salary level increases the level of satisfaction increases. By observation (eyeballing the plotted points) the research could also suggest that the relationship is likely to be described by a straight line equation[50].

Excel provides a method of quickly fitting a curve to the data. By right clicking on one of the data points a menu appears and if the option **Add Trendline** is chosen then the researcher may choose a trend line from a range offered by the software. In this case a **Linear** trend line should be selected and a line will be drawn on the graph as is shown in Figure 3.4.

---

[50]Of course no cause and effect relationship can be deduced from this graph. The direction of causality is up to the judgement of the researcher based on theory and experience.

3.5   Fitting the curve

Curve fitting is an important aspect of regression analysis and Excel is helpful with this.

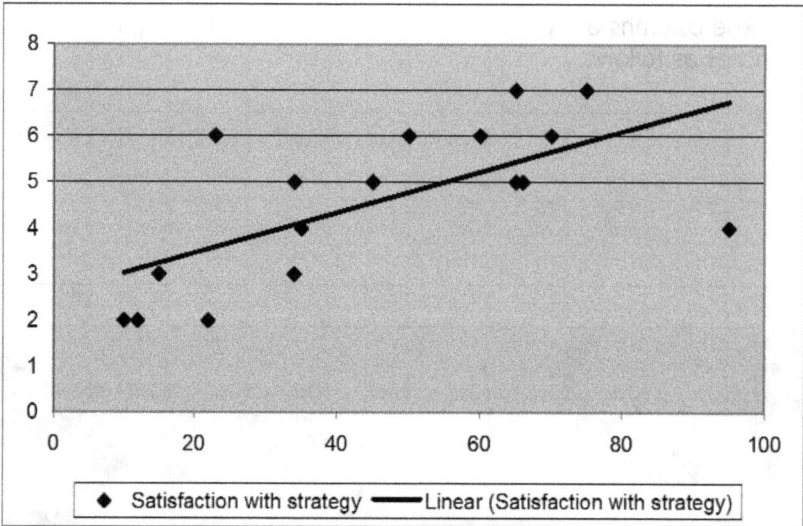

Figure 3.4: A scatter diagram with a quick trend line

By the way, the data point at an income of £95k could be an outlier and should be investigated as such to see how it affects the slope estimate. There is also another potential outlier at salary level £23k. The inclusion of an outlier can have a significant effect on the slope of the line and this question needs to be addressed early in this process. A description as to how to assess and handle outliers is provided in an earlier section.

A next step which may be taken is to determine the equation of the straight line which would "best" describe the relationship between these two variables[51]. This may be achieved in Excel in a number of different ways. The quickest way is to use the trendline command as described above. In this approach having selected **Add Trendline** and **Linear** it is then necessary to select **Options.** Within the options sub menu tick the boxes for **Display equation on chart** and **Display R-squared value on chart**.

---

[51] The best fitting line is determined by the method of least squares and is often referred to as the least squares line.

The equation representing the line and the value of the R^2 will be displayed on the screen as shown in Figure 3.5.

3.6 Quick formula

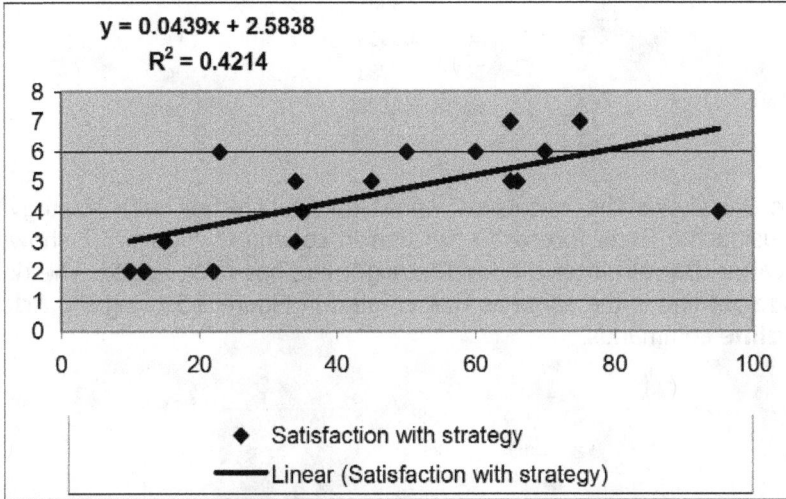

Figure 3.5: A scatter diagram with a trend line and equation and R^2

Another approach available in Excel is the use of the =forecast() function. The mathematics behind the =forecast() function is based on the equation for a straight line which is y=βx+c. This is the usual way of denoting a straight line[52]. In this equation β is the slope of the line and c is the intercept of the line with the Y-axis. In the literature the parameter β is referred to as a regression coefficient.

Using the regression equation y=0.0439x+2.5838 from Figure 3.5 above we may now calculate some of the values on this graph, by replacing x with the given values below. The results are shown below.

---

[52]Formally the equation y=βx+c should be stated as y=βx+c+e where e is a random error.

	A	B	C
1	x	y	
2	10	3.0228	
3	20	3.4618	
4	30	3.9008	
5	40	4.3398	
6	50	4.7788	
7	60	5.2178	
8			

Figure 3.6 shows the calculated values for "satisfaction with strategy" after using the Excel forecast() function in column C. Figure 3.7 shows the scatter diagram after the fitted straight line has been added. The fitted straight line is the same as that created in Figure 3.5 using the **Add Trendline** commands.

	A	B	C	D	E	F
1						
2	Salary	Satisfaction with strategy	Linear regression estimate	Slope (β)	Intercept (c)	
3	10	2	3.02	0.0439	2.5838	
4	12	2	3.11			
5	15	3	3.24			
6	22	2	3.55			
7	23	6	3.59			
8	34	5	4.08			
9	34	3	4.08			
10	35	4	4.12			
11	45	5	4.56			
12	50	6	4.78			
13	60	6	5.22			
14	65	5	5.44			
15	65	7	5.44			
16	66	5	5.48			
17	70	6	5.66			
18	75	7	5.88			
19	95	4	6.76			
20						
21	The formula in C3 is =FORECAST(A3,$B$3:$B$19,$A$3:$A$19)					
22	This is copied through to G19					
23	The formula in D3 is =SLOPE(B3:B19,A3:A19)					
24						
25	Another way to calculate the linear regression estimate in C3 is					
26	=$D$3*A3+$E$3 and this formula can be copied to C19.					
27						

Figure 3.6: The original data with the Simple Linear Regression line

As has already been mentioned in Excel there are various ways of establishing the estimate of the least squares line. The =forecast() function calculates the values for this estimate directly. However, the regression may also be calculated by using the =slope() function which calculates the value of β and using the =intercept() function to calculate the value of c. If the slope and the intercept are calculated separately then the equation, $y=\beta x+c$ needs to be entered into a cell and this formula copied for as many cells as there are data points. It is useful to calculate the estimates for the least squares line using both methods as a cross- check that the correct result has been obtained.

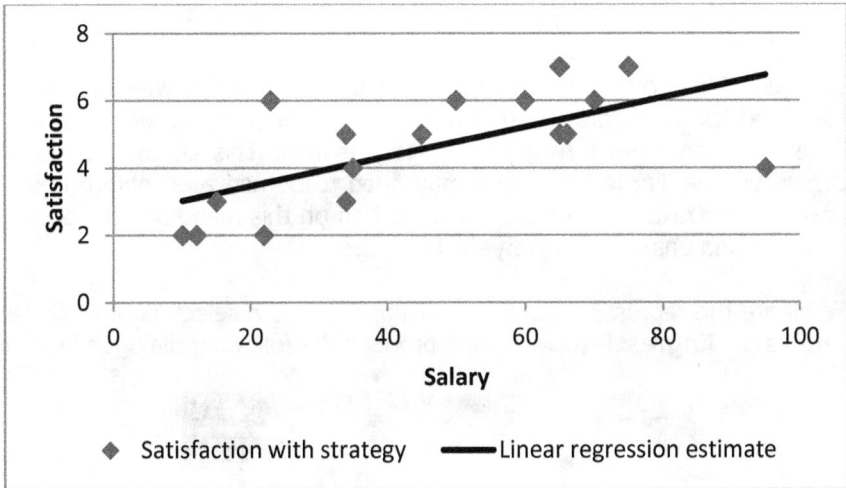

Figure 3.7: Original data with the fitted least squares line[53]

Goodness of fit
Taking the approach described here the following six steps are used to assess the regression model in terms of goodness of fit.

Step 1: Determine the value of the r and the r^2
The researcher will now want to know how good a fit this least squares line is, and this will be measured by the correlation coefficient between the actual values of "satisfaction with strategy" and the predicted values of "satisfaction with strategy" as obtained from the fitted least squares line. In Excel this is calculated using the =correl() function or by using the **Tools - Data Analysis - Regression** commands, which will be discussed later.

---

[53] Notice that the two potential outliers are highly visible.

In this example the value of the correlation coefficient (r)[54] is 0.649. The question is then whether this calculated correlation (multiple R in Excel) is a satisfactory level of fit[55].

In practice assessment of goodness of fit is usually done through the square of the correlation coefficient (r^2) which in this example has the value of 0.421 as per Figure 3.5 and is the R^2 in the Excel output. R^2 is interpreted as a measure of the extent to which the variability in the dependent variable is explained by the regression model. From this result we can conclude that the independent variable "salary" explains 42% of the variability in the "satisfaction with strategy" scores thus leaving 58% of the variability in "satisfaction with strategy" scores unexplained[56].

In Figure 3.8 a comprehensive set of statistics is provided which includes the r and the R^2 as discussed above. This has been produced using the Excel command **Data Analysis – Regression.** This command is accessed via the **Tools** menu and may need to be activated before being available. If **Data Analysis** is not an option on this menu select **Tools - Add-ins** and enable the **Analysis Toolpak**.

To create the regression output shown in Figure 3.8 select **Tools - Data Analysis - Regression**, which will produce the following dialogue box:

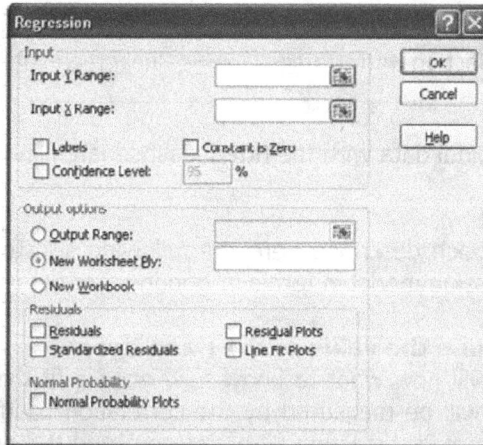

---

[54] In the simple linear regression case the r is the correlation coefficient between Y and X. In this case r will be equal to R which is the correlation coefficient between the estimated Y and the estimated Y from the fitted regression model.
[55] Although this depends on the sample size, values of r below 0.3 (or r^2 0.09) should not be regarded as a fit that will have value in a practical sense.
[56] The unexplained variance could be due to random error or to other predictor variables which have not been indentified and included in the model.

Enter the location of the dependent variables (Y-range) and the independent variables (X-range) and specify where the output is to be placed – in this case in a New Worksheet. One clicking OK the Summary Output in Figure 3.8 is produced.

	A	B	C	D	E	F	G	H	I
1	SUMMARY OUTPUT								
2									
3	*Regression Statistics*								
4	Multiple R	0.649118							
5	R Square	0.421355							
6	Adjusted R Square	0.382778							
7	Standard Error	1.333811							
8	Observations	17							
9									
10	ANOVA								
11		*df*	*SS*	*MS*	*F*	*gnificance F*			
12	Regression	1	19.43189	19.43189	10.92262	0.00481			
13	Residual	15	26.68576	1.779051					
14	Total	16	46.11765						
15									
16		*Coefficient*	*andard Err*	*t Stat*	*P-value*	*Lower 95%*	*Upper 95%*	*ower 95.0%*	*pper 95.0%*
17	Intercept	2.583829	0.68737	3.759007	0.001896	1.118734	4.048925	1.118734	4.048925
18	Salary	0.043911	0.013286	3.304938	0.00481	0.015592	0.07223	0.015592	0.07223
19									

Figure 3.8: Summary output from the **Data Analysis - Regression** command.

Hypothesis testing for the regression model

Step 2: Perform a hypothesis test to explore if there is predictability in the model.
A logical question to ask is whether the model does explain a statistically significant proportion of the variance in the dependent variable. This involves a test of significance on the R^2. Stated formally this will appear as follows:-

Null Hypothesis H_0: There is no predictive ability in the model
Alternative Hypothesis H_1: There is predictive ability in the model

Step 3: Here we will test the hypothesis at the 5% level of significance ($\alpha=5\%$).

Step 4: In the ANOVA table in Figure 3.8 the P-value associated with the Null Hypothesis is 0.0048 which is less than the traditionally used level of 0.05 for alpha. The rule for using the P-value discussed in Part 2 was – *If the P-value is low then the hypothesis must go* (i.e. the hypothesis can be rejected). Here the P-value is lower than the required significance level.

Step 5: This supports the rejection of the Null Hypothesis and thus there is evidence that the model has predictive ability.

In the ANOVA table the next figure which should be consulted is the significance of the F statistic for the regression model. This statistic is used to assess the overall significance of the fit of the regression model. It is used to test whether the R^2 value is statistically significant. In this example the F-statistic is 10.92 and its associated significance level is 0.0048. The reported significance value can be interpreted as indicating a highly significant statistical fit. The fit can be said to be significant at the 0.48% level. This means that there is only a 0.48% chance that the regression model has no predictive value.

Step 6: Examine estimates of the slope and the intercept

In addition Excel goes on to provide more data concerning the slope of the straight line as well as an estimate of the Intercept. The slope estimate β is 0.04 and the intercept c (also called the constant) estimate is 2.58. The column labelled P-value indicates the statistical significance of the regression coefficients and is based on the t-test. The t-test is used to establish whether the regression coefficient is significantly different from zero. If it is statistically different from zero then its associated variable is a highly statistically significant predictor of the dependent variable. The P-value for the intercept[57] is 0.001 (0.1%) and for the slope is 0.005 (0.5%). Thus both are highly significant[58]. Notice that the P-values[59] are both well below the 5% level of significance.

3.7   Residuals

Another issue which needs to be addressed is the question of Residuals. In this case the Residual is defined as the difference between the actual (observed) "Satisfaction with Strategy" score and the estimated "Satisfac-

---

[57] In practice the significance of the intercept may not be of concern as it could be seen as merely a mathematical adjustment which has no physical interpretation.

[58] If the P-value is less than 0.001 then the result is regarded as very highly significant, If the P-value is less than 0.01 then the result is regarded as highly significant, If the P-value is less than 0.05 then the result is regarded as significant.

[59] The P-value which is another name for the probability value may be defined as the largest level of significance at which we would not reject the Null Hypothesis. The advantage of the P-value is that it allows us to test an hypothesis without first having to specify a value for α. If the P-value is 0.15 it means that the probability of erroneously rejecting the Null Hypothesis is 15% which is generally regarded as too high. This means that if the hypothesis is rejected then we are likely to experience 15 cases in a 100 where it was wrong to so do.

tion with Strategy" score. This is calculated by =C3-B3 in cell D3 and the result needs to be copied for the length of the column.

	A	B	C	D	E
1					
2	Salary	Satisfaction with strategy	Linear regression estimate	Residuals	
3	10	2	3.02	1.02	
4	12	2	3.11	1.11	
5	15	3	3.24	0.24	
6	22	2	3.55	1.55	
7	23	6	3.59	-2.41	
8	34	5	4.08	-0.92	
9	34	3	4.08	1.08	
10	35	4	4.12	0.12	
11	45	5	4.56	-0.44	
12	50	6	4.78	-1.22	
13	60	6	5.22	-0.78	
14	65	5	5.44	0.44	
15	65	7	5.44	-1.56	
16	66	5	5.48	0.48	
17	70	6	5.66	-0.34	
18	75	7	5.88	-1.12	
19	95	4	6.76	2.76	

Figure 3.9: The residuals – estimated value minus the actual value

If the estimates of the "Satisfaction with Strategy" are unbiased then the Residuals should be randomly distributed around a value of Zero. The quick ways of "eyeballing" this is to plot the Residuals as a scatter diagram. This is shown in 3.10.

The residual plot is used to assess whether the fitted line is appropriate. A random pattern for the residuals indicates an acceptable fit. Patterns in the residuals may be an indication that the addition of one or more independent variables to the fitted model is likely to result in an improvement. This plot is particularly useful in fitting a multiple regression model as described below.

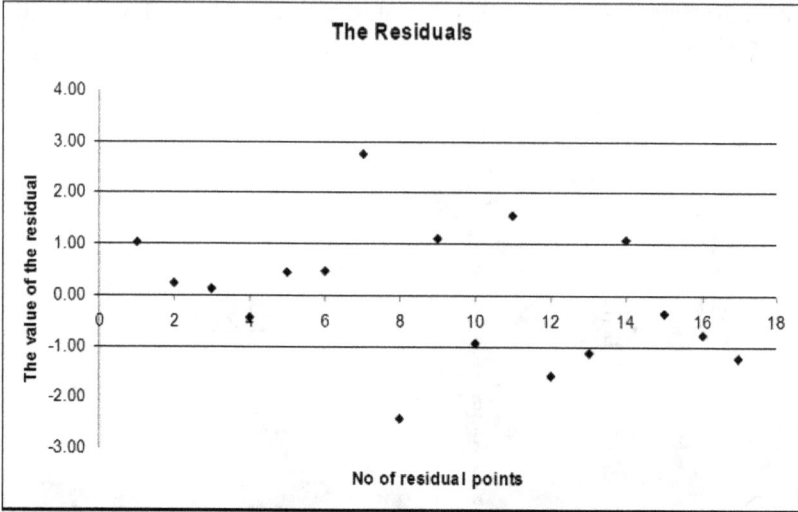

The Residuals

Figure 3.10: A scatter diagram of the residuals[60]

3.8 Removing outliers

Apparent outliers should not be removed from the data unless there is an obvious reason why they should not be considered part of the data set. Outliers which are the result of errors in data collection or data capture should be removed. Outliers which distort the purpose of a survey may be omitted. An example of this might be a study to ascertain the average income of a middle-class area. It could happen that in such an area there is one multimillionaire. In such a study it may well be appropriate to omit such a person from the study. The removal of outliers can make a significant impact on the results of the analysis of the data. It is crucial that inconvenient data points are not casually omitted.

Eyeballing the data in Figure 3.7 it will be seen that there are two possible outliers. These are the data points representing the salary of 22 matched with the satisfaction score of 2 and the salary of 95 matched with the satisfaction score of 4. If the two possible outliers are removed then the fit of the regression model changes and the regression analysis report in Figure 3.11 is obtained[61].

---

[60] The horizontal axis in this graph is the actual "Satisfaction with Strategy" scores.

[61] Strictly speaking one outlier at a time should be removed and the analysis stops when an "acceptable" fit is achieved. Clearly experience and judgements plays a large role in this process.

	A	B	C	D	E	F	G	H	I
25	Regression analyis without the outliers								
26	SUMMARY OUTPUT								
27									
28	*Regression Statistics*								
29	Multiple F	0.902164							
30	R Square	0.813899							
31	Adjusted I	0.799584							
32	Standard E	0.791241							
33	Observati	15							
34									
35	ANOVA								
36		*df*	*SS*	*MS*	*F*	*Significance F*			
37	Regressio	1	35.59452551	35.594526	56.854621	4.24901E-06			
38	Residual	13	8.138807825	0.6260621					
39	Total	14	43.73333333						
40									
41		*Coefficients*	*Standard Error*	*t Stat*	*P-value*	*Lower 95%*	*Upper 95%*	*Lower 95.0%*	*Upper 95.0%*
42	Intercept	1.423362	0.460276277	3.0924068	0.0085711	0.428995072	2.417728	0.42899507	2.417727953
43	X Variable	0.070896	0.009402405	7.5402003	4.249E-06	0.050583354	0.091209	0.05053335	0.091208674

Figure 3.11: Regression analysis without the outliers

Note the regression coefficient r = 0.902 and coefficient of determination r^2 =0.813.

One of the only justifiable reasons for treating these data points as out-liers (if it is clearly not a bogus data point) is if it could be argued that the individuals involved were not actually typical of the population from which the sample was to be drawn. Even in this case the outlier should not be automatically rejected. Rather the research question needs to be consulted to see if the outlier is useful in answering the question.

3.9 Multiple linear regression

Should the degree of fit resulting from the simple linear model be deemed inadequate, one or more additional independent variables can be added to the model in order to improve the degree of fit. In this example two possible additional independent variables are "length of service in the organisation" and "age next birthday". Before these can be added to the model it is important that the researcher is able to justify why there could be a relationship between the dependent variable and these new vari-ables. Remember this technique does not necessarily suggest that there is a cause and effect relationship between the variables.

These additional variables are shown in Figure 3.12.

▲	A	B	C	D	E
1					
2	Salary	Length of service	Age next birthday	Satisfaction with strategy	
3	10	3	55	2	
4	15	4	54	3	
5	35	5	50	4	
6	45	4	45	5	
7	65	6	45	5	
8	66	8	41	5	
9	95	9	43	4	
10	23	1	30	6	
11	12	2	59	2	
12	34	1	40	5	
13	22	3	60	2	
14	65	3	25	7	
15	75	4	23	7	
16	34	4	60	3	
17	70	5	33	6	
18	60	6	35	6	
19	50	7	33	6	
20					

Figure 3.12: Three independent variables and one dependent variable

As the data sorting, graphing procedures and the use of the =forecast() function are exactly the same they will not be repeated for the other two independent variables. However the results of the =correl() are different and are worthy of separate comment and discussion.

The challenge is to decide which independent variables to include in the model. For the additional independent variables to be useful predictors they need to be correlated with the dependent variable.

The correlation between "length of service" and "satisfaction with strategy" is found to be 0.160. The r^2 is therefore .0256, which implies that length of service as a predictor of satisfaction with strategy has low predictive value. This r^2 suggests that the variable "length of service" will explain less than 3% of the variation in the "satisfaction with strategy" scores. Turning to the other potential predictor of "satisfaction with strategy", namely "age next birthday", its correlation coefficient with "satisfaction with strategy" is found to be -0.962[62]. Note that in this case the correlation coefficient is negative. The value of the correlation coefficient here suggests on average a high degree of correlation but as the value is negative it indicates that the older the individual the less satisfied he or she is likely to be with the strategy. It needs to be remembered once again that this does not in itself suggest any cause and effect relationship.

Another challenge is to ensure that the independent variables measure different things. In other words the independent variables are not too highly correlated with themselves. This inter item correlation between the independent variables is also referred to as multicollinearity.

If two or more variables are too highly correlated (r> 0.7) with one another then consideration should be given to including only one of the variables as an independent variable. In order to explore the relationship among the independent variables correlation coefficients are calculated for "Salary" to "Length of Service" and "Salary" to "Age" and "Length of Service" to "Age". These are shown in Figure 3.13.

	I	J	K	L	M	N	O	P
1								
2		Correlation Sal to Sat	Correlation LoS to Sat	Correlation Age to Sat	Correlation Sal to Los	Correlation Sal to Age	Correl LoS to Age	Corr Sat to Est
3	Correlations	0.649	0.161	-0.962	0.695	-0.617	-0.110	0.649
4								

Figure 3.13: Inter item correlations for the 3 independent variables

3.10 Multicollinearity

The numeric values shown in Figure 3.13 above represent the multicollinearity between the independent variables and can be portrayed diagrammatically to provide a clearer view of how the variables are related to each other. From Figure 3.14 it is possible to access the pool of predictors of "Satisfaction with Strategy".

---

[62] A correlation coefficient of -0.962 will strike the researcher as being unusually high and this should trigger further study to ascertain if there is any special reason for this.

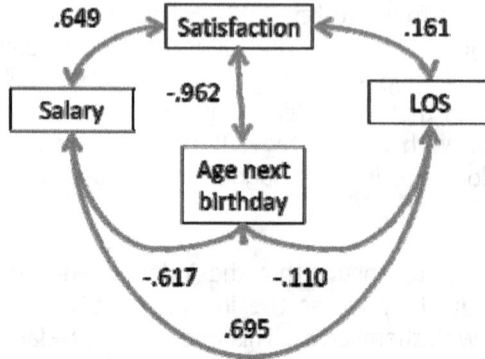

Figure 3.14: The diagrammatic representation of the inter-item correlations of the variables in the model

It can be seen that the correlation coefficients for "Salary" to "Length of Service" (0.695) and "Age" to "Salary" (-.617) are high. On the other hand the correlation coefficients for "Length of Service" to "Age" (-0.110) is relatively low and this suggests that there is no relationship here. Earlier it was established that "Length of service" was not correlated to "Satisfaction with Strategy" and so is eliminated as an independent variable. This suggests that "Age" and "Salary" could both be considered for inclusion in a regression model to predict and/or explain "Satisfaction with Strategy". When the regression model includes two or more independent variables it is referred to as a multiple regression model.

When there are multiple independent variables or predictors and one dependent variable it is sometimes useful to consider the combined effect of the multiple independent variables. The process by which this is done is referred to as multiple linear regression and in Excel this is calculated by using the **Tool – Data Analysis – Data – Regression** command.

When this is executed Excel produces the data in Figure 3.15.

The form of the equation for linear multiple regression is

$$y = \beta_1 x_1 + \beta_2 x_2 + \ldots + \beta_k x_k + c_k$$

	A	B	C	D	E	F	G	H	I
1	SUMMARY OUTPUT								
2									
3	Regression Statistics								
4	Multiple R	0.764811							
5	R Square	0.584936							
6	Adjusted R Square	0.525642							
7	Standard Error	1.169303							
8	Observations	17							
9									
10	ANOVA								
11		df	SS	MS	F	gnificance F			
12	Regression	2	26.97589	13.48794	9.864883	0.002122			
13	Residual	14	19.14176	1.367269					
14	Total	16	46.11765						
15									
16		Coefficient	andard Err	t Stat	P-value	Lower 95%	Upper 95%	ower 95.0%	pper 95.0%
17	Intercept	3.236194	0.663513	4.877366	0.000244	1.813101	4.659287	1.813101	4.659287
18	Salary	0.070375	0.016205	4.342804	0.000675	0.035619	0.105132	0.035619	0.105132
19	Length of service	-0.42169	0.179522	-2.34895	0.034031	-0.80672	-0.03665	-0.80672	-0.03665
20									

Figure 3.15: Multiple linear regression analysis output

The first comment which needs to be made is that the correlation coefficient (R) is 0.964. This is an improvement on the Simple Linear Regression which was first applied. Similarly the coefficient of determination (R^2) is higher than that calculated with one variable. An R^2 of 0.930 shows that the two independent variables may be considered to explain 93% of the variation in the dependent variable which is 37% more than the one-variable regression model[63]. Now 7% of the variation in the dependent variable remains unexplained.

Adding additional variables to a regression model will always show an improvement in the R^2 and the adjusted R^2 is provided to take this tendency into account.

Note the significance of the F-statistic is high and therefore the corresponding P-value is small.

---

[63] One of the issues which need to be considered is the order in which the variables are introduced into the model. In this example if Age had been used in the simple linear regression model the amount of variation explained in the satisfaction scores by this variable alone would have been 92.5%. This level is nearly as much as that explained by the use of the multiple regression model above (using two variables) and therefore there is a question of whether the formulation of the multiple regression model was necessary.

As specified our model may now be considered to provide a good fit. The next step is to look at each independent variable to establish their significance in predicting satisfaction.

Referring to Figure 3.15 the significance (that is the P-value) of X, the first variable which is the salary has a P-value of 0.34 which is not statistically significant at the 5% level. This suggests that salary does not contribute significantly when used in conjunction with age next birthday. In the case of multiple regression analysis age next birthday has a P-value of 0.000 which is very highly significant at the 5% level.

The reason for this is that the two predictors salary and age next birthday are highly correlated (correlation is -0.617) and therefore inclusion of both variables in the model is not necessary. Additionally it should be noticed that age next birthday alone explains 92.5% of the variation in the satisfaction scores.

3.11 Plotting the residuals

In the same way as residuals were calculated for simple linear regression we may calculate residuals for multiple linear regression as shown in Figure 3.16.

	K	L	M	N	O
4					
5	Salary	Age next birthday	Satisfaction with strategy	Estimated by Multiple Linear Regression	Residuals
6	10	55	2	2.840727832	-0.8407278
7	15	54	3	2.998634314	0.00136569
8	35	50	4	3.630260238	0.36973976
9	45	45	5	4.329021075	0.67097893
10	65	45	5	4.450049833	0.54995017
11	66	41	5	4.966698437	0.03330156
12	95	43	4	4.886891554	-0.8868916
13	23	30	6	6.110628813	-0.1106288
14	12	59	2	2.342233542	-0.3422335
15	34	40	5	4.900701715	0.09929828
16	22	60	2	2.27509863	-0.2750986
17	65	25	7	7.003035663	-0.0030357
18	75	23	7	7.318848626	-0.3188486
19	34	60	3	2.347715885	0.65228411
20	70	33	6	6.012098521	-0.0120985
21	60	35	6	5.696285559	0.30371444
22	50	33	6	5.891069763	0.10893024

Figure 3.16: Calculated residuals for multiple regression

Plotting the residual values on an X,Y axis is useful to see if there is any trend among them.

From an eyeballing of Figure 3.17 the residuals appear to be randomly distributed.

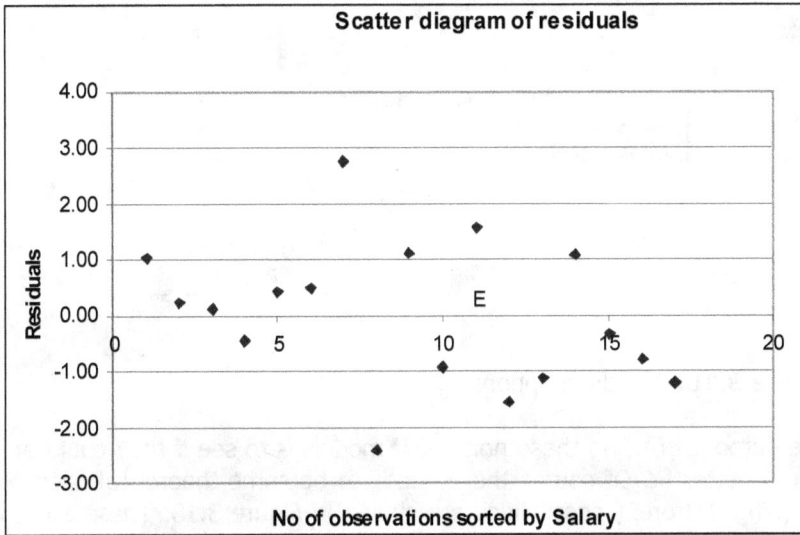

Figure 3.17: Scatter diagram of the residuals

3.12 Curve fitting

One of the important features of Excel is the facility to consider a number of different types of curves which could be used to understand the data. Under the **Trendline Options,** as shown in Figure 3.18, six different alternatives are supplied. The options within the **Type** page are Exponential, Linear, Logarithmic, Polynomial, Power and Moving Average. There is also a further Options page with further functionality and this is shown in Figure 3.19.

In addition there is an option which allows forecast both **Forward** and **Backward**.

3.13 Some non-linear lines

Figures 3.20, 3.21, 3.22 and 3.23 show the graphs that these options produce together with the formulae which underpin these graphs.

Figure 3.24 shows a moving average graph which may also be used as well as the forecast feature available in Excel as shown in Figure 3.25.

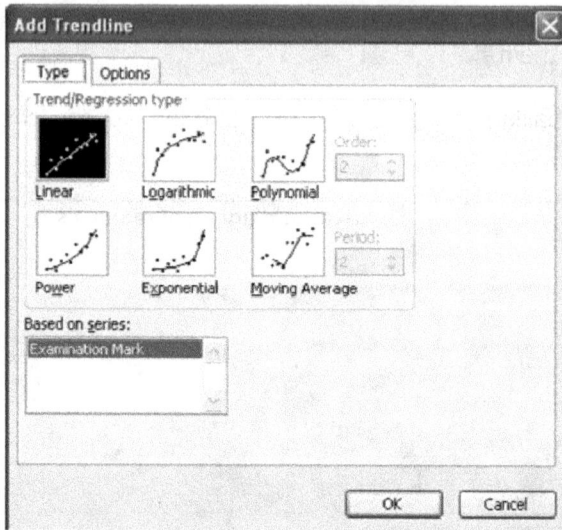

Figure 3.18: Trendline options

The purpose of using these non-linear models is to see if they could provide a better fit. Of course there needs to be some theoretical basis for
so doing. Different possibilities are shown in Figure 3.18. These are the
most commonly encountered models that after suitable transformation
are amenable to estimation by means of linear regression techniques and
examples of these are shown in the following Figures.

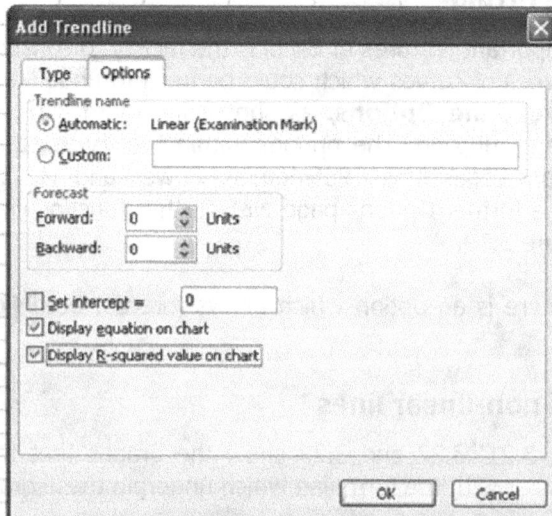

Figure 3.19: More Trendline options within the Options section

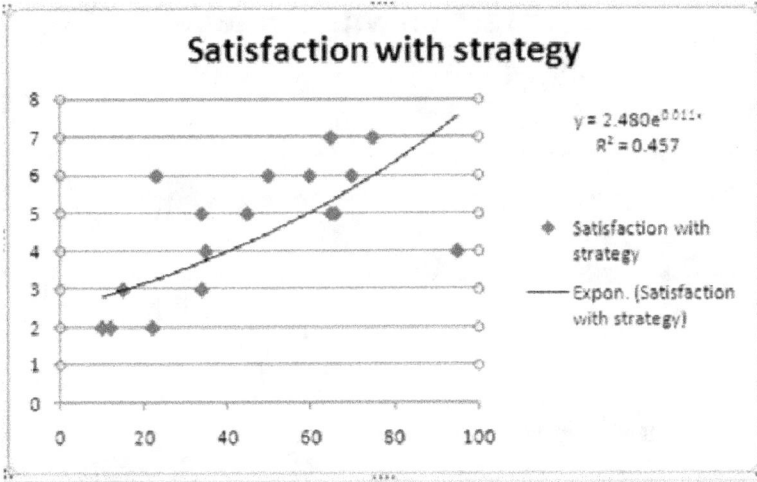

Figure 3.20: An exponential curve

It is interesting to be able to see how different models may be used within a regression context with the same data set. The nature of the model should be determined by theoretical considerations as well as perhaps the data itself so as to guide the researcher in the choice of the independent variable domain.

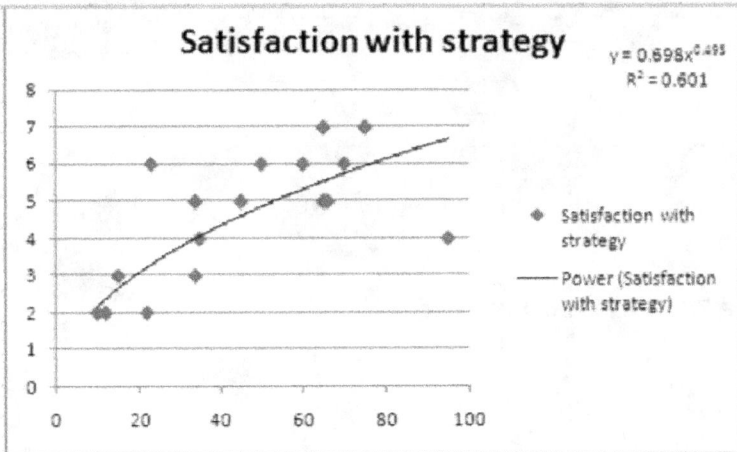

Figure 3.21: A power curve

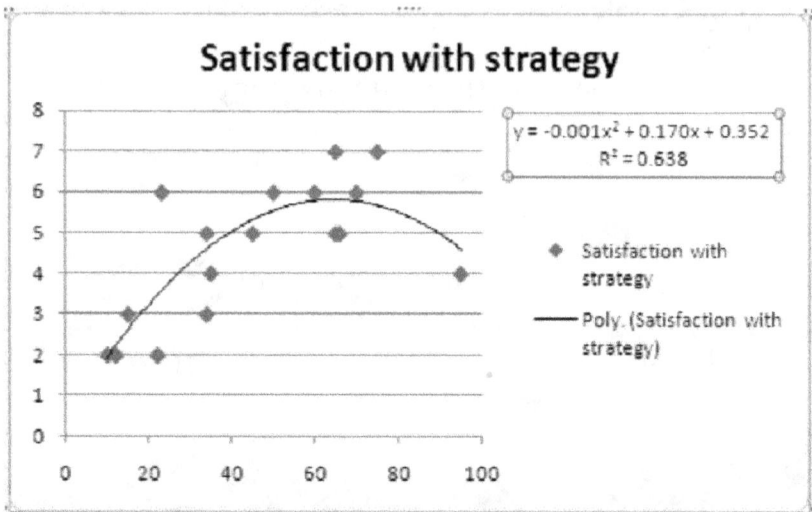

Figure 3.22: A polynomial curve

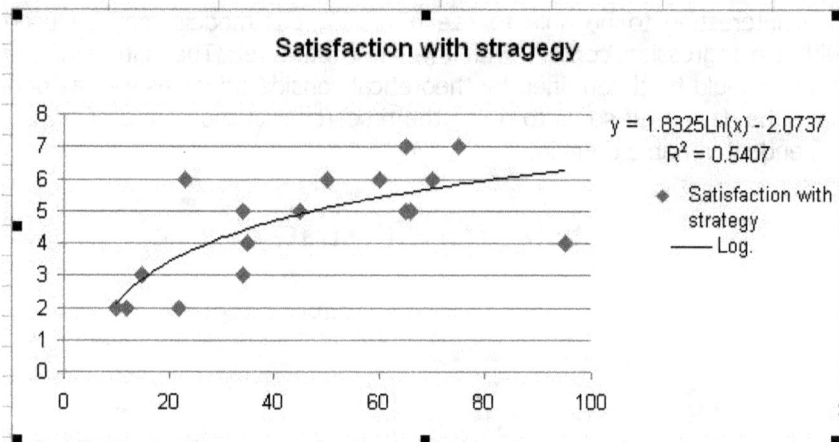

Figure 3.23: A logarithmic curve

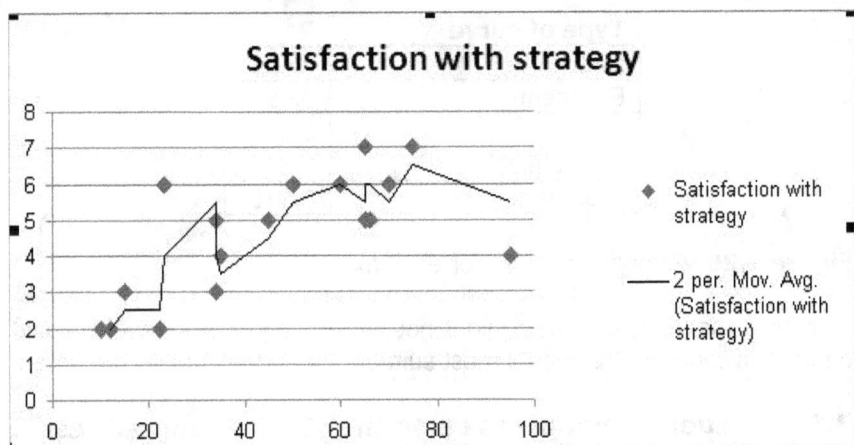

Figure 3.24: Two month moving average

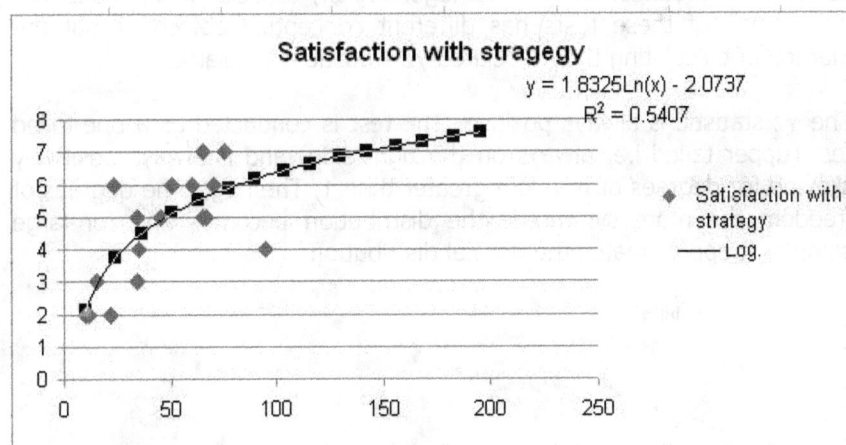

Figure 3.25: A forecast forward using the Options Forward commands

3.14 Compare the R^2

Considering the different models that are available within Excel we may compare the goodness of fit using the R^2. Figure 3.26 below shows these and from this you can see that the polynomial[64] gives the highest R^2

---

[64] It should be noted that in Figure 3.25 the last data point in the data set plays a large part in influencing the goodness of fit. If this data point is omitted as an outlier then the decision will be different.

Type of curve	R^2
Liner	0.421
Exponential	0.457
Power	0.601
Polynomial	0.638
Logarithm	0.541

Figure 3.26: Comparing the R^2 for each model

Of course the value of the R^2 might not be the only criterion which could be used in choosing the model most suitable for understanding the data.

3.15 Categorical variables using the $\chi^2 \cdot$ Chi-squared test

The χ^2 test is one of the most widely used approaches for testing hypotheses using categorical variables. χ^2 tests are sometimes referred to as tests of goodness of fit, homogeneity or, association or independence. Each of these tests has different conceptual objectives but the method of calculating the associated χ^2 statistic is the same.

The χ^2 statistic is always positive. The test is conducted as a one-tailed test (upper tailed i.e. always on the right side) and is always positively skewed for degrees of freedom greater than 1. The larger the degrees of freedom the more symmetric the distribution becomes and for large samples it approximates the normal distribution.

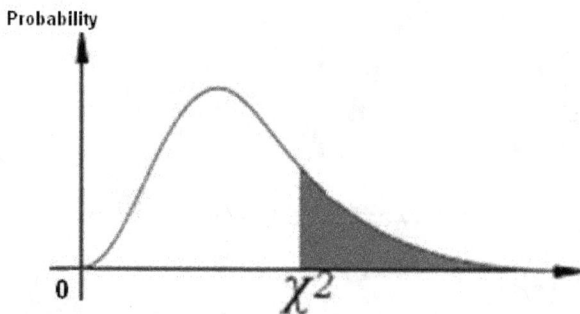

Figure 3.27: A χ^2 probability distribution with probabilities on the Y axis and χ^2 values on the x-axis.

The basis of the χ^2 test is the comparison of the data frequencies observed with the data frequencies expected under the assumption of the Null Hypothesis. Large discrepancies between these two lead to the rejection of the null hypothesis.

To repeat large differences between the observed and the expected lead to the rejection of the Null Hypothesis. A sample of $\chi 2$ critical values is provided in Figure 3.28. A more complete set of $\chi 2$ critical values at various levels from 0.50 to 0.005 levels can be seen in Appendix 3.

V\area	.500	.250	.100	.050	.025	.010	.005
1	0.45494	1.32330	2.70554	3.84146	5.02389	6.63490	7.87944
2	1.38629	2.77259	4.60517	5.99146	7.37776	9.21034	10.59663
3	2.36597	4.10834	6.25139	7.81473	9.34840	11.34487	12.83816
4	3.35669	5.38527	7.77944	9.48773	11.14329	13.27670	14.86026
5	4.35146	6.62568	9.23636	11.07050	12.83250	15.08627	16.74960
6	5.34812	7.84080	10.64464	12.59159	14.44938	16.81189	18.54758
7	6.34581	9.03715	12.01704	14.06714	16.01276	18.47531	20.27774
8	7.34412	10.21885	13.36157	15.50731	17.53455	20.09024	21.95495
9	8.34283	11.38875	14.68366	16.91898	19.02277	21.66599	23.58935
10	9.34182	12.54886	15.98718	18.30704	20.48318	23.20925	25.18818

Figure 3.28: Part of a χ^{2} (Chi-squared) table showing one-tailed critical values for levels of significance ranging from 0.50 to 0.005

3.16 An application of goodness of fit

Consider the following example. It is desired to test at the 5% level of significance if there is bias in a six-sided die. The first step is to obtain data, so the die is rolled 120 times. The number of times each face of the die has been produced i.e. 1 to 6 has been recorded and inserted in the observed column C of the spreadsheet in Figure 3.29.

If the die is unbiased then each of the six outcomes is equally likely and therefore the probability of each outcome is one of six. Over 120 rolls of the die the expected outcome for each number is 20 times.

Figure 3.29 shows the results of observing the roll of such a die.

	A	B	C	D
1	The Chi Squared Test			
2		Data Points	Frequency	
3		1	20	
4		2	20	
5		3	18	
6		4	17	
7		5	23	
8		6	22	
9			120	
10	Degrees of freedom		5	
11				

Figure 3.29: The results of casting a die 120 times

The steps required to calculate the $\chi 2$ are as follows:

Step 1: State the Null and Alternative Hypotheses:

The Null Hypothesis is:
H_0: The die is unbiased or more formally the probabilities of the different outcomes are equal.

The Alternative Hypothesis is:
H_1: The die is biased and the probability of the outcomes are not equally likely.

Step 2: Set the significance level equal to 5%.

Step 3: Calculate the expected frequencies (values). In the sample above if the die is unbiased than we would expect to find each of the six numbers appearing approximately 20 times. In a simple example such as this the expected value is intuitive but this is not always the case. If the expected frequency is not intuitive then it is calculated as:

Expected frequency = (probability of occurrence X sample size)

For example in Figure 3.29 the expected frequency for obtaining the number 1 on a die is = 1/6*120=20

	A	B	C	D	E	F
1	The Chi Squared Test					
2		Data Points	Frequency	Expected Frequencies		
3		1	20	20		
4		2	20	20		
5		3	18	20		
6		4	17	20		
7		5	23	20		
8		6	22	20		
9			120			
10						

Figure 3.30: The expected frequencies for casting a die 120 times.

Step 4: The $\chi 2^{\cdot}$ is calculated using the formula:

$$\chi^2 = \sum \frac{(O-E)^2}{E}$$

This formula is applied in Figure 3.31 below. In column E the (O-E) is calculated. In column F the result of the (O-E) is squared and in column G this number is divided by E and the $\chi 2$ is calculated in cell G9 as the sum of the items in column G.

Step 5: Calculate the degrees of freedom which is the number of categories minus 1 and in this case this is (6-1) =5.

	A	B	C	D	E	F	G
1	The Chi-Squared Test						
2		Data points	Observed O	Expected E	(O-E)	(O-E)^2	(O-E)^2/E
3		1	24	20	4	16	0.8
4		2	27	20	7	49	2.45
5		3	12	20	-8	64	3.2
6		4	17	20	-3	9	0.45
7		5	18	20	-2	4	0.2
8		6	22	20	2	4	0.2
9			120				7.3
10	Degrees of freedom		5				

Figure 3.31: Calculating the $\chi 2$

Step 6: Consult the tables or use the =chiinv() function in Excel.

For a significance value of 5% and df=5 the Critical-$\chi 2$ is 11.07.

Step 7: Compare the calculated statistic (Calc-χ2) to the table or Critical or Theoretical (or Excel) statistic.

If the calculated statistic is greater than the table statistic then the hypothesis may be rejected. Otherwise the Null Hypothesis should not be rejected i.e.

If Calc-χ2 >Critical-χ2 reject the hypothesis

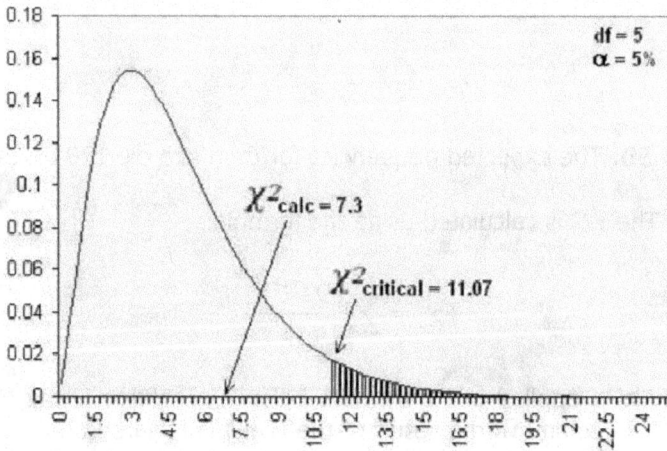

Figure 3.32: Chi square distribution with df=5 and α=5%

As 11.07 is greater than 7.3 this does not allow the Null Hypothesis to be rejected at the 5% level of significance.

3.17 χ2 as a test of independence

Another example of χ2 is to test for the independence of choice. If the recruiting department selects new graduates from four universities A, B, C and D in the following numbers 20, 30, 25 and 40, can it be said that there is no bias for a particular university at the 5% level of significance? The data is entered into a spreadsheet as shown in Figure 3.33.

	A	B
1	University	Observed
2	A	20
3	B	30
4	C	25
5	D	40
6	Total	115

Figure 3.33: Graduates recruited from 4 different universities

Step 1: State the Null Hypothesis:

H_0: There is no preference for a particular university

The Alternative Hypothesis is:

H_1: There is a preference for a particular university

Step 2: Calculate the expected frequencies (values).

The number of observations is summed. If there is no bias for a particular university then the number recruited from each university should be the same and equal to the total number recruited times the probability of selecting the university. With 4 universities then the probability is 0.25 for each university and the expected frequencies are calculated as shown in Figure 3.34, using $\frac{1}{4} \times 115 = 28.75$.

Level of significance $\alpha = 5\%$

Step 3: Again the $\chi 2'$ is calculated using the formula:

$$\chi^2 = \sum \frac{(O-E)^2}{E}$$

This formula is applied in Figure 3.34 below. In column D the (O-E) is calculated. In column E the result of the (O-E) is squared and in column F this number is divided by E. The $\chi 2$ is calculated in cell C10.

Step 4: Calculate the degrees of freedom which is the number of categories minus 1 and in this case this is (4-1) =3. The result is shown below in Figure 3.34 in cell C8.

	A	B	C	D	E	F
1	University	Observed	Expected	O-E	(O-E)^2	(O-E)^2/E
2	A	20	28.75	-8.75	76.5625	2.663
3	B	30	28.75	1.25	1.5625	0.054
4	C	25	28.75	-3.75	14.0625	0.489
5	D	40	28.75	11.25	126.5625	4.402
6	Total	115			Total	7.609
7						
8	df		3			
9	Significance level		5%			
10	Test Calculated		7.609			
11	Critical Value		7.815			
12						
13	Decision	Do not reject null hypothesis at significance level 0.05				
14						
15	C10 = SUM(F2:F5)					
16	C11 = CHIINV(C9,C8)					
17	B13 = IF(C10>C11, "Reject null hypothesis", "Do not reject null					
18	hypothesis") &" at significance level "&C9					

Figure 3.34: Calculating the Calc-$\chi2$ and Critical-$\chi2$ values

Step 5: Consult the tables or use the =chiinv() function in Excel.

The critical $\chi2 \cdot$ value derived from the tables or Excel for the statistic at 5% is 7.81.

Step 6: Compare the calculated test statistic to the table (or Excel) statistic.

The rule is....**if Calc-$\chi2$ >Critical-$\chi2$ reject the hypothesis.**

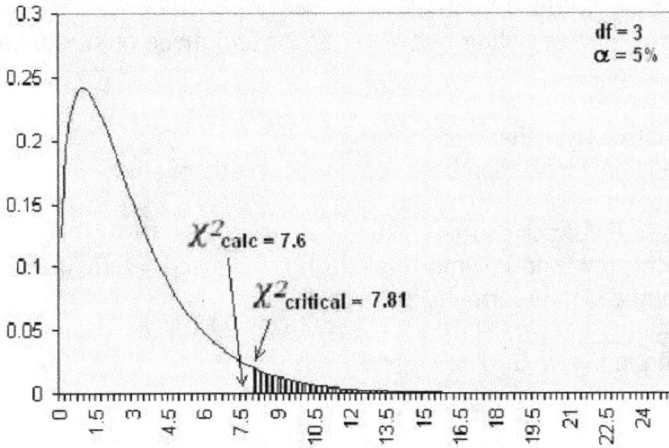

Figure 3.35: Chi square distribution with df=3 and α=5%

As 7.609 is less than 7.815 at the 5% level of significance this does not allow the Null Hypothesis to be rejected.

3.18 $\chi2$ as a test of association

There are several more steps involved in the use of the $\chi2$ as a test of association and the following example illustrates these.

The data below represents the number of responses to a survey. There were 340 respondents of which 205 were males and 135 were females. Of the 205 males 85 were part-time workers. Of the 135 females 70 were part time. Here there is one sample which addresses the relationship between categorical response variables namely gender and mode of study.

These are shown in Figure 3.36.

The research question is – *Is there an association between gender and work status (part-time and/or full-time work) at the 5% level of significance?*

	A	B	C
1		Part-time	Full-time
2	Males	85	120
3	Females	75	60
4			

Figure 3.36: Data supplied for gender and work status

Step 1: State the Null Hypothesis.

H_0: There is no association between gender and mode of study i.e. they are independent

The Alternative Hypothesis is:

H_1: There is an association between gender mode of study

Step 2: Level of significance = 5%.

Calculate the row and column totals using either the =sum() function or by compiling a simple formula, and copying it..

This is seen in Figure 3.37.

	A	B	C	D
1		Part-time	Full-time	Total
2	Males	85	120	205
3	Females	75	60	135
4	Totals	160	180	340

Figure 3.37: Data and sums of rows and columns

In this application of the· $\chi 2$ having summed the rows and columns it is now necessary to perform some additional calculations. These calculations are on the basis of the Null Hypothesis that the two variables are independent. Expected frequencies (values) are produced using probabilities. The following calculations show how the expected frequency for being a male and a part time worker is arrived at.

The probability of a male = $\dfrac{205}{340}$

The probability of a part time worker = $\dfrac{160}{340}$

The probability for a male and a part time worker = $\dfrac{205}{340} * \dfrac{160}{340}$

thus the expected frequency for this group is

$$= 340 * \frac{205}{340} * \frac{160}{340}$$

$$= 205 * \frac{160}{340}$$

$$= 96.47$$

Note the calculation $205 * \dfrac{160}{340}$ gives a clue to the quick way of working out the expected frequencies. Thus the expected frequency is:

$$Expected\ Frequency = \frac{(row\ total) * (column\ total)}{(grand\ total)}$$

For cell B9 the calculation (formula) is = D3* B5/D5
For cell B10 the calculation (formula) is = D4*C5/D5 etc.

Figure 3.38 shows the results of these calculations for the completed table of expected frequencies using a similar procedure.

	A	B	C	D
1	Observed			
2		Part-time	Full-time	Total
3	Males	85	120	205
4	Females	75	60	135
5	Totals	160	180	340
6				
7	Expected frequency			
8		Part-time	Full-time	Total
9	Males	96.47059	108.5294	205
10	Females	63.52941	71.47059	135
11	Totals	160	180	340

Figure 3.38: Calculation of the expected frequencies

Note that the totals for the expected and observed frequencies in rows 5 and 11 are the same.

Step 3: The $\chi 2$ is now calculated by summing the four new expected frequencies by rows and columns as shown in Figure 3.38.

Because there are only two categories in this example Yates' Correction is applied. Yates' Correction requires 0.5 to be subtracted from the absolute value of the difference between the observed and the expected values. Thus the O-E in the usual equation becomes =abs(O-E)-0.5

Step 4: Calculate the degrees of freedom. The degrees of freedom are defined as the number of rows minus 1 times the number of columns minus 1. In this case the result is 1.

Step 5: Calculate the $\chi 2'$ with Yates' Correction by applying the formula:

$$\chi^2 = \sum \frac{(|O - E| - 0.5)^2}{E}$$

to each of the points in the 2X2 matrix and then summing the four new values.

Step 6: Compare the calculated statistic Calc-χ2 and Critical-χ2 statistic.

The rule is....**if Calc-χ2 >Critical-χ2 reject the hypothesis.**

In Figure 3.39 the calculated $\chi 2 ^{\cdot}$ is 5.93, which exceeds the table value at the 5% level (3.84). This may be interpreted as – We may reject the Null Hypothesis if we are prepared to be wrong 5 times in a hundred. Figure 3.40 shows the chi square distribution graphically.

	H	I	J	K	L	M
1	Observed					
2		Part-time	Full-time	Total		
3	Males	85	120	205		
4	Females	75	60	135		
5	Totals	160	180	340		
6						
7	Expected frequency					
8		Part-time	Full-time	Total		
9	Males	96.47059	108.5294	205		
10	Females	63.52941	71.47059	135		
11	Totals	160	180	340		
12						
13	Degrees of freedom		1			
14						
15	Level of significance		5%			
16						
17	Calculating the Chi-squared					
18		Part-time	Full-time	Total		
19	Males	1.363881	1.212339	2.57622		
20	Females	2.071078	1.840959	3.912037		
21	Totals	3.434959	3.053297	6.488257		
22						
23	Chi-squared calculated value		6.488257			
24						
25	Chi-squared critical value		3.841459			
26						
27	I9 = K3*I5/$D$5; J9 = K3*J5/$D$5					
28	I10 = K4*I5/$D$5; J10 = K4*J5/$D$5					
29	I19 = (ABS((I3-I9))^2/I9); J19 = (ABS((J3-J9))^2/J9)					
30	I20 = (ABS((I4-I10))^2/I10); J20 = (ABS((J4-					
31	J10))^2/J10)					
32	K23 = SUM(I21:J21);					
33						
34						

Figure 3.39: Estimate of the χ2 after applying Yates' correction.

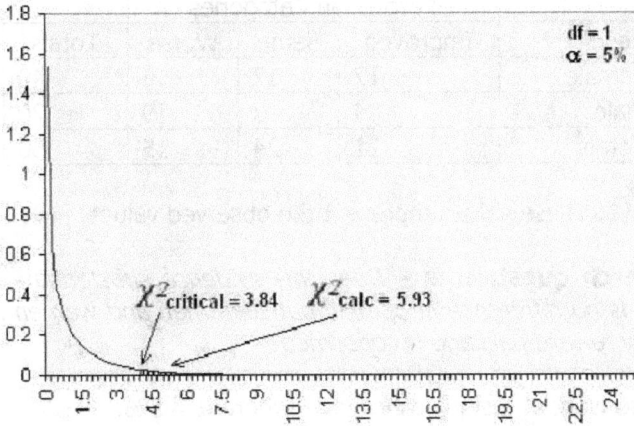

Figure 3.40: Chi square distribution with df=1 and α=5% after applying Yates' correction

3.19 A test for homogeneity

In order to make inferences about two groups, male and female with respect to a single categorical response variable in this case concerning the perception of a new reward package compared to an old one we can make use of the test for homogeneity.

Here the gender variable identifies two independent samples of staff, one for male staff and a separate sample for female staff. This is the grouping variable.

In both of these samples the respondents are asked to state whether they believe the new reward package has left them with improved conditions, the same conditions, or worse conditions. This is the response variable.

The objective of this study is to determine whether the true proportion of responses within each of the categories of the response variable can be considered to be equal.

Let's say that the management of University A wants to see if the score for a new reward package offered is independent of the employee's gender. Therefore a random sample of men and women indicated their view on the new reward package in relation to the old one as follows:

Result	Perception Categories			Totals
	Improved	Same	Worse	
Female	17	17	6	40
Male	4	7	9	20
Totals	21	24	15	60

Figure 3.41: These values represent the observed values.

The research question is - *Does this evidence substantiate the fact that there is no difference in opinion between men and women in so far as this new reward package is concerned?*

You want to work at a significance level where α = 5%.

Steps in the Solution

Step 1: State the Null Hypothesis
H_0: There is no difference between male and female perceptions in the proportion of responses across all the categories concerning the reward package.

The Alternative Hypothesis is:
H_1: There is a difference between male and female perceptions in the proportion of responses across all the categories concerning the reward package.

Step 2: State the level of significance at which you want to work.
Level of significance α = 0.05 or 5%

Step 3: Decide on the test statistic.
Chi-square test statistic is chosen.

Step 4: Calculate the expected values:

Using the quick formula

$$Expected\ Frequency = \frac{(row\ total) * (column\ total)}{(grand\ total)}$$

The expected values for each cell are calculated as follows:-

Females that consider the new package improved: (40x21)/60 = 14
Females that consider the new package same: (40x24)/60 = 16

Females that consider the new package worse: (40x15)/60= 10
Males that consider the new package improved: (20x21)/60 = 7
Males that consider the new package same: (20x24)/60 = 8
Males that consider the new package worse: (20x15)/60= 5

The table of expected frequencies is shown in Figure 3.44:

Expected Frequencies

Result	Perception Categories			Totals
	Improved	Same	Worse	
Female	14	16	10	40
Male	7	8	5	20
Totals	21	24	15	60

Figure 3.42: The calculated expected frequencies

Step 5: Within each category we must calculate the difference between the observed values and the expected values (the calculated values).

Females that consider the new package improved: $\dfrac{(17-14)^2}{14} = 0.643$

Females that consider the new package same: $\dfrac{(17-16)^2}{16} = 0.063$

Females that consider the new package worse: $\dfrac{(6-10)^2}{10} = 1.6$

Males that consider the new package improved: $\dfrac{(4-7)^2}{7} = 1.286$

Males that consider the new package same: $\dfrac{(7-8)^2}{8} = 0.125$

Males that consider the new package worse: $\dfrac{(9-5)^2}{5} = 3.2$

The calculated chi square is equal to the sum of the above values:
    $\chi 2 = 0.643+0.063+1.6+1.286+0.125+3.2$
    $\chi 2 = 6.916$

Step 6: Use the test statistic (remember the degrees of freedom).

    df = (no of rows − 1) x (no of columns − 1)
    df = (2-1) x (3-1)
    df = 2

From chi square ($\chi 2$) tables or from Excel we see that $\chi 2$ (α = 0.05) = 5.991. As our calculated $\chi 2$ = 6.916 the test statistic is significant and the Null Hypothesis can be rejected. Therefore the alternative hypothesis can be accepted with 95% confidence that men and women employed in University A have different views with regards to the new reward package. The results of the chi-square test using Excel are summarised in Figure 3.43

	A	B	C	D	E	F
1	Observed	Categories				
2	Result	Improved	Same	Worse	Totals	
3	Female	17	17	6	40	
4	Male	4	7	9	20	
5	Totals	21	24	15	60	
6						
7	Expected	Categories				
8	Result	Improved	Same	Worse	Totals	
9	Female	14.0	16.0	10.0	40	
10	Male	7.0	8.0	5.0	20	
11	Totals	21	24	15	60	
12						
13	χ^2 results					
14	df	2				
15	Significance level	5%				
16	p-value	0.031				
17	Calculated chi square	6.916				
18	Critical chi square value	5.991				
19	Decision	Reject null hypothesis at significance level 0.05				
20						
21	B14 = (COUNTA(B2:D2)-1)*(COUNTA(A3:A4)-1)					
22	B16 = CHITEST(B3:D4,B9:D10)					
23	B17 = CHIINV(B16,B14)					
24	B18 = CHIINV(B15,B14)					
25	B19 = IF(B17>B18,"Reject null hypothesis", "Do not reject null					
26	hypothesis") & " at significance level "&B15					

Figure 3.43 Excel spreadsheet with Chi-Square results.

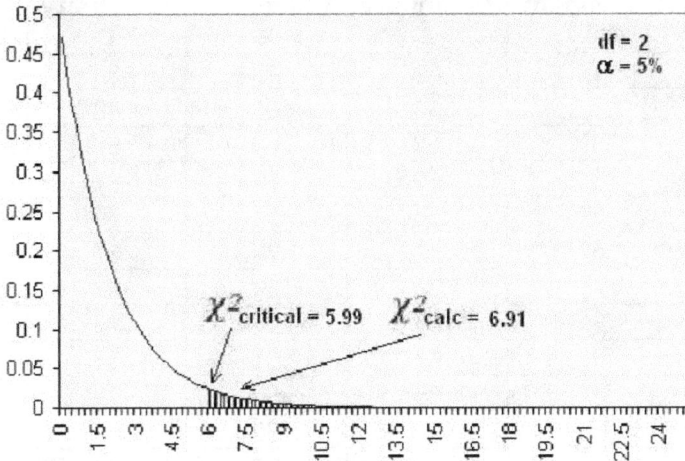

Figure 3.44 Chi square distribution with df=2 and α=5%.

3.20 One-way ANOVA: Three Independent Samples[65]

The one-way ANOVA is an extension of the 2 sample t-test. The one-way ANOVA for independent sample is an extension of the two way test for independent samples. In the one-way ANOVA it is possible to simultaneously test for the equality of three or more groups means with respect to a single quantitative response variable. The independent variable designates the groups and is therefore categorical.

The basic premise is that if the population means for the groups are different this can be established through the variation between the sample means for the groups. If the variance between the group means is small relative to the variation within the groups, then we conclude that the sample means are equal. Otherwise we conclude that they are not equal.

3.21 A three sample application

The senior management of the University A claim that on average their reward package is better than the reward package offered by their competitors University B and University C. Within each university, the 15 employees were randomly chosen and asked to score the reward package on a 100 point scale where 100 is the best score and 0 is the poorest. The following scores were obtained.

---

[65] Apart from three independent samples it is possible to have repeated measures ANOVA which is not addressed here.

Respondent	University A	University B	University C
1	81	43	65
2	48	63	48
3	68	60	57
4	69	52	91
5	54	54	70
6	62	77	67
7	76	68	83
8	56	57	75
9	61	61	53
10	65	80	71
11	64	50	54
12	69	37	72
13	83	73	65
14	85	84	58
15	75	58	58

Figure 3.45 Three independent samples

In this case we have what we call a "one way ANOVA"or "Single Factor ANOVA". That is, there is one factor (reward package) we are looking at across the three universities.

Research question is: *Does this evidence supplied in Figure 3.47 sub-stantiate University A's claim?* You want to work at a significance level of 5%.

Steps in the Solution

Step 1: State the Null Hypothesis and the Alternative Hypothesis.
We will test the Null Hypothesis that there is no difference between the means scores for the reward packages offered by all three universities, against the Alternative Hypothesis that University A's reward package is better than University B's and University C's reward package:

The Null Hypothesis $\quad\quad$ $H_0: \mu_1 = \mu_2 = \mu_3$
The Alternative Hypothesis $\quad$ $H_1: \mu_i \neq \mu_j$ for at least 1 pair $i \neq j$

Step 2: State the level of significance at which you want to work.

Level of significance $\alpha = 0.05$ or 5%

Step 3: Decide on the test statistic.

F-statistic is chosen using Excel's **Data Analysis Toolkit**. Click on **Tools** and choose **Data Analysis**. Under Data Analysis, choose the appropriate type of ANOVA. (Sometimes the data analysis routines have not been activated in the spreadsheet. Where this is the case it is necessary to first click on **Add-ins** and then select **ANOVA** and click **OK**.)

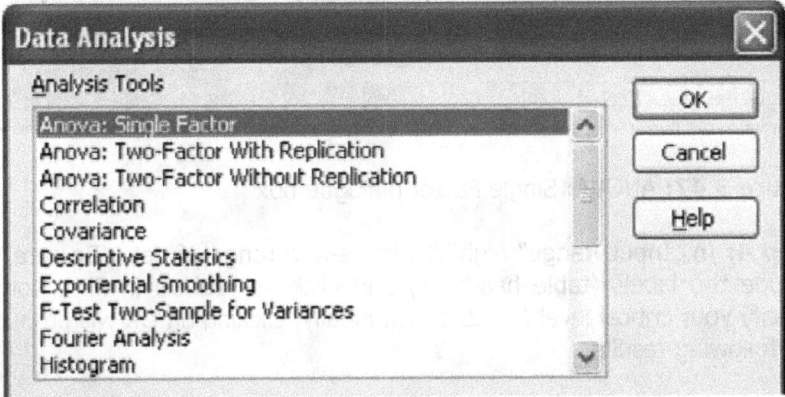

Figure 3.46: Excel Data Analysis Toolkit options

There are three types of ANOVA. "Single factor" ANOVA is the same as "one-way" ANOVA. That is what we have in this example, since we are only considering one factor (reward package) across the three universities. Excel can handle any number of groups as long as they are in columns.

Two Factor without Replication - This performs an analysis of variances between two or more data sets. This should be used when you only have one sample from each data set.

Two Factor with Replication - This performs an analysis of variances between two or more data sets. This should be used when you have more than one sample from each data set.

After choosing ANOVA: Single Factor you will see

	A	B	C	D	E	F	G	H
3	University A	University B	University C		Anova: Single Factor			
4	81	43	65		Input			
5	48	63	48		Input Range:	$A$3:$C$18		OK
6	68	60	57		Grouped By:	⊙ Columns		Cancel
7	69	52	91			○ Rows		Help
8	54	54	70					
9	62	77	67		☑ Labels in first row			
10	76	68	83		Alpha: 0.05			
11	56	57	75					
12	61	61	53		Output options			
13	65	80	71		○ Output Range:	$E$3:$D$18		
14	64	50	54		⊙ New Worksheet Ply:			
15	69	37	72		○ New Workbook			
16	83	73	65					
17	85	84	58					
18	75	58	58					

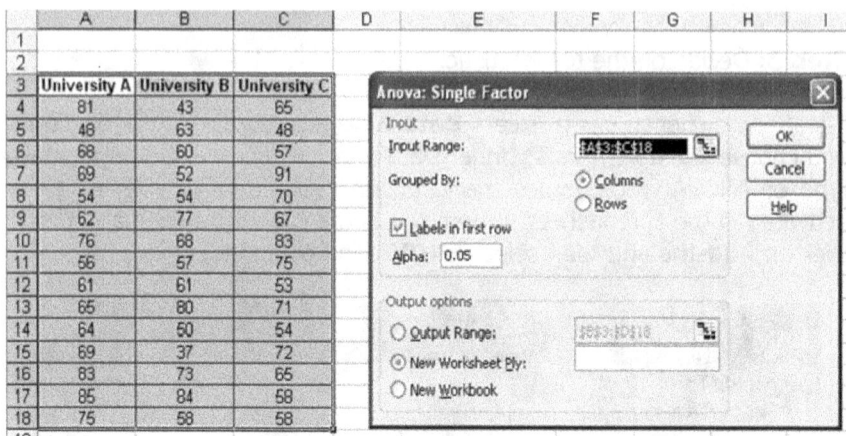

Figure 3.47: ANOVA: Single Factor dialogue box

Step 4: In "Input Range" highlight the entire range of data. Be sure to include the labels (table headings) and click on "Labels in First Row". Specify your critical level (see Step 2). Finally, clicking on OK will produce the following results.

Anova: Single Factor

SUMMARY

Groups	Count	Sum	Average	Variance
University A	15	1016	67.73333	117.6381
University B	15	917	61.13333	179.981
University C	15	987	65.8	137.1714

ANOVA

Source of Variation	SS	df	MS	F	P-value	F crit
Between Groups	345.3778	2	172.6889	1.191532	0.313814	3.219942
Within Groups	6087.067	42	144.9302			
Total	6432.444	44				

Figure 3.48: Excel spreadsheet with ANOVA results

Step 5: As we can see, the mean level of scores reported by University A's employees (67.73) is higher than that of either University B's employees (61.13) or University C's employees (65.8).

But are these differences statistically significant? According to the test result Calc-F = 1.191532 and the Critical-F= 3.219. Therefore we fail to reject the Null Hypothesis.

The Null Hypothesis was that all 3 of these universities' means were equal. Apparently, the differences we saw in this sample were simply due to random sampling error. There is no evidence to support the University A claim.

3.22 Summary-Part 3

Three important techniques have been addressed in this Part of the book and these have been as follows:-

1. Regression analysis
2. $\chi 2$ Chi-square
3. ANOVA

This is an introduction to the use of regression analysis in the academic research environment. It is not intended to be a definitive account of regression analysis but it is comprehensive enough to show the power of the tool and this has been demonstrated using a spreadsheet. Thus in a sense this is both an exposition of the statistical technique and the spreadsheet in which the analysis has been performed.

Regression is a particularly powerful technique and there are many incidences in which it may be useful in academic research. In some respects it is deceptively easy to calculate the numbers. It is much more challenging to understand what the numbers might actually mean.

However it needs always to be remembered that although there may be a high correlation between the dependent and the independent variables it may not be assumed from the mathematics alone that there is any cause and effect relationship between the variables.

Also addressed in this Part of the book is the $\chi 2$ (Chi-square). This is one of the most frequently used probability density functions in inferential statistics for the social science researcher. A number of different applications of the $\chi 2 \cdot$ test of significance have been discussed in this section.

List of Excel functions used in this Part of the book.

Functions	Result
=forecast()	Calculates data required to produce a linear regression line.
= slope()	Calculates the β value of the linear regression formula $y=\beta x+c+e$
=intercept()	Calculates the intercept (the value of x if y is zero) of a linear regression line.
=chiinv()	Calculates the inverse of the one-tailed probability of the $\chi 2$ ·distribution.
=chitest()	Returns the test for independence of chi-square distribution.

More details of these functions are provided in the Help command within the spreadsheet.

Self test 3

No.	Question	Answer
1	Distinguish between dependent and independent variables	
2	What is the role of cause and effect regression modelling?	
3	How do correlation and regression differ?	
4	What is the difference between r and r^2?	
5	What do we mean by the inter-item correlations of the variables?	
6	What is a $\chi2$ distribution?	
7	Explain how to calculate the *expected frequencies* when performing a Chi-squared analysis.	
8	What is meant by the critical value of the $\chi2$'?	
9	Define a contingency table?	
10	What is Yates' Correction?	

11	What is meant by homogeneous frequencies?	
12	What is a test of association?	

Assignment No 3

Using your own data set create a regression model and write a report as to what may be deduced from the model.

Additional exercises

1. Using the data supplied below establish if there is an association between height and age next birthday.

Height in inches	Age next birthday
60	12
62	13
63	12
61	14
60	13
65	14
67	14
58	12
59	13
60	15
64	15
65	13
64	12
66	14
65	15
62	16
61	16
60	15
55	15
68	13

2. Using the data supplied below comment on the association between interest in gardening and age next birthday as seen through these

data. The interest in gardening is scored on a 1 to 200 point scale where 1=no interest at all and 200 = most interested.

Interest in Gardening	20	21	21	25	25	26	27	28	31	33	36	42	42	45	48	49	52	55	55	55
Gender	m	f	m	f	f	f	f	f	f	m	f	f	f	f	m	m	f	f	f	m
Age next birthday	46	41	40	43	41	46	46	40	40	43	50	47	48	40	48	42	50	41	47	50
Interest in Gardening	56	58	60	60	62	64	65	67	68	70	72	73	73	73	75	76	76	78	82	84
Gender	m	f	f	m	f	m	m	f	m	f	m	f	f	m	f	m	m	m	f	f	m
Age next birthday	42	49	47	45	40	50	49	47	43	50	42	42	43	40	45	48	49	50	48	47
Interest in Gardening	85	92	97	103	106	107	109	109	110	110	111	112	113	116	128	128	129	134	134	135
Gender	f	f	m	m	f	m	f	m	m	m	m	m	f	f	m	m	m	m	m	m
Age next birthday	50	47	42	43	50	45	50	44	43	40	48	47	43	44	40	44	42	40	42	42

3. A new machine recently purchased is still subject to being fine tuned by the engineers. As part of this exercise they have been experimenting with different speeds at which it can produce widgets. It has been observed that the faster the machine runs the more widgets it produces which require quality control attention. The following data has been collected:-

No of Widgets per minute	No of widgets requiring attention
20	5
22	5
24	4
26	5
28	3
30	7
32	8
34	9
36	10
38	15
40	20

Is there a relationship between the number of widgets per minute and the number of widgets requiring attention? Use Excel to produce a linear regression model and display this on a scatter diagram. Assess the goodness of fit of the regression model.

4. As a result of a special appeal for funds to build a new research centre the university received 25 donation cheques. The appeal fund manager wondered if there was any association between the amount donated and the grades obtained by the donors when they were students. She consulted the university records and was able to obtain the final degree grades for the alumni and she matched the grades and the amount of the donations as follows:-

Grades	Donation
3	500
2	700
1	1200
2	750
2	750
2	600
2	900
3	500
3	400
3	200
3	100
1	2000
1	1750
3	400
3	500
2	850
2	900
2	500
1	2500
1	2250
1	1750
1	1500
1	2000
1	1500
1	1000

Using Excel functions what can be said about the association between the grades and the amounts donated?

5. Using Excel functions and commands develop a model which is able to provide an understanding of the implications for running the new machine at different speeds.

6. The following are the results of three different teachers who teach advanced mathematics.

	A	B	C	D
1				
2		Teacher A	Teacher B	Teacher C
3	Passed	55	39	66
4	Failed	4	7	10
5				
6				

Test the hypothesis that the proportions failed by the teachers are equal at the 5% level of significance.

7. The analysis of voting patterns after the election suggest that there was a significant difference between the way employed and unemployed people voted.

The following are the numbers estimated by the constituency office. Is there evidence to support the view that there is an association between work status and voting patterns at the 5% level of significance?

	A	B	C
1		Supports the government	Against the government
2	Employed	33,500	250
3	Unemployed	2900	150
4			

8. The following statistics were collected by the Citizens' Advice Bureaux in each of the three cities.

	A	B	C	D
1	Serious Crime Reported			
2		Dublin	London	Paris
3	1	32	67	48
4	2	44	70	46
5	3	30	50	49
6	4	36	72	41
7	5	37	54	39
8	6	43	67	50
9	7	44	53	43
10	8	40	68	41
11	9	39	56	44
12	10	42	53	50
13	11	43	74	43
14	12	35	52	41

Paris claims to be the city with the least serious crime. Does the evidence support this claim at the 5% level of significance?

Part 4

Making Statistics Work

There is more to statistics than simply knowing how to use the formulae.

Readers will now be aware of a number of important concepts in statistics as well as how to apply these using Excel. What has been covered so far has been neither conceptually difficult nor with the use of a spreadsheet have the calculations been burdensome.

However, being able to use statistics effectively is not just about knowing how to perform the techniques. Statistics is a science and an art which requires a thorough understanding of what we can expect to learn from numbers, and where we are likely to encounter the limitation of such knowledge.

This final part of the Introduction to Statistics using Microsoft Excel addresses these issues.

Making Statistics Work

4.1 Some Basic Issues

Having experienced some of the techniques in descriptive and inferential statistics it is now important to stand back and reflect on some of the macro issues which need to be considered before, during and after any statistical analysis should be undertaken.

In the research context statistics is only of use as a tool to assist our understanding and explanation of data which might contribute to answering our research questions. Statistics alone does not answer any of our questions.

We try to understand the phenomenon we are researching by obtaining data about various characteristics of situations which are often complex. These characteristics may be regarded as variables and the data we collect are values for these variables. Data only takes on meaning in terms of our cognitive capacity i.e. we give meaning to the data which requires us to identify and understand the possible inferences that the data might be able to offer. This requires us to be aware of the circumstances in which the data occurs and what the origins of these circumstances are. Because data is an abstraction we cannot be certain that our understanding of it is correct.

4.2 Seeking patterns

In pursuit of our understanding we are often looking for patterns. It has been said that *Human beings are pattern-seeking creatures*. Patterns may take various forms and may involve a few or many variables. Patterns will be seen as differences, similarities and sources of variation in the variables we are studying. But patterns alone are not good enough. As researchers we are often interested in attributing meaning to patterns. It is only our intellect which may confer meaning to patterns. Neither statistics, nor mathematics nor computers can do this. It is correct to say that an advanced application of computer science is pattern recognition but this field of study is still in its early stages and even when computers will be able to recognise patterns with little or no error, it will still take another major break through in technology for computers to be able to associate meaning with patterns.

4.3 Data is an abstraction

Data is an abstraction. Data we obtain is not the situation itself and thus data is never an end in itself nor can it give us a complete picture. Paulos

(1998:p30) said that "*Mathematics is also beautiful, but it is aesthetic, minimalist and austere, can blind one to the messiness and contingencies of the real world*". This comment is also true for data and statistics. It is easy to fall into the trap of acting as though statistical artefacts such as data points themselves or specific statistics are somehow more than conceptual abstractions for understanding an often highly complex world. To know that someone has been born in 1944, weighs 100kg and has 5 years of tertiary education does not tell us much about him/her. To know that the average person's year of birth is 1940, weighs 90kg and has 3 years of tertiary education does tell us quite a lot more. But care has to be taken not to assume that this extra data will lead to any great understanding. The importance which is sometimes given to data can be seen in an English piece of slang. The following is sometimes said "*OK, lie to me if you like, but I've got your number*", meaning that the speaker understands what is really going on, behind the lie. It is indeed curious that the word number is used here. Why not use, "*I've got your colour or I've got your shape, or I've got your essence?*" The high status given to numbers has been a part of our culture for a long time. In modern times Lord Kelvin in the 19th century said:

> *When you can measure what you are speaking about, and express it in numbers, you know something about it; but when you cannot measure it, when you cannot express it in numbers, your knowledge is of a meagre and unsatisfactory kind.*

According to Rowland (2001) Galileo had earlier remarked:

> *Philosophy is written in this grand book the universe, which stands continually open to our gaze, but the book cannot be understood unless one first learns to comprehend the language and to read the alphabet in which it is composed. It is written in the language of mathematics, and its characters are triangles, circles, and her geometric figures, without which it is humanly impossible to understand a single word of it; without these, one wanders about in a dark labyrinth.*

But our romance with numbers and mathematics actually goes back much further to ancient times. Plato is reputed to have written over the door of the Academy, his school in Athens, "*Let no man ignorant of geometry enter here*". And Plato's attitude was simply an extension of the thinking of the pre-Socratics and especially Pythagoras, who believed that everything in the world could be thought of and explained in terms of numbers. Today we understand that the complexity of the world requires multiple ways of understanding of which numbers, mathematics and statistics are but one. This is true in all fields of study including physical science, life science and social science.

4.4   Types of data

Even when the use of numbers, mathematics and statistics is the most appropriate approach to be successful it is important that the right type of data be collected or produced. There are many ways of classifying data. There are primary and secondary data. There are observational and experimental data. There are quantitative and qualitative data. There are nominal, ordinal, interval and ratio data. There is historic and current data. There are naturally occurring data and there is derived data. Each of these has a different use in research and the researcher needs to be aware of their uses and limitations. Choosing the wrong data type to answer a research question will lead to disappointing results. In addition the integrity of the data is an issue. In this context integrity is difficult to define but it certainly involves issues related to the type of data collected, how it was collected and how it was captured in order to be processed. Increasingly ethics considerations are important in this respect. Data needs to be valid and reliable and the data needs to be accurate within acceptable limits. Validity refers to the data which is being collected actually matching what the researcher was intending to collect. Reliability means that if the data was collected again the researcher would obtain approximately the same results. If the data does not comply with these requirements it will not be credible and thus the research findings may be regarded as spurious or even wrong.

4.5   Underpinning assumptions

Part of the issues of being valid and reliable is the underpinning assumption of the distribution from which the data was obtained. If Z-score testing or t-testing is to be performed, for example, then the data should have been obtained by way of a random sample. It is often difficult to obtain a random sample. When this is the case then a compromise is sometimes made. The researcher admits that the sample is not random but asserts that the sample is representative of the population being studied. Of course it may not be easy to convince recipients of the research that an adequately representative sample was found.

The purpose of the random sample is to try to eliminate unacceptable bias. When the researcher suggests that the sample is representative then he/she is also asserting that bias has been taken out of the situation. It is important to note that if you wish to study the attitudes of men as apposed to women or the behaviour of 60 year olds then you need to obtain a sample of men and a sample of 60 year olds and these may be regarded as biased samples. This type of bias is necessary to answer the research questions. Another complicating fact is that statistical tests may require the assumption that the population from which the data has been drawn is normally distributed. In practice populations are seldom perfectly normally distributed and a decision has to be made if the data is sufficiently close to a normal distribution so that the technique is valid. Researchers sometimes claim with some justification that the chosen technique is adequately robust so that not normally distributed data will suffice.

4.6 The research question

In research another key consideration is: *Is the data collected appropriate for answering the research question?* As research questions differ considerably the type of data required to answer them will also differ substantially. Studying processes which improve the productivity in a manufacturing situation will often require data which reflects production levels before and after a change in process. This type of data might or might not be available. Studying how the chairman of the board of directors of a bank is selected might require in depth discussions with a number of relevant senior directors. In the first example here the data will probably take the form of units produced per hour while in the latter example the data will be the considered view of the "*king makers*" in the organisation. Statistical techniques may be applied in both these situations. In the first example both descriptive and inferential statistics may be appropriate while in the second example it is likely that only descriptive statistics will be used. But this cannot be said with certainty until the actual data is to hand and closely examined.

4.7 Quantitative and qualitative data

If you wish to undertake statistical analysis on qualitative data (and sometimes on quantitative data) then there are concerns regarding coding. There are two issues here which are the degree of granularity required and the scales used to summarise the results of the coding. If a transcript of the data supplied by an informant is being coded then one of the first considerations is to establish the issues which the researcher is seeking to explore. Some research may examine high level concepts such as strategy and leadership and in this case it is possible that only a small number of different codes are required. On the other hand the research could be addressing the detail of how certain processes are monitored and controlled. In this type of enquiry a large number of different issues could be identified and thus a large number of codes could be required. Too many codes will take longer to analyse and may produce an over diffuse picture.

When you are coding you also normally need to establish a scale and then you need to decide if you want your scale to run from 1 to 10 or 1 or 5 or some other number set. There are traditions in statistics which may direct you to a particular scale such as the Likert scale which is usually based on 1 to 7. If you wish to compare the answers of two or more different questions then it is useful although not absolutely necessary to have the same set of scales for the questions involved.

An important issue is whether you are using questions which produce nominal or ordinal or interval or ratio data. Nominal data which is sometimes called (not strictly correctly) categorical data provides the smallest opportunity for statistical analysis. As a result of the use of a question requiring a nominal type answer such as what is your home language the analyst can provide counts and percentages. Nominal data may also be used in non-parametric statistical tests such as the chi-square test (based on counts) but in general these techniques tend to be of less value than the techniques which may be used with other categories of data.

For example averages and ranges based on nominal data have no meaningful interpretation. Ordinal data in which numbers are selected to state a hierarchy of preference (such as in the case of the Likert scale) or some other variable, provides more opportunity for analysis but is still restricted. Some researchers argue there should be no restriction in the way ordinal data should be analysed and they could be used in conjunction with the full range of statistical techniques. It is the view of some researchers that as long as there are 5 or more categories in an ordinal type question it may be treated as interval data.

Two other types of data which are interval (quantitative data or metric data) and ratio data refer to measurements on a continuous scale. These data types allow a much wider range of analysis and for the purposes of most research activities may be treated in the same way.

Another way of looking at the classification data is that if the numbers are assigned to the outcomes of events by the researcher then they are considered qualitative e.g. Male =1 and Female=2 or if a preference ranking is used where 1=most preferred and 7 = least preferred.

Quantitative data is when numbers result from a reading of a measuring instrument. In this case there are two types of data. The first is where difference between points on the scale have meaningful interpretation but ratios have not e.g. a centigrade temperature range shows that 20 degrees is the same distance from 30 degrees as 50 degrees is from 60 degrees. But we cannot say that 40 degrees is twice as hot as 20 degrees. This is because the zero is chosen arbitrarily. The other quantitative scale is referred as the ratio scale and this scale allows not only differences but also ratios for meaningful interpretation. Thus we can say that Jones with a million pounds is only half as wealthy as Smith with 2 million pounds. In this case the zero has a physical interpretation.

Quantitative data can be discreet or continuous for example the number of goals scored in a football match is both discrete and continuous.

The issue of sample size is often of concern. If data is assumed to be generated by a normal distribution and a test is to be performed concerning the mean of the distribution then if the standard deviation is known a Z-test can be performed irrespective of the sample size. If the standard deviation is unknown then it has to be estimated by the sample standard deviation and the resulting test statistic is assumed to follow the t-distribution. If the sample size is in excess of 30 then t-test results will coincide with the z-test to a satisfactory level of approximation.

In a similar way specific sample sizes are often recommended for regression analysis (5 data points or cases per parameter to be estimated), Chi-squared tests (an expected frequency of 5 or more per cell) and ANOVA (approximately 10 data points per group). In general larger sample sizes are helpful to the researcher and may reduce the variations which will be implicit in any estimation (Fowler et al. 2002). Large samples improve statistical confidence but there is a diminishing return effect and the researcher needs to be careful of this. In the end sample size is often related to credibility of the research and thus there may be a reasonable amount of flexibility in this regard. Ultimately the sample size issue is related to the need to limit the chance of random variation and if this is of key importance then the requirement is as large a sample as is practicable. If the chance of random variation is not central then a more relaxed attitude may be taken to sample size. In general if your sample size is small then you will need to observe a large difference from the hypothesised value before any significance may be attributed to it. On the other hand if your sample size is large then it is possible for a small difference to be significant. Sometimes the term practical significance as opposed to statistical significance is an important consideration.

4.8 An art and a science

Statistics is both an art and a science. The science of statistics relates to the mathematical formulae which are rigorously derived from basis axioms as well as judgements as to how to achieve the objectives of the research. Art of statistics refers to ex-ante choices and ex-post interpretations. The formulae used by statisticians may de derived using well established mathematics to produce algorithms in various circumstances to deliver appropriate statistics. The art in statistics is to do with choosing the right statistical approach to help answer a particular question. This can be challenging. Sometimes there are a number of different techniques which could to the same job but one or more could be better than the rest. Another aspect of the art of statistics is the fact that experience is a key part of the work of a researcher. Many decisions are required and the following are some of them:-

1. Is the research question answerable?
2. Does the data required to answer the question exist and if it does, is it possible to acquire it?
3. What are the most appropriate tools with which to analyse the data?
4. How is the rigour of the analysis ensured?
5. How are the results of the analysis to be interpreted?
6. How can the interpretations be converted into relevant practical guidelines or policies for the stakeholders?

Each of these questions deserves detailed attention from the researcher. The above areas requiring judgements may be regarded as requiring high level decisions. There are also a number of other detailed decisions which in the main relate to whether to include suspect data in your analysis or how to cope with a small data set. Examples of these are:

1. What can be done to accommodate partially completed questionnaires?
2. How to cope with outliers?
3. What to do when there is a high non-return or refusal rate?
4. Is the sample size adequately representative?

There will inevitably be questions in a questionnaire which certain informants will not complete. There are ways of coping with this situation, some of which have been discussed elsewhere in this book and a judgement has to be made as to which approach to take.

4.9 Outliers are problematic

The issue of outliers is always a thorny one. It is possible to categorise outliers as either bogus data which means that an error occurred in some part of the data collection and capture process or as a valid data point which requires consideration. A bogus data point needs correcting or omission from the data set and the judgement here is straight forward. If on the other hand an outlier is a valid data point, such as, if you are trying to calculate the mean income of a middle class suburb and there happens to one billionaire living within its boundaries then you have to decide how to handle this occurrence. The rule here is that you need to revert to the research question. If you want to calculate the mean income for the purposes of some general hypothesis testing then you will possibly or even probably omit this data point. If on the other hand you are compiling some descriptive statistics you could include the data point and use the median as your average.

4.10 Small number of responses

When only a small number of questionnaires are returned a judgement has to be made as to whether or not to proceed with the research. A high refusal rate can invalidate the whole research project and make any attempt to produce results suspect. It is clearly a painful decision to have to abandon a research project. Pre-testing and field testing of research should help reduce the incidences of this type of problem.

4.11 Judgements to be made

These types of judgements should be made without the biases of the researcher playing too large a role. A useful rule-of-thumb is that the simplest techniques which can deliver an answer should be used. Sophistication or complexity for its own sake should be avoided. This is nothing more than the application of Occam's Razor. It is also worth remembering the comment of Gould (1997), not a professional statistician himself, who remarked:

> Our searches for numerical order lead as often to terminal nuttiness as to profound insight.

Paulos (1998), a professional mathematician, cautioned against the unthinking use of mathematics by saying:

> Being able to manipulate symbols and objects like a sidewalk card shark does not necessarily imply any understanding of underlying mathematical principles.

Although Paulos is clearly correct there are not many *sidewalk card sharks* in research and those who try to impress through their knowledge of statistics are relatively easy to identify. A considerable amount of research requires only relatively simple statistics. These are normally adequate and are well within the grasp of most researchers or students. The 80/20 rule often applies in this respect and although advanced statistical procedures do deliver more insights much of what is mostly needed may be obtained without them.

4.12 Personal data

Another important factor which needs to be considered is whether the data we seek is too personal. Some respondents to questionnaires refuse to state their age. Some will refuse to state their income. Questions related to political affiliation and religion are often problematic to mention only a few relatively simple data collection issues which arise from time to time. If you want to study subjects' honesty then there are great obstacles to be overcome. It is today ethically unacceptable to conduct a research study on individuals who have not been fully informed that they are the objects of the study and who do not know the purpose of the study. This means that studies such as those carried out by Milgram (1963)[66] and Zimbardo (1971)[67] are not possible today.

Worth emphasising again is that it is important that care needs to be taken throughout the whole research process and that data should be inspected with a critical eye to ensure its validity, reliability and its integrity. Data needs to be understood for what it is – an abstraction which may facilitate understanding and sometimes this point is missed.

Bernstein (1996) was pointing to how data can take on a life of its own when he said:

> *Our lives teem with numbers, but we sometimes forget that numbers are only tools. They have no soul; they may indeed become fetishes.*

4.13 The status of data

The danger of data, especially computer generated data, being raised to a status beyond its true level of importance is a continuous worry which all researchers have to address. Stephen Levitt who is an astute observer

---

[66] Milgram conducted an experiment which was inspired by the Adolph Eichmann trial in which the accused said that he was only following orders. Milgram encouraged individuals to inflict pain on subjects who exhibited the symptoms of acute distress. In fact the apparent victims were acting. This was kept secret from those administering the punishments who reported considerable levels of stress.

[67] Zimbardo divided a group of students into two subgroups. One of the subgroups was designated as prison wardens and dressed as such and the other as prisoners. Real policemen arrested the prisoners and conducted them to jail where they were clothed in prison uniforms. The group who were designated as prison wardens began to behave in a cruel and arbitrary way to the students who were prisoners to such an extent that the experiment had to be abandoned.

of the social and economic world takes what can only be a controversial view which was declared by the New York Times Magazine (2005) as follows:

> Steven Levitt may not fully believe in himself, but he does believe in this: teachers and criminals and real estate agents may lie, and politicians, and even CIA analysts. But numbers don't.

At best Levitt's view displays a partial truth but it vastly underestimates the complexity of the world which is represented by the abstractions which we call data. It also neglects to mention the fact that researchers have agendas which impact the way data is perceived and these agendas are not always obvious to the users of the research output. Disraeli showed his awareness of this when he said that, *There are lies, dammed lies and statistics*. For completeness it has to be said that the same criticism made concerning quantitative research may be levelled at qualitative research i.e. all researchers have an agenda.

It is far better to take a much more critical stance and ensure that the numbers have a clearly articulated basis on which they stand. Paulos (1998) summarises this well when he says:

> Without an ambient story, background knowledge, and some indication of the providence of the statistics, it is impossible to evaluate their validity. Common sense and informal logic are as essential to the task as an understanding of the formal statistical notions.

It is easy to see that the theory and practice of statistics underpins much of contemporary research. But it is not the only way to research. Even when quantitative research using statistics is the preferred approach considerable care has to be taken that these techniques are applied in an appropriate way. It has to be understood that contrary to the aphorism *"The facts speak for themselves"*, this is not the case. When Dickens (1989) said in Hard Times *"Facts alone are wanted in life........... Stick to Facts, sir!"* he was practising his skill of irony. Facts, data, statistics always need interpretation and this is probably the part of any research study which requires the greatest level of skill.

None of the above should detract from the most important role of statistics in our research. Essentially the message is that it is necessary to approach the subject reflectively and to make sure that data and data analysis are conducted in a professional manner.

4.14 Knowledge acquired

There are four categories of knowledge which may be acquired through the study of statistics. These are the following:

1. The language of statistics;
2. Skills needed to acquire data and statistical techniques used to analyse them;
3. Interpretation of the results of the analysis and;
4. A mind set which has been referred to as statistical thinking.

The language of statistics is the key to learning about the subject and the learner starts to acquire the new vocabulary from the beginning. Without knowing the meaning of the words little or no progress can be made. This is one of the reasons that a comprehensive glossary is supplied with this text. Although knowing the meaning of the words is a *sine qua non,* there is yet another step required where an understanding of the nature of the concepts is acquired.

Skills in using the techniques of statistics come with practice as mentioned elsewhere in this book. Skill with statistics comes in part with use of the commands and functions associated with the data input, analysis and reporting. But knowing which buttons to press is not enough. Understanding the thinking behind the commands and functions is what is required. Furthermore the techniques, commands and functions need to be reinforced in the mind of the learner through regular use.

Interpretation of the results of research is largely a question of judgement and this is obviously contingent on experience with the use of statistics.

4.15 Thinking Statistically and Statistical thinking

Thinking statistically has been described in the prologue and it is quite a different matter to statistical thinking. Statistical thinking is about having the ability and the inclination to apply the tools and techniques which have been addressed in this book to everyday problems which the reader might face. It is also about becoming aware of the need for data as a way of understanding problems and finding solutions to them. To this end statistical thinking requires an understanding of the different types of data and what information we can obtain from them (Hoerl and Snee, 2002). The term evidence based learning, evidence based management and evidence based research reflect the current importance given to data.

Thinking statistically and statistical thinking together enhance our understanding that there is always a degree of variability in data and thus it is seldom possible to provide data with anything which resembles complete accuracy. There are very few things in life about which we can be certain and the recognition of this opens up new horizons. Incomplete information is the most usual set of circumstances which we all face, including researchers and as a result we have to understand how to cope with risk and uncertainty.

Statistical thinking allows us to realize that although we cannot achieve great accuracy in terms of our measurement or prediction of a single event or even a set of events we can be quite confident that we can understand how such events vary and we can estimate the likelihood of different outcomes with considerable precision.

In general being involved with statistics provides a different mindset which allows you to look at the world with a fuller understanding of the objects and processes therein.

References

Bernstein P, 1996, Against the Gods, John Wiley and Sons, New York P7

Bram U, (2013), Thinking Statistically, CreateSpace Independent Publishing Platform.
http://www.abebooks.com/servlet/BookDetailsPL?bi=14067701880&searchurl=an%3Duri+bram%26sts%3Dt

Chance B L, (2002), Components of Statistical Thinking and Implications for Instruction and Assessment, Journal of Statistics Education Volume 10, Number 3

Dickens C, 1989, Hard Times, Oxford University Press, bk. 1, Ch. 1, first published 1854, words spoken by Mr Thomas Gradgrind

Fowler J, P Jarvis, M Chevannes, 2002, Practical Statistics for Nursing and Health Care, John Wiley & Son, Chichester

Gould S J, Questioning the Millennium, p36, Vintage, London, 1997

Hoerl R and R Snee, 2002, Statistical Thinking – Improving Business Performance, Duxbury, CA

Kelvin http://www-history.mcs.st-andrews.ac.uk/Quotations/Thomson.html 10 July 2006

Milgram S, 1963, The man who shocked the world, http://www.psychologytoday.com/articles/pto-20020301-000037.html

Paulos J, 1998, Once Upon A Number, p14, The Penguin Press, London

Roosevelt FD, http://en.wikipedia.org/wiki/First_inauguration_of_Franklin_D._Roosevelt , found March 3 2015

Rowland W, Galileo's Mistake, Thomas Allen Publishers, Toronto, 2001

The New York Times, 2003, Magazine, August 3, Cited in Levitt S and S Dubner , Freakonomics, Allen Lane, London

Thomson William, Lord Kelvin, Found at http://www.todayinsci.com/K/Kelvin_Lord/KelvinLord-Quotations.htm spoken in 1883, found March 3 2015

Wild C J, and Pfannkuch M, (1999), "Statistical Thinking in Empirical Enquiry," International Statistical Review, 67, 223-265.

Zimbardo P, 1971, The Stanford Prison Experiment,
http://www.prisonexp.org/

Appendix 1: Probabilities for the standard normal distribution

For a given z, the table gives P(Z≤ z)

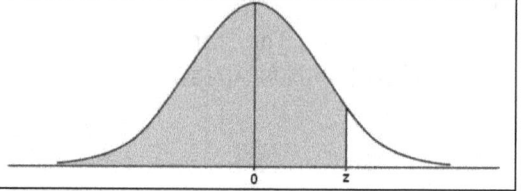

z	0.0	0.01	0.02	0.03	0.04	0.05	0.06	0.07	0.08	0.09
0.0	0.5000	0.5040	0.5080	0.5120	0.5160	0.5199	0.5239	0.5279	0.5319	0.5359
0.1	0.5398	0.5438	0.5478	0.5517	0.5557	0.5596	0.5636	0.5675	0.5714	0.5753
0.2	0.5793	0.5832	0.5871	0.5910	0.5948	0.5987	0.6026	0.6064	0.6103	0.6141
0.3	0.6179	0.6217	0.6255	0.6293	0.6331	0.6368	0.6406	0.6443	0.6480	0.6517
0.4	0.6554	0.6591	0.6628	0.6664	0.6700	0.6736	0.6772	0.6808	0.6844	0.6879
0.5	0.6915	0.6950	0.6985	0.7019	0.7054	0.7088	0.7123	0.7157	0.7190	0.7224
0.6	0.7257	0.7291	0.7324	0.7357	0.7389	0.7422	0.7454	0.7486	0.7517	0.7549
0.7	0.7580	0.7611	0.7642	0.7673	0.7704	0.7734	0.7764	0.7794	0.7823	0.7852
0.8	0.7881	0.7910	0.7939	0.7967	0.7995	0.8023	0.8051	0.8078	0.8106	0.8133
0.9	0.8159	0.8186	0.8212	0.8238	0.8264	0.8289	0.8315	0.8340	0.8365	0.8389
1	0.8413	0.8438	0.8461	0.8485	0.8508	0.8531	0.8554	0.8577	0.8599	0.8621
1.1	0.8643	0.8665	0.8686	0.8708	0.8729	0.8749	0.8770	0.8790	0.8810	0.8830
1.2	0.8849	0.8869	0.8888	0.8907	0.8925	0.8944	0.8962	0.8980	0.8997	0.9015
1.3	0.9032	0.9049	0.9066	0.9082	0.9099	0.9115	0.9131	0.9147	0.9162	0.9177
1.4	0.9192	0.9207	0.9222	0.9236	0.9251	0.9265	0.9279	0.9292	0.9306	0.9319
1.5	0.9332	0.9345	0.9357	0.9370	0.9382	0.9394	0.9406	0.9418	0.9429	0.9441
1.6	0.9452	0.9463	0.9474	0.9484	0.9495	0.9505	0.9515	0.9525	0.9535	0.9545
1.7	0.9554	0.9564	0.9573	0.9582	0.9591	0.9599	0.9608	0.9616	0.9625	0.9633
1.8	0.9641	0.9649	0.9656	0.9664	0.9671	0.9678	0.9686	0.9693	0.9699	0.9706
1.9	0.9713	0.9719	0.9726	0.9732	0.9738	0.9744	0.9750	0.9756	0.9761	0.9767
2	0.9772	0.9778	0.9783	0.9788	0.9793	0.9798	0.9803	0.9808	0.9812	0.9817
2.1	0.9821	0.9826	0.9830	0.9834	0.9838	0.9842	0.9846	0.9850	0.9854	0.9857
2.2	0.9861	0.9864	0.9868	0.9871	0.9875	0.9878	0.9881	0.9884	0.9887	0.9890
2.3	0.9893	0.9896	0.9898	0.9901	0.9904	0.9906	0.9909	0.9911	0.9913	0.9916
2.4	0.9918	0.9920	0.9922	0.9925	0.9927	0.9929	0.9931	0.9932	0.9934	0.9936
2.5	0.9938	0.9940	0.9941	0.9943	0.9945	0.9946	0.9948	0.9949	0.9951	0.9952
2.6	0.9953	0.9955	0.9956	0.9957	0.9959	0.9960	0.9961	0.9962	0.9963	0.9964
2.7	0.9965	0.9966	0.9967	0.9968	0.9969	0.9970	0.9971	0.9972	0.9973	0.9974
2.8	0.9974	0.9975	0.9976	0.9977	0.9977	0.9978	0.9979	0.9979	0.9980	0.9981
2.9	0.9981	0.9982	0.9982	0.9983	0.9984	0.9984	0.9985	0.9985	0.9986	0.9986
3	0.9987	0.9987	0.9987	0.9988	0.9988	0.9989	0.9989	0.9989	0.9990	0.9990

Appendix 2: Student's t-distribution showing one-tailed critical values

Given A, the table gives the value of k for which $P(T>k)=A$ where T follows a t-distribution with v degrees of freedom.

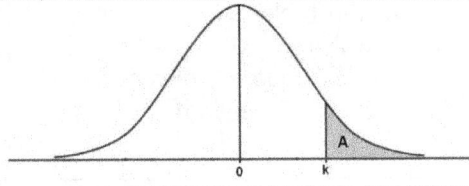

v	0.1	0.05	0.025	0.01	0.005	0.0025	0.001	v
1	3.077685	6.313749	12.70615	31.82096	63.6559	127.3211	318.2888	1
2	1.885619	2.919987	4.302656	6.964547	9.924988	14.08916	22.32846	2
3	1.637745	2.353363	3.182449	4.540707	5.840848	7.4532	10.21428	3
4	1.533206	2.131846	2.776451	3.746936	4.60408	5.59754	7.17293	4
5	1.475885	2.015049	2.570578	3.36493	4.032117	4.773319	5.893526	5
6	1.439755	1.943181	2.446914	3.142668	3.707428	4.316826	5.207548	6
7	1.414924	1.894578	2.364623	2.997949	3.499481	4.029353	4.785252	7
8	1.396816	1.859548	2.306006	2.896468	3.355381	3.832538	4.500762	8
9	1.383029	1.833114	2.262159	2.821434	3.249843	3.689638	4.29689	9
10	1.372184	1.812462	2.228139	2.763772	3.169262	3.581372	4.143658	10
11	1.36343	1.795884	2.200986	2.718079	3.105815	3.496607	4.024769	11
12	1.356218	1.782287	2.178813	2.68099	3.054538	3.428451	3.929599	12
13	1.350172	1.770932	2.160368	2.650304	3.012283	3.372479	3.852037	13
14	1.345031	1.761309	2.144789	2.624492	2.976849	3.325695	3.787427	14
15	1.340605	1.753051	2.131451	2.602483	2.946726	3.286041	3.732857	15
16	1.336757	1.745884	2.119905	2.583492	2.920788	3.251989	3.686146	16
17	1.333379	1.739606	2.109819	2.56694	2.898232	3.222449	3.645764	17
18	1.330391	1.734063	2.100924	2.552379	2.878442	3.196583	3.610476	18
19	1.327728	1.729131	2.093025	2.539482	2.860943	3.1737	3.579335	19
20	1.325341	1.724718	2.085962	2.527977	2.845336	3.1534	3.551831	20
21	1.323187	1.720744	2.079614	2.517645	2.831366	3.13521	3.527093	21
22	1.321237	1.717144	2.073875	2.508323	2.818761	3.118839	3.504974	22
df	0.1	0.05	0.025	0.01	0.005	0.0025	0.001	df
23	1.319461	1.71387	2.068655	2.499874	2.807337	3.103996	3.484965	23
24	1.317835	1.710882	2.063898	2.492161	2.796951	3.090536	3.466776	24
24	1.317835	1.710882	2.063898	2.492161	2.796951	3.090536	3.466776	24
25	1.316346	1.70814	2.059537	2.485103	2.787438	3.078203	3.450186	25
26	1.314972	1.705616	2.055531	2.478628	2.778725	3.066889	3.43498	26
27	1.313704	1.703288	2.051829	2.472661	2.770685	3.056521	3.42101	27
29	1.311435	1.699127	2.045231	2.46202	2.756387	3.03804	3.396271	29
29	1.311435	1.699127	2.045231	2.46202	2.756387	3.03804	3.396271	29
30	1.310416	1.69726	2.04227	2.457264	2.749985	3.029782	3.385212	30
40	1.303076	1.683852	2.021075	2.423258	2.704455	2.971174	3.306923	40
50	1.298713	1.675905	2.00856	2.403267	2.677789	2.936977	3.261375	50
60	1.295821	1.670649	2.000297	2.390116	2.660272	2.914567	3.231689	60
70	1.293763	1.666915	1.994435	2.380802	2.647903	2.898742	3.210807	70
80	1.292224	1.664125	1.990065	2.373872	2.638699	2.886954	3.195237	80
90	1.291029	1.661961	1.986673	2.368497	2.631568	2.877896	3.183231	90
100	1.290075	1.660235	1.983972	2.364213	2.625893	2.870656	3.173773	100
v	0.1	0.05	0.025	0.01	0.005	0.0025	0.001	v

Appendix 3: Chi-squared χ^2 Distribution showing one-tailed critical values

Given A, the table gives the value of k for which P(X>k)=A where X follows a chi-squared distribution with v degrees of freedom.

V \ A	.500	.250	.100	.050	.025	.010	.005
1	0.45494	1.32330	2.70554	3.84146	5.02389	6.63490	7.87944
2	1.38629	2.77259	4.60517	5.99146	7.37776	9.21034	10.59663
3	2.36597	4.10834	6.25139	7.81473	9.34840	11.34487	12.83816
4	3.35669	5.38527	7.77944	9.48773	11.14329	13.27670	14.86026
5	4.35146	6.62568	9.23636	11.07050	12.83250	15.08627	16.74960
6	5.34812	7.84080	10.64464	12.59159	14.44938	16.81189	18.54758
7	6.34581	9.03715	12.01704	14.06714	16.01276	18.47531	20.27774
8	7.34412	10.21885	13.36157	15.50731	17.53455	20.09024	21.95495
9	8.34283	11.38875	14.68366	16.91898	19.02277	21.66599	23.58935
10	9.34182	12.54886	15.98718	18.30704	20.48318	23.20925	25.18818

Appendix 4: Statistical Add-in Packages for Excel

Name of Add-in	URL
statistiXL	http://www.statistixl.com/
SolverStat	http://www.freewebs.com/solverstat/solverstat/solverstat.htm
Fatesoft	http://www.fatesoft.com/excel/
XLSTAT	http://www.xlstat.com/
DigDB	http://www.digdb.com/
Analyse-it	http://www.analyse-it.com/
Xcelential	http://www.ozgrid.com/excel-add-ins/Xcelential.htm
@RISK5.5	http://www.palisade.com/risk/
PHStat2	http://www.prenhall.com/phstat/
VBA	http://www.fontstuff.com/VBA/vbatut03.htm
ASAP	http://www.asap-utilities.com/
SQL-Excel	http://www.sq
DPLOT	http://dplot.com/exceladdin.htm
Price Grabber	http://www.pricegrabber.co.uk/search_noresults.php/ form_keyword=excel+add+in/st=query
Decompiler	http://www.straxx.com/excel/decompiler/xla_decompile.html

Index

www.ingramcontent.com/pod-product-compliance
Lightning Source LLC
Chambersburg PA
CBHW070408270326
41926CB00014B/2759